To my beautiful, fierce sister Selemawit Terrefe, who insists that we fight to chart a path for our flights into Revolutionary Love.

CONTENTS

PART III: COMMUNITIES IN CONFLICT AND CARE

Foreword

Da'Shaun L. Harrison

I used to sign all of my emails to Black folks with "Revolutionary Love" in hopes that it would signify to the reader that I was invested in their life and livelihood and committed to our collective struggle for freedom. Signing my emails this way was intended to act as a subtle indication that the individual(s) on the receiving end of the email could find community with/in me. "Revolutionary Love" acted as a stand-in for "Black Love," which I understand to be a commitment to our freedom and to the destruction of the conditions under which the Black is subjugated. In this way, I see Black Love not just as the existence of Black subjects in relationship to each other, but also as an entity that should necessitate the destruction of anti-Blackness on which a need for Black (or Revolutionary) Love exists.

Eventually, I stopped signing my emails that way because the phrase began to mean something else to me. I started to interrogate the idea of love and of revolution more deeply. In doing so, I found that love, at least as it is used hegemonically, does not function in this way; that Love—Black, Revolutionary, or otherwise—is often used as a way to asphyxiate our desire to revolt and rebel. It allows for us to believe that there can be something subtle about revolution, which is ultimately a call to/for death. Love works to ensure that our desire to see to the end of our suffering becomes quelled by postulations of a "better" world being possible without the destruction of anti-Blackness, which is the destruction of the world. It is presented as something more powerful than revolution, thus assisting in the destabilization of our movements and our commitment to our collective liberation.

Joy James writes that "Revolutionary Love for justice and equity has a self-acknowledged vulnerability: no amount of compassion and love has historically demystified the majority's reactionary and predatory fetishes for racial, sexual, and class domination, and its suspicions and hostilities toward the 'other.' Revolutionary Lovers are a distinct minority." This quote, and what follows it in James's book, moves me to understanding Revolutionary Love in a much different way. Through my reading of James's work, Revolutionary Love becomes the force through which I understand death to be an essential and vital part of revolution. Said differently, dying for the revolution is a necessary part of struggle, in one way or another, and Revolutionary Love—this unrequited political will—is the catalyst.

This means that death and dying do not always come by way of murder in the streets by the police or other white supremacists, but through attempting to divest from *all* of the structures that wield power over us—and doing so earnestly. Revolutionary Love calls us to acknowledge that the state and the state's violence are only a fragment of the sadistic nature of anti-Blackness; that our struggle for liberation cannot and must not be limited to critiques of state power, but rather must extend to the metaphysical, global structure that is anti-Blackness, through which the state apparatus *maintains* its power. It is a call to sacrifice; to sacrifice our lives, our relationships, our time, our livelihoods with the understanding that nothing is guaranteed in return.

When we die for the sake of revolution, the contradictions of anti-Blackness are heightened. Anti-Blackness relies on the existence and the subjugation of the Black subject to maintain its power while also requiring, or giving way to, our physical and social deaths. In this way, Revolutionary Love functions as a prompt that cues us into action that leads to the forced collapse of anti-Blackness. Revolutionary Love justifies and pulls us closer to bypassing or undermining the rules of the state, of power, of capitalist violence, and helps to determine what these rogue acts can look like. James's work makes me excited about the real possibilities of Revolutionary Love. If Revolutionary Love is about political will and the will to die for revolution, then this phrase that functions as both instructional and thematic lends itself as a tool for how to end the precariousness of our being and our suffering.

Through this book, James leads us to acknowledging that community is a requisite for structuring any analysis that is competent and adept; that as we deepen our relationship with community, we must also begin to welcome the contradictions of our words and our thoughts. If we take this work seriously, James and her invitation into the minds of the communities with which she thinks will deepen our understanding of Revolutionary Love, and of death and dying, and of the sociopolitical animus to accelerate the precarity of anti-Blackness and anti-Black violence.

That is the urgency of this text: to invite us into an understanding that revolution requires us to die, and to do so in more ways than one. Revolutionary Love is not about being invested in our lives, but rather it is about being invested in and knowledgeable about our deaths. It is not about the romanticized fantasy and hallucinations shared by many revolutionaries about being at war with the state, but rather it is about the death of Desire, and of our desires. It is not about Black Love, or any romantic, familial, or platonic love at all. It is about sustained movements, political will, and laboring for the sake of revolution to kill the very things designed to kill us. It requires that we die to this world.

This book, and James's work more largely, is indispensable. James offers a pivotal analysis in the midst of a sociopolitical climate where accelerating the contradictions of anti-Blackness is not only inevitable, but one of the most pertinent demands in modern history.

Preface: Oshun's Flight

I do not seek to represent or dishonor any spiritual or religious traditions. If I err, please forgive. I merely note that thirst compels this writing.

I heard one story about the African orisha Oshun. I do not recall all the details so I embroider here to make my own political-ethical points. According to the griot, as the ambitious lofty conspired to overthrow the creator, they mocked Oshun who had refused to join in a coup or genuflect as a member of the political demimonde. Angered by the upstarts' challenges to authority, and the disorder of things, Spirit—Olodumare—withdrew protections. Waters in skies and on lands dried up.

Oshun sided with the lower castes, dispossessed masses, animals and creatures dying from malnourishment, parched and perched amid poisoned and absent waters. Oshun so loved the world. Only the embodiment of the beauty of rivers and streams dared to fly to the heavens to petition Spirit for redress and aid for those suffering cracked earth under dry, burning skies. As Oshun flew closer to Spirit, the radiating sun took its toll. Their beautiful peacock-like feathers began to smolder, then burn and fall. Despite the agony, Oshun focused on the desperation of those left behind and so reached their destination.

Shorn of beautiful feathers, scorched and scarred with the ashen appearance of a gray vulture, Oshun stumbled from the torturous flight to approach Spirit. Oshun bowed. Spirit observed, then agreed to listen to Oshun petition on behalf of those betrayed by life, abandoned by gods, bereft with broken defenses, and left to ward off "leadership" alien to the needs of the mass.

Was it compassion or grace that led to respite from desertification? Or, was the catalyst the beautiful boldness wielded by a defiant orisha compelled to care? Whatever the motivation, Spirit heard risk, love, and courage in the pleadings; and ceased to punish the mass for the crimes of arrogant challengers who sought to dethrone—and to imperialize— misery. Thwarted but unpunished, destructive wannabe gods continued to transgress for accumulations. Unforgiven, they were mostly forgotten except by the dishonored and desperate who recalled and recoiled from their violence. Ignoring the imbalance on the scales of justice, the heavens granted relief from pain by releasing rain to all as Spirit met our desperate needs for flowing waters.

The path of a worthy returnee is a painful sojourn. Oshun flew into scorching skies seeking to sabotage predators and authoritarianism and to serve the people. Taking flight as warrior, Oshun navigated sacrificial labor. Carried by the echo of protective spirits, Oshun's heartbeat became a radar for struggle. With(out) feathered beauty, their persistence fueled Revolutionary Love. Thus, the orisha returns wearing the radiance of agape. Reverence seeps through the labors of saints, ancestors, healers, doulas to fall upon captive communities and kin.

Survivors battle catastrophes unleashed by would-be gods—rapists, capitalists, overseers, imperialists, traffickers, abortion bounty hunters, prison guards, environmental desecrators, military-mercenaries, death squads. Survivors willing to hear the echoes of griot speaking love also coordinate flights and fights to ensure that—even when muddied—we remain within sacred waters.

Is Oshun's flight as tortured messenger a form of the Captive Maternal? Or is their labor to give birth to community care a "gift" from a transcendent deity? Are deities captives to agape? Do they (un)willingly suffer or are they emotionally and spiritually compelled to sacrifice? Can all forms of communities—deified, (de)humanized, demonized, cyborg— generate or produce Captive Maternals? Oshun is a sovereign. Sovereigns suffer, yet are captive to love. In the presence of agape, battles for life ensue.

*

The dread doula Ominira Mars tracks within struggling communities the emotions found in Oshun's flight. Mars's essay "Dear Mariame Kaba, Hope Is Not a Discipline" opens with a quote from the US-American organizer and educator Mariame Kaba, who has made significant contributions to abolitionism: "Hope doesn't preclude feeling sadness or frustration or anger or any other emotion that makes total sense. Hope isn't an emotion, you know? Hope is not optimism. Hope is a discipline . . . we have to practice it every single day."[1] In some ways, Kaba echoes Rev. Martin Luther King Jr.'s 1955 speech in Holt Street Baptist Church four days after Rosa Parks refused to relinquish her seat to a white man on a segregated Montgomery, Alabama bus on December 1, 1955: "My friends, there comes a time when people get tired of being trampled over by the iron feet of oppression . . . when they get tired of being plunged across the abyss of humiliation, where they experience the bleakness of nagging despair . . . Now let us go out to stick together and stay with this thing until the end . . . yes it means sacrificing at points. But there are some things that we've got to learn to sacrifice for."

Beneath Kaba's quote, Mars posts:

Hope requires complete trust and confidence; it requires faith.

Faith grounds.

Faith is the foundation upon which both our desires and expectations reside.

Faith is at the root of our ability to hope.[2]

Reflecting on Kaba's contributions, conceding that hope is not an emotion, Mars describes hope as "a phenomenon of many emotions coexisting together." Mars asserts that we must recognize the impossibility of any project to render hope a "discipline" because hope as "(cap)ability" accrues through "power, privilege," yet systemic abuse, without transformative accountability or strategic efficacy to address anti-Blackness, capitalism, and neocolonialism, leads people to lose faith in institutions and prominent leaders; hence, Mars argues, those lacking *"power, privilege, and/or capacity to hope . . .* become incapable of hope":

> Hope as a discipline becomes restrictive, monotonous, exhausting. We must be able to occupy a multifaceted consciousness and way of reasoning with what could be that makes room for both the pragmatic and the impossible. We must practice a regenerative and expansive hope, or else hope becomes contained only by what we assume and/ or are told is not possible.[3]

Mars asserts that the capacity to "imagine beyond the carceral status quo" depends not on "liberatory imaginings" but on a "faith" that we can materialize what we imagine. Asserting that learning "hope as a discipline" mandates that we "lower our expectations of liberation," Mars quotes Nicholas Brady: "paradoxically, the most hopeful people are those who have no hope in the system." Mars argues: "We should not and will not discipline ourselves into hope. We will not build more tolerance for disappointment in violent institutions and systems built upon our erasure and pain. We will not police our doubt." To move forward rather than become stuck in despondency or defeat, Mars advocates that we "embrace despair not as an end or an arrival point," but as a "bridge" constructed without binaries.[4] This suggests to me that confidence shaped by skills and strategies is developed in communal *struggles* and also builds organizing that can frame and sustain movements. Such struggles are energized and amplified by engineering Revolutionary Love, not as "scientific" but as *sentient*. The spiritual nature of that love is embodied in agape disciplined by political will. Political will sustains this form of love even when one wishes its dissipation or dissolution in order to dodge the entanglements and suffering of liberation struggles. There exists the possibility that *despair*, rather than leading to nihilism or passivity and indifference, could be a key catalyst to confrontational change. How else could Mamie Till-Mobley disturb psyches across the globe by demanding and obtaining an open-casket for the September 3, 1955 funeral—and allowing photographers to capture the horror-as-catalyst—for her fourteen-year-old son Emmett, who was sexually assaulted, tortured, and mutilated before being murdered by white supremacists on August 28, 1955? Mamie Till-Mobley *despaired*. On December 1, 1955, Rosa Parks expressed aspects of that despair and rage with rebellion when, reportedly while thinking of Emmett, she refused to give up her seat to a white man on a segregated bus. Catalysts in struggle that foment resistance are not always sparked by hope.

As do Marxists, materialists, and activists, Mars asserts that "one cannot 'discipline' themselves into the phenomena of hope without concrete material change."[5] Hence, absent "concrete material change," influencers and celebrities, as well as religious and community leaders, cannot discipline communities into hope when there are no material conditions to sustain it. Building on Mars's contributions, I would however argue that it is *struggle* rather than "change" that serves as the catalyst for "disciplining" strategies. Struggles in the later stages of the Captive Maternal's evolution lead to maroon camps or autonomous zones, sanctuaries and enclosures that make "hope" a possibility and a stable accelerant for liberation struggles. "Hope" can be used to extinguish revolutionary struggle, according to Mars, when leadership and platforms with the capacity to "discipline hope" often "depend on teaching self-regulatory violence to their 'followers'":

> However, hope as a "discipline" in the face of ongoing systemic and institutional abuse (and modest material change) requires the weight of the psychological and/or emotional consequences of our conditions, and the task of nurturing feelings of "productive" expectation (in the midst of our ongoing suffering) dependent exclusively upon self-discipline. Hope should not be contingent upon

me (or those of us on the very margins) being able to (self) regulate/discipline in the face of violence; there is no honor, healing, and spaciousness in that.[6]

Reading Mars, I hear the generative and see the void as shaped by communal dialogue and interrogation, as well as negotiations structuring theory, politics, and strategies to further liberation movements through community connectors. In my graduate studies, I learned that democracy is based in discursive communication for the common good, according to the European political theorists Jürgen Habermas and Hannah Arendt. Yet in Indigenous and diverse cultures, deities precede the demos. The recognition of their political will—if it has validity—is based not on their superpowers but on their capacity to receive and return love.

Oshun took flight not because they loved in the abstract and from on high, but because they reciprocated the love they received, not from other deities but from the mass. Neither pity nor emotional grandeur fueled Oshun's flight. Gratitude did. Oshun returned the love given by the mass that taught Oshun how to love. The origin story of Spirit within revolutionary struggle is the agency of the mass catalyzed by the gravitas of loss—healthy childhoods, clean air, fresh water, freedom, dignified life and death. Whatever Oshun's capacity, the political will of the people to endure and love shaped their flight plan. Oshun was the messenger; the message delivered was "Pursue Revolutionary Love."

For this writer, it is irksome that the image on this book's cover is catalogued as "Unidentified, *Fan for an Osun Priestess*, 19th–20th century, Yoruba Peoples; The New Orleans Museum of Art: Museum purchase, Françoise Billion Richardson Fund, 90.306." Despite the "government name" issued by the museum and the capture of culture under colonization, this is not a plummet because we retain the capacity to reclaim and name Black beauty and Black Love as we continue to seek sovereign and communal freedom.

Notes to Preface

1 Kaba quoted in Ominira Mars, "Dear Mariame Kaba, Hope Is Not a Discipline," *Medium*/Patreon, May 2, 2022, https://www.patreon.com/posts/dear-mariame-is-65935224.
2 Ibid.
3 Ibid.; emphasis in original.
4 Ibid.
5 Ibid.
6 Ibid.

Introduction:
Where Is Revolutionary Love?

"Where is Revolutionary Love?" The answer depends in part upon where you are standing and with whom. This endeavor did not start as an attempt to write a book.

My book *Shadowboxing: Representations of Black Feminist Politics* was published over two decades ago and offered an appreciation and a critique of Black feminisms (in the plural). The appreciation was for the radicals who were willing to become organizers, not intending to assimilate or accumulate in a racially driven empire stoked by predatory capitalism and violence. The Black radical feminists I admired were not "managerial"; hence they merged with the mass of people, particularly those dispossessed, exploited, impoverished and trafficked into prisons, jails, psych wards, foster care, and underground economies.

Over the last decade, I have begun to think about what I call "Captive Maternals," the agender or nongendered caretakers with diverse political agendas discussed throughout this book. What struck me was their capaciousness and capacity, the space they hold inside for struggle, contradictions, and betrayals.

The co-authors of this text are pedagogic podcasters, analysts, organizers, teacher-students. They are largely Captive Maternals and overwhelmingly radical. They are not managerial; they do not present themselves as leaders who are aligned with the state and (non)corporate entities that have flooded hundreds of millions—if not billions—of dollars into representing or managing "Black lives." The 2012 vigilante murder of Trayvon Martin, the 2014 police executions of Eric Garner, Tamir Rice, and Michael Brown, the 2015 deaths of Sandra Bland and others, the 2020 police murder of George Floyd that incited protests worldwide, reveal state violence against the most vulnerable: the impoverished, imprisoned, and rebellious who seek or demand human and civil rights.

Without the deaths, protests, rebellions, and labor of intellectual, political, and spiritual communities there would be no writing that reflected the intense energy and focus of this collective literary collaboration shaped by agape and organizing. This book—with one contributor's name on the cover—brings collective analyses to the table to be studied and dissected for resistance to white supremacy, femicide, filicide, genocide, ecocide. I am grateful to be in dialogue with interlocutors who, on my best days, are also part of my collective. Although we lack the intimacy and emotional connections of a "crew," we share political kinship and similar desires to contest a rapacious, imperial state garbed in the trappings of a violent overlord.

The contributors to this book cannot fully define Revolutionary Love; yet, we pursue it. When we retreat from searching for it, we stagnate or stumble. On our best and worst days and nights, an elusive Revolutionary Love might be the one tangible link that holds us together as communities despite the precarity and the predatory powers arrayed against freedom in balance with all life forms.

The United States has influenced the world with cultural commodities, militarism, and racial capitalism historically built through anti-Black and anti-Indigenous genocides and enslavement, and extractive accumulations and anti-Blackness. From these zones of struggle, this book seeks international alliances and solidarity in order to curtail wars, exploitation, and imprisonment. Here, theorists demand and strategize for international justice and freedom. Some are organizers and intellectuals on the ground working with vulnerable communities; others are academics working to curtail class divisions and to serve as allies for those facing the brunt of repression.

One basic tenet throughout this text is that force in opposition to enslavement, exploitation, and extermination is not another form of violence; it is self/familial/communal defense. Working analyses that offer material, emotional, psychological protections to the vulnerable should be honed in collective dialogues and debates. A caretaker discourse is not sufficient, although it is helpful and therapeutic. To confront cooptation and coercion from state and (non)profit corporations, donors, and political parties requires critical building blocks that foster dialogue, debate, and transformational politics and maneuvers that stabilize Revolutionary Love.

We organized the book into three sections, focusing on precarity, power, and communities. We needed specificity: in reviewing the contributions from varied resistance sectors, we noted that activism was central, and decided that despite the disagreements and conflicts among "progressives" we would center on activism because we knew it to be indispensable in the material and spiritual worlds that we inhabit, worlds where betrayals strongly register against the revolutionary and radical paths.

In Part I, "Precarity in Activism," chapter 1, "Revolutionary Love Resists Democracy," reflects on Black culture, specifically US Black music, as a mainstay in our resistance to predatory violence and consumption. Nina Simone, Sly and the Family Stone, War: these and other musical wizards with spiritual powers blossomed in the 1960s and early 1970s when Black rebellions were clearly in resistance to state violence before cooptation, COINTELPRO, and the monetization of Black death which led to the rise of movement millionaires. "'Sorrow, Tears, and Blood' Disavows the Talented Tenth," chapter 2, was published during the height of the militant faction of Black Lives Matter protests and organizing, and points to international connectors with Black/African culture as exemplified in the musician Fela Kuti's "Sorrow Tears & Blood." Chapter 3, "Seven Lessons in One Abolitionist Notebook: On Airbrushing Revolution," looks back on my organizing as an untenured assistant professor in the late 1990s, as academic abolition began to solidify through elite universities or research institutes and with the backing of liberal nonprofits and university funders. "Anti-Racist Algorithms in Abolition Alchemy," chapter 4, notes another misperception or distortion of political struggle: the positioning of the academy as a training ground for liberators or radical abolitionists. Organizers appear on campuses largely as consumers, students, workers, or allies. However, the mission of the public university as an extension of government and the private college as a corporate entity, is not structured to be aligned with radical activism or abolition. Important diversity efforts can easily become distanced from or offer distorted representations of freedom strategies for impoverished workers, laborers, imprisoned, children, LGBTQ+, fe/males, Blacks, Indigenous.

Within the academy, struggles are also studied through blueprints from the past. The Black Panther Party—increasingly enshrined in symbolism and Panther-adjacent romanticism through Hollywood film and publications—can also be read in critical analyses from those with experiential knowledge. K. Kim Holder, a former New York Harlem Panther trained by Assata Shakur, offers through his 1990 dissertation a political schematic for two chapters that emphasize community connections, interconnectedness, and caretaking, as well as critiques of the state's attempts to destabilize Revolutionary Love embodied in Panther community care networks. Chapters 5 and 6 respectively—"The Limitations of Black Studies" and "Power and the Contradictions of Communal Socialism"—co-authored with Holder, reflect his original experiences and analyses as a Panther.

Part II, "Power in Structures," begins with an interview-dialogue with the public philosopher George Yancy, "Reaching beyond 'Black Faces in High Places,'" that critiques the 2020 election of President Joe Biden and Vice President Kamala Harris—the first Black woman to hold the second highest position in US government. The interview scrutinizes the liberal or progressive embrace of an anti-revolutionary, former prosecutor, whose narratives on Blackness and South Asian identity echoed a refrain for Black struggle but offered no concrete strategy or advocacy to counter US genocidal violence and economic violence abroad and at home.

Home, the training ground for politics and love, connection and alienation, can also be a zone of distortion and violence as reflected in chapter 8, "Political Theory in the Academy," a dialogue with Carlotta Hartmann of People for Womxn* in Philosophy. Chapter 9, "Captive Maternals, the Exonerated Central Park Five, and Abolition," explores in a wide-ranging conversation with Chris Time Steele of *Time Talks* how personal experiences shape epistemology and how academic structures reinterpret radicalism into conventional progressivism rather than resistance to state violence.

Chapter 10, "(Re)Thinking the Black Feminist Canon," with Paris Hatcher, summarizes a segment of a Black Feminist Future conference on the contributions and complexities of Black feminism. Chapter 11, "How the University (De)Radicalizes Social Movements," with Rebecca A. Wilcox of the Political Theology Network, focuses on graduate students and community organizers, rising generations of intellectuals seeking to push beyond convention and academic innovations.

The close reading and analysis by community-radical thinkers in chapter 12, "Angela Davis Was a Black Panther (AKA 'Pragmatism vs Revolutionary Love')," with *The Black Myths Podcast*, convinced me that community intellectuals should be teaching my college courses. The hosts Too Black and Ryan parse out the details and debate over whether or not Davis was a *member* rather than an important ally for the Black Panther Party for Self Defense (distinct from the Black Panther *Political* Party, a study group, identified in her autobiography—Davis asserts that she was a "Panther" although her political biographer only identifies her as a member of the BPPP).[1]

Part III, "Communities in Conflict and Care," reveals how strangers in strange lands attempt to cross oceans or continents of thought and politics to reconcile our disagreements and confirm our commitments to revolutionary struggles and communities. In "Troubling Black Feminisms," chapter 13, for *The Malcolm Effect* podcast, Momodou Taal and Khadijah Anabah Diskin presented queries and analyses that led me to hold on to the analytical concept of the Captive Maternal but also to reaffirm that Black feminism as a global endeavor can disrupt land and water theft, child disappearances, femicide, and forced birthing. Chapter 14, "The Plurality of Abolitionism," is anchored by the theories of the *Groundings* podcast led by Felicia Denaud and Devyn Springer and rooted in the brilliance and compassion of Walter Rodney, the Guyanese historian, intellectual, and freedom fighter who was assassinated in 1980.[2] In chapter 15, "On the Rise of the Black Bourgeoisie," Jason Myles and Pascal Robert of the *This Is Revolution* podcast (aired with The Real News Network) emphasize the under-analysis of class struggle in critiques of racism and white supremacy. Our discussions, which were not always aligned with the same critique, focused on gender, race, and leadership, and the complexities of anti-Blackness and revolutionary struggle. Jared Ware and Joshua Briond of *Millennials Are Killing Capitalism* sent a dozen questions to review before hours of discussion and debate on their podcast while referring to and riffing on notes. Unsurprisingly, their work ethic proved that we needed two chapters to contain the debates and agreements and solidarity in struggle by which we bonded: chapters 16 and 17 —"We Remember the Attempts to Be Free: Part I" and "We Remember the Attempts to Be Free: Part II"—with Briond and Ware close this book on collective thinking and struggle.

This book began with the love and spirit of Orisha and ancestors; it concludes with the love and spirituality of revolutionary youth. The conclusion, inspired by a post that a Panther veteran shared on Facebook—is a reminder about the important role of memory linked to those who survived the FBI's lethal Counterintelligence Program (COINTELPRO), conducted to discredit and undermine domestic political organizations, especially those that fought imperial and colonial violence. Despite my aversion for Facebook, Twitter, and global megamedia corporations in general, I am grateful for this restored snapshot of Revolutionary Love imprinted on history through the photo of and text by "Peaches," the imprisoned teen Panther enveloped in love as political will. Half a century after she penned her public letter, I was tutored by the "Agape of Peaches."

Notes to Introduction

1   The book review by Keeanga-Yamahtta Taylor, "'Hell, Yes, We Are Subversive': The Legacy of Angela Davis," *New York Review of Books*, September 4, 2022, valorizes Davis without acknowledging contradictions, betrayals of radicalism, or naming Davis's co-defendant Ruchell Magee who remains incarcerated at the age of eighty-three.

2   See Richard Gray, "The Death of Walter Rodney," *History Today* 30, no. 9 (September 1980), https://www.historytoday.com/archive/death-walter-rodney.

Part I
Precarity in Activism

1 Revolutionary Love Resists Democracy

I have never considered United States democracy to be trust-worthy. Though preferable to a formal dictatorship, it often seems to function as a racist-classist-misogynist-transphobic Ponzi scheme for elite accumulations and unregulated warfare and war-profiteering. After centuries of genocide and racial enslavement, the US denies those most in need—most deserving—of reparations, restitution, respect, and sovereign autonomy. Insulted with exhortations to "try harder" to prove our worth, chastised for going "too left" in our search for social justice, we are called upon to "save" democracy from authoritarianism and repression.

Given the long history of US volatility and racist violence, those attentive to white-supremacist and fascistic ideologies were dismayed but not surprised at the January 6 breach of the Capitol Building. A militarized mob endeavored to block the certification of the Biden–Harris election and harm, if not kill, elected officials seeking to uphold constitutional norms. (The following month, the Senate acquitted Donald Trump of inciting sedition that inflicted trauma, injuries, and the loss of life.) White-supremacist politicians, citing the betrayal of Reconstruction and Black equality as a template, coupled with violent Trump loyalists to derail a peaceful transfer of power. Viewers watched in real time the preceding rally coordinated by Trump, its anti-Black and neo-Nazi themes, as evangelical reactionary conservatism and Confederate flags were working their ways into the history books.[1] Later during hearings, the public would learn that civilians had planned to assassinate Vice President Mike Pence, a white ultra-conservative/reactionary determined to certify the presidential election based on votes. The president is determined not by the popular vote but by the Electoral College—the Three-fifths Compromise of the US Constitution, through mass rape/reproduction, created a representative democracy in which the Thirteenth Amendment to ban chattel slavery codified enslavement to incarceration and thereby enabled voter suppression of poor, working-class, and racially stigmatized peoples. Eliminating the Electoral College as well as the penal exception to the Thirteenth Amendment, and overturning *Citizens United v. Federal Election Commission*, whereby the Supreme Court transposed the "political personhood" granted in the Fourteenth Amendment from the emancipated to the corporations, would be the tools required for fundamental change. However, in order to truly confront repression, we must pursue Revolutionary Love.

Revolutionary Love is difficult to define. Distinct from personal or familial love, it originates from a desire for the greater good that entails radical risk-taking for justice. Revolutionary Love is not romantic or charming. It neither romanticizes nor projects celebrities or politicos as surrogates for radical activism. Worship within a "cult of personality" is not an expression of Revolutionary Love. Seeking equity and securing basic needs (housing, food, education, healthy environments), despite constant frustrations and betrayals is a sign of faithfulness. Despite the hostilities of well-funded anti-revolutionary and counter-revolutionary organizing to maintain predatory hierarchies and police forces, communities are invested in preserving the theory and analyses of the Illinois Black Panther leader Fred Hampton, a Revolutionary Lover who maintained that "the greatest weapon is political education."[2] Revolutionary Love is the portal for lifelong education.

Revolutionary Love for justice and equity has a self-acknowledged vulnerability: no amount of compassion and love has historically demystified the majority's reactionary and predatory fetishes for racial, sexual, and class domination, and its suspicions and hostilities toward the "other." Revolutionary Lovers are a distinct minority. Millions appalled by Trump and the Capitol breach—quite possibly aided by police[3]—prefer civic duty, conformity, or consensus-building as more acceptable than Revolutionary Love for equity and liberation. Conventional Democratic politics and policies have historically proven insufficient to stop white-supremacist violence against Black elected officials or Black environmental naturalists.[4]

During enslavement, ungendered Captive Maternals found their generative powers—their intellectual, emotional, and physical capacities—stolen and repurposed to build and stabilize a social order and governance that deny Black humanity.[5] Thus, a racially fashioned democracy stabilized and accumulated through predatory extraction and its residue of Black depletion and death. The transformative powers of Revolutionary Love—rooted in suprarational politics, not in the quid pro quo politics that consistently fail to meet the needs of vulnerable masses—can develop on community-focused training grounds—even within an imperial racial order. Patrice Lumumba understood Revolutionary Love as he led a freedom movement in the Congo; Ernesto "Che" Guevara, another Revolutionary Lover, who mourned Lumumba's assassination, castigated the UN for failing to protect Lumumba from assassination (reportedly with the assistance of the CIA). Guevara asserted, "At the risk of seeming ridiculous, let me say that the true revolutionary is guided by a great feeling of love. It is impossible to think of a genuine revolutionary lacking this quality." The revolutionary Fannie Lou Hamer, as a sharecropper, intellectual, and militant organizer for the Student Nonviolent Coordinating Committee (SNCC) and the Mississippi Freedom Democratic Party, was not assassinated as were Lumumba and Guevara, but was brutalized and sexually assaulted by US police forces.[6] The risks and sacrifices for Revolutionary Love are inherent in the struggle against neo-fascism and repression. Risk-taking veteran activists, such as Dhoruba Bin Wahad, note that if "BLM" meant "Black Liberation Movement" there would be more focus on revolutionary concepts than corporate donors. Those guided

by love rather than hate are confronted not only with the
human rights violations of US domestic policy, but also with
US betrayals in foreign policy; the Black Alliance for Peace,
for instance, has drawn our attention to the Biden–Harris
administration's neo-imperial politics on the coup in Haiti.[7]
Just Security notes that the Biden administration's support for a
violent dictator in Haiti destabilized the country.[8] Meanwhile,
United States Africa Command, known as AFRICOM, and
imperialist foreign policies are part of the bipartisan war
machine.[9] Reactionaries and centrists attack radicalism that
challenges US policies for such violations.

If through Revolutionary Love we develop the communal structures, political will, and emotional intelligence
to sustain longevity in struggle, then we build capacity to
embrace and learn from the survivors of genocide, enslavement, political imprisonment, and mass incarceration. We all
need self-respect and self-defense; this democracy is not engineered to meet our needs—hence the organic development of
Revolutionary Love addresses our needs. White-supremacist
violence followed the election of Barack Obama. It still stalks
the Biden–Harris administration and Georgia's Black and
Jewish Democratic senators, Raphael Warnock and Jon Ossoff.
Elected officials have security details and designated police for
protections. Non-wealthy communities, particularly activists
guided by Revolutionary Love, do not—and thus are preyed
upon not just by civilians but also by police forces. Voter suppression against Black people (from gerrymandering to "Stop
the Steal" myths) will continue along with ideologically and
racially driven police and vigilante violence.

Captive Maternals—nongendered entities who function as caretakers and nurturers, protectors of communities,
raising future generations—move from conflicted caretakers
to protesters who build movements, only to later transition
into maroons who build freedom schools and community
aid; or inevitably, war resistors who risk everything for freedom. Consider that 2021 was the fiftieth anniversary of the

September 1971 Attica Prison rebellion. Treated as subhuman, Attica's incarcerated rebels, as Captive Maternals, transitioned from caretakers whose labor allowed the prison to function into movement activists for human rights. For a brief time, with a feeling of "freedom," they formed a maroon camp (with medical care and political education) within the prison. Inevitably, they became war resistors who perished or survived to be tortured (and later killed) when the state retook the prison through warfare.[10] That is a legacy that we can study as stages in Revolutionary Love—conflicted caretakers; movement activists; maroon communities; war resistors. The year 2021 was also the seventieth anniversary of the Civil Rights Congress's petition to the United Nations, *We Charge Genocide*, based on the UN Genocide Convention and currently studied by activists to petition for US human rights.[11] We have an amazing legacy to study and to stitch together.

The Legacy of Cultural Rebellion

Our culture of resistance is a mainstay for resilience in the face of formidable opposition. We all need self-respect and self-defense; this democracy is not engineered to meet our needs.

The most incandescent forms of Revolutionary Love often circulate through spirituality within popular culture. In 1962, during a "civil war" against Southern US Jim Crow laws, Nina Simone sang "Sinnerman," in which she begs the Lord to hide her (presumably from lynching) only to be told to "go to the Devil"; facing the Devil in abandonment, she cries to the Lord for power (presumably Black Power). In 1969, Sly and the Family Stone's "Thank You (Falettinme Be Mice Elf Agin)" chronicles racist policing while embracing self-love in resistance: "Lookin' at the devil, grinnin' at his gun / Fingers start shakin', I begin to run / Bullets start chasin', I begin to stop / We begin to wrestle, I was on the top . . . / Dying young is hard to take, but selling out is harder." In 1971, the Family Stone's "It's a Family Affair" describes the microcosm of polarized society and state: "One child grows up to be / Somebody that just loves to learn / And another child grows up to be / Somebody you'd just love to burn."

Political hymns soothe and inspire. During New York City's pandemic and state abandonment, I heard War's "Slippin' into Darkness" playing on the phone of a young Black "essential"—but for state and corporations too often "expendable"—frontline worker standing at a subway entrance. The counsel of lyrics crafted decades before he was born spoke of intergenerational love and struggle: "Slippin' into darkness, yeah / When I heard my mother say / I was slippin' into darkness / When I heard my mother say / Hey, what'd she say what'd she say / You've been slippin' into darkness (Wo ho ho ho) / Pretty soon you gonna pay, hey."

Practice increases skill. Combined with Revolutionary Love, we grow power through mutual aid, political education, the release of the incarcerated, and community control over police. Love, vulnerability, and agency mitigate apathy, depression, and aggression; promote viaducts into structures that fuel transformative power—the powers protecting the masses, nature, and animal life forms. Resisting violent inequities, liberationists, and anti-racist allies, inspired by Revolutionary Love, construct small drawbridges and maroon sanctuaries to enable survival with vitality, strategies, and security.

Notes to Chapter 1

1   Jason Stanley, "Movie at the Ellipse: A Study in Fascist Propaganda," *Just Security*, February 4, 2021, https://www.justsecurity.org/74504/movie-at-the-ellipse-a-study-in-fascist-propaganda/.
2   See Flint Taylor and Jeff Haas, "New Documents Suggest that J. Edgar Hoover Was Involved in Fred Hampton's Murder," *Truthout*, January 19, 2021, https://truthout.org/articles/new-documents-suggest-j-edgar-hoover-was-involved-in-fred-hamptons-murder/; and Eddie Conway, "The Government Murdered Fred Hampton: Will It

Ever Be Held Accountable?," The Real News Network, February 15, 2021, YouTube video, https://www.youtube.com/watch?v=YQvNcrcYa3A.

3   A&S Communications Staff, "Police 'Unprepared' and Possibly 'Complicit' in Capitol Breach," The College of Arts & Sciences, Cornell University, January 7, 2021, https://as.cornell.edu/news/police-unprepared-and-possibly-complicit-capitol-breach.

4   See Zinn Education Project, "This Day in History—Nov. 10, 1898: Wilmington Massacre," accessed July 8, 2022, https://www.zinnedproject.org/news/tdih/wilmington-massacre-2/; and Ed Pilkington, "The Day Police Bombed a City Street: Can Scars of 1985 Move Atrocity Be Healed?," *Guardian*, May 10, 2020, https://www.theguardian.com/us-news/2020/may/10/move-1985-bombing-reconciliation-philadelphia.

5   See Joy James, "The Womb of Western Theory: Trauma, Time Theft, and the Captive Maternal," *Carceral Notebooks* 12 (2016); available online, https://www.thecarceral.org/cn12/14_Womb_of_Western_Theory.pdf, accessed October 26, 2022.

6   See Tasha Fierce, "Sister Soldiers: On Black Women, Police Brutality, and the True Meaning of Black Liberation," *bitchmedia*, February 11, 2015, https://www.bitchmedia.org/article/sister-soldiers-black-lives-matter-women-activism.

7   Black Alliance for Peace, "For Biden Administration, Black Lives Don't Matter in Haiti!—A BAP Statement on Haiti," February 12, 2021, https://blackallianceforpeace.com/bapstatements/bidendoesntcareabouthaiti.

8   Pierre Esperance, "An Appeal to President Biden: Change Course on Haiti Now," *Just Security*, July 9, 2021, https://www.justsecurity.org/77374/an-appeal-to-president-biden-change-course-on-haiti-now/.

9   See e.g. David Chrisinger, "The Surge Nobody's Talking About: The US War in Somalia," *The War Horse*, June 25, 2020, https://thewarhorse.org/the-surge-nobodys-talking-about-the-u-s-war-in-somalia/.

10   See Orisanmi Burton, *Tip of the Spear* (Berkeley, CA: University of California Press, 2023); and the 2021 PBS documentary *Eyes on the Prize: A Nation of Law? (1968–1971)*.

11   Civil Rights Congress, *We Charge Genocide: The Historic Petition to the United Nations for Relief from a Crime of the United States Government against the Negro People* (New York: Civil Rights Congress, 1951): available online, https://babel.hathitrust.org/cgi/pt?id=mdp.39015074197859, accessed 8 July 2022.

"Sorrow, Tears, and Blood" Disavows the Talented Tenth

Everybody run run run
Everybody scatter scatter
Some people lost some bread
Someone nearly die
Someone just die
Police dey come, army dey come
Confusion everywhere
Hey yeah!
Seven minutes later
All don cool down, brother
Police don go away
Army don disappear
Them leave sorrow, tears, and blood
—Fela Kuti, "Sorrow Tears & Blood"

In the first decades of the twenty-first century, the men, women, and children detained, imprisoned, or slain by US police in excessive and grotesque uses of force remain disproportionately Black.

Those killed by police are remembered as innocent civilians, hapless citizens whose lives are traumatized or taken by the racist fear and arrogance of white police and vigilantes authorized to kill with impunity. As martyrs they have no public histories of known organizing or family connections to social justice movements. Yet, their deaths sparked mobilizations, protests, lobbying, and legislation for reform. The homicides of Black Americans by self-deputized whites or white police include the slayings of Sean Bell, Oscar Grant, Trayvon Martin, Akai Gurley, Eric Garner, Michael Brown, Yvette Smith, Aiyana Stanley-Jones, Tamir Rice, John Crawford III, and Tarika Wilson, who died holding her fourteen-month-old son, Sincere, who was also shot but survived. Police and vigilantes have largely not been held accountable for these homicides by the state or police departments, unions, district attorneys, grand juries, and sizable segments of the public. It is that lack of accountability before the law (federal investigations still pending in some cases) for criminal acts by police that incites outrage. That rage sparked protests by multiracial, diverse protestors and organizers.

Conventional progressive leadership and radical confrontations with police and state-sanctioned violence are rarely in alignment during protest movements; this schism reflects divisions among activists and organizers. Fractionation divides leadership from below while top-down or elite leadership from above garners financial donors and government allies. From "the bottom," recognizing betrayals, street and low-income organizers create new forms of political agency and community engagement without financial support and at times, despite the opposition, receive state and nonprofit funding for movement-making.

Spokespersons for the families of those slain by state employees have emerged as national personalities against torture and police violence. Initially, they seem to have deflected attention from formal civil rights leadership privy to corporate-state power. However, there is a long history of diverse actors for rights embedded in one movement. The professionalization of civil rights through philanthropy dates back more than a century. It increased during the Southern civil rights movement in the mid-twentieth century, and today shapes leadership for the reform of mass incarceration in alignment with liberal perspectives on social change. That leadership is now being contested not only by those who deny the existence of white supremacy as a structured evil and so oppose rights (from voting rights to the rights of the impoverished and imprisoned), but also those who find deficient "deliverables" of professional liberal and neo-radical leadership, embedded in corporate-state structures, resistant to change "from below."

The consumer advocate Ralph Nader observed that being raised in American culture often means "growing up corporate."[1] For Blacks, "growing up corporate" in America means training for the elite "talented tenth" with expectations of "Black excellence." One need not be affluent to grow up corporate; one need only adopt a managerial style. When merged with radicalism, the managerial ethos produces a neo-radicalism that, as a form of commercial "left" politics, emulates corporate structures and behavior. As corporate funders finance "radical" conferences and "lecture movements," democratic power-sharing diminishes. Radical rhetoricians and political managerial vanguards supplant grassroots organizers.[2] This elite could either join or expand upon the street protests and prayer vigils. But it would not be allowed to *lead* the grassroots movement that exploded in Ferguson, Missouri. For that movement had a proximity to sorrow, tears, and blood, and the conditions of subjugation tied to a non-celebrity queerness, Blackness, and maternal femaleness familiar with trauma and poverty. Uprisings are not the same as movements; they often refuse gestures of welcome to those considered "outsiders." The civility of muted applause can be easily replaced with jeers towards elites and police. It is insufficient to be in favor of civil rights; one must be in favor of *following*—rather than attempting to lead or control protests in the streets and speech on screens— the most disenfranchised groups.

There is always pushback against unauthorized activism. Police spectacles of racist denial challenged demonstrations against police violence: white NYPD supporters take selfies wearing "I Can Breathe" T-shirts, mocking the shirts donned by protestors of Eric Garner's death by chest compression and chokehold; police wives protest with placards reading "Blue Lives Matter" ("*White* Lives Matter" might have been seen as too provocative), mimicking the "Black Lives Matter" coda.[3]

Others still translate the coda into "All Lives Matter," deflecting from Black vulnerability and agency. For spectacles to usurp the public stage and deflect from serious debates, there must be spectators and performers. For debates to dominate the public arena and foster strategies and the implementation of useful plans, there must be leadership based on democratic power that moves beyond the elites. Such leadership would not be self-serving or pragmatically opportunistic, with a vision limited by liberalism or neo-radicalism; such leadership would be inspired by an agitated mass that might or might not see eye-to-eye with parvenu (Ivy League-trained) or pariah (lesser-educated) professional leaders.

Leadership has to deliver in order to command loyalty. The rise and fall of funding for social welfare programs seems to follow at times the rise and fall of riots, as the political scientist Frances Fox Piven and the sociologist and activist Richard Cloward have argued.[4] Funding in the absence of incisive analyses and agency is not sufficient to distract from traumatizing spectacles replayed constantly through memories and on screens. Narratives and visuals radicalized segments of the public (some prepared by academic texts on mass incarceration). Michael Brown's body lies in the streets for hours without comfort from and to family.[5] Tamir Rice stomps on snowballs; points a toy gun at the sky and several pedestrians; sits under a gazebo by himself; stands up as a police car races into the park towards the pavilion and child; seconds later, Police Officer Timothy Loehmann shoots Tamir. Police offer no assistance to the dying twelve-year-old, yet tackle his teen sister as she runs to his aid and handcuff her in the back of the police car. A federal detective passing by gives the CPR that police are not legally obligated to administer. The boy dies.[6] Eric Garner pants "I can't breathe" nearly a dozen times while white men pin him to the concrete;[7] later only Ramsey Orta, the Latino friend of Garner, who filmed, denounced, and shared the killing with the public is indicted, on an alleged gun-possession charge. John Crawford III, toy gun in hand, does pre-Christmas shopping in Walmart, in an aisle where families stand unalarmed at their carts, and is shot moments later by Ohio police in a state that legalizes unconcealed weapons[8] (elsewhere in the store, running, frantically escaping gunfire, a white shopper, Angela Williams, suffers a fatal heart attack later ruled a homicide).

Graphic illustrations of ghosting Black life and collateral damage to non-Black life coexist with data on incarceration and policing that is less visibly embodied but equally disturbing. There are over 2 million people incarcerated in the United States.[9] The US has less than 5 percent of the global population but 20 percent of its prisoners; Blacks make up nearly 40 percent of the incarcerated, according to the Federal Bureau of Prisons.[10] Racial disparities abound: whites are five times more likely to use drugs, yet Blacks are ten times more likely to be imprisoned for drugs; Blacks' state prison sentences for drug offenses are only slightly less than the sentences whites serve for violent offenses (five years plus). Penal captivity stabilizes the middle class and upper class with job security that factory work and industry can no longer provide. For example, the former African-American president of the largely Black and brown correction officers' union for New York City's Rikers Island jail, Norman Seabrook, built a comfortable lifestyle through overseeing a large complex known for its brutality, particularly against youth of color, before being imprisoned in 2019 for corruption.[11] New York's former governor, Andrew Cuomo, authorized legislation to ban housing teenagers in adult prisons and people under twenty-one in solitary confinement. New York is one of the few states to treat teens as adults and has consequently seen the rise of teen suicides in captivity as youth too poor to post bail wait for trials under horrendous conditions.[12] Policing and incarceration also provide economic growth for investors and professional critics. Interracially and intraracially, violence and economic exploitation are unevenly distributed. Strategies to redress these inequities often seem superficial and underfunded, yet progressives are told to work harder for change. Of course, this state of affairs, this crisis in transformative leadership, did not happen by accident.

Robber Barons and Talented Tenths

During Reconstruction—the period 1863–77 following the American Civil War in which slavery was abolished constitutionally via amendments, except as punishment for a crime— the convict leasing system of forced penal labor emerged after the emancipation proclamation with the December 6, 1865 ratification of the Thirteenth Amendment to the US Constitution (which abolished slavery except for those duly convicted of a crime). Under the convict leasing system, Blacks were essentially worked to death; with a life expectancy shorter than that of the plantation—they died for mining, lumber, and the industrialization of the South. White philanthropists fractionated Black leadership, and filled a void the federal government had created by reneging on its protection of Black life under Reconstruction. The key promise here was safety from racial terrorists, and the ability to work freely. As the sociologist and historian W.E.B. Du Bois notes in *Black Reconstruction in America: 1860–1880* (1935), with its chapters on the "Black proletariat" and the reinstitution of slavery and historical propaganda, misery followed emancipation; federal intervention in the South was in favor of capital, not the worker or laborer or neo-slave.[13]

Robber barons expanded their great wealth (J.P. Morgan had been a war profiteer during the Civil War).[14] Wealthy philanthropists, understanding themselves to be without peers, offered themselves as role models and tutors. They ruled empires securitized by a state that would not police them, but that would deploy violence against those who resisted racial capital. That historical trajectory continues, protected by a buffer zone funded by corporate wealth.

They took a fraction of that wealth accrued from the

postbellum Black slavery of penal servitude (legalized through the Thirteenth Amendment) and endowed educational industries to train the talented tenth. The Black talented tenth has its prototype in every ethnic and racial grouping. Philanthropy fractionated Black leadership, but not just Black leadership. The corporate leaders Rockefeller, Carnegie, Cornell, and others funded colleges and universities (most carry their names) that are predominately white and work to maintain a social order controlled by corporate elites who redirect law, government, and police-military power in their favor.[15] Their training of the educated class would influence the multiple fractions of leadership that constituted a complex opposition to racism and poverty.

The American Baptist Home Mission Society (ABHMS), funded by corporate magnates in 1832, coined the term "talented tenth" in 1896.[16] Martin Luther King Jr.'s alma mater, Morehouse College, is named in honor of the ABHMS secretary Henry Morehouse. The equally prestigious Spelman College in Atlanta is named for the wife of John D. Rockefeller, Laura Spelman Rockefeller. In theory, the worst effects of racist oppression and poverty are mitigated by the philanthropic intervention of capitalists. In practice, their wealth, derived from exploitation and degradation of workers and neo-slaves, uses police-military violence and law for maintenance and expansion. The Fourteenth Amendment, designed for emancipated Blacks, gradually was interpreted by the judiciary to grant political personhood to corporations; thus the US Supreme Court, and also local, state, and federal courts, protected corporate interests and the exploitation of labor.

With the 1903 publication of "The Talented Tenth" in *The Souls of Black Folk*, W.E.B. Du Bois became temporarily a promoter of a talented tenth of "race" men and women modeling the path for a democracy against the "color line." This formally educated Black leadership cadre based in elitism and race management, funded by Blacks as well as state largesse and private benefactors, was trained to remain at Southern, historically Black colleges, in order to serve as both a model for minorities and a buffer zone between emancipated Blacks and the white elite and middle class. Outmigration, desegregation, and affirmative action liberated it and likely diluted its historical mandate as recognized "race leadership." Filtered increasingly through mainstream colleges and universities, the mandate of service trumped activism, particularly radical activism, which seemed unscholarly and "biased."[17]

Many conveniently forget that Du Bois later dismissed the talented tenth as opportunistic and self-serving, and why he recanted.[18] With Fisk degrees and a Harvard PhD, Du Bois had an inside track on the talented tenth. Lesser-educated Blacks might idealize this formation as a set of important celebrities (albeit minor ones in relation to artists, entertainers, and sports heroes). Liberal whites and the tenth themselves might view them, as Du Bois once did, as a "credit to their race," working in the interests of progress. But elites are human; they work within political economies. They have desires and needs; and they want to be paid.

In some ways, Du Bois committed caste suicide as an academic and a mainstream progressive intellectual. Notwithstanding his judgmental study on impoverished Blacks in Philadelphia in which classism shaped dismissive attitudes towards working class and impoverished communities,[19] as he stood closer in solidarity to mass Black suffering, he developed a critical understanding of the (self-)conceit of fractionated leadership, seeing the tenth as a byproduct of racial capitalism and consumerism. His memoirs note that when the US government targeted him for his communism and internationalism, the Black middle class strayed while Black trade unionists stayed with him. He reflects upon his ouster from the National Association for the Advancement of Colored People (NAACP), due to his advocacy for economic justice, lamenting the absence of radical peers. This is sadly ironic, given his marginalization years earlier of the anti-lynching crusader and investigative journalist Ida B.

Wells from the founding of the NAACP. Wells's affinity for, and proximity to, Black suffering was embedded in an incendiary pen and voice as noted in her *Southern Horrors: Lynch Law in All Its Phases* (1892).[20] She once disguised herself as a laborer to enter prisons to take the testimonies of Black males awaiting legal lynching. Wells had fractionated the talented tenth by being an immensely talented, largely self-taught intellectual, traumatized by family loss into a confrontational radicalism at odds with more affluent and assimilated Blacks. She was neither corrupted nor coopted by formal power. Her fraction of the talented tenth was outside of officialdom. Unauthorized, it was marginalized for an affinity to the needs of the most vulnerable, poorer Blacks for whom Wells had great demands, but also much respect, too much to try to manage them. Wells's resistance, depicted in *Crusade for Justice: The Autobiography of Ida B. Wells* (1928), became an art form, an impressive shield against state-sanctioned violence impeding grassroots struggles.[21]

On Anniversaries

In 1965, Martin Luther King Jr. and President Lyndon Johnson represented an interdependent relation between the government and the civil rights movement that led to the signing of the 1965 Voter Rights Act[22] (weakened in 2013 by the Supreme Court decision *Shelby County v. Holder*). Over the course of his remaining years, King became more closely aligned with grassroots activists and publicly rejected capitalism and the imperialist US war in Vietnam (55,000 Americans and 2–3 million Vietnamese died as the war drained public coffers of funding for the "Great Society" programs). Consequently, King's political and economic support from government, corporate funders, and the middle class (Black and non-Black) dissipated. Like Ida B. Wells, King had fractionated the talented tenth with the desires of poor and colonized people. In 1968, the Poor Peoples Campaign, co-led by King, followed the 1963 March on Washington, DC (originally designed for jobs and freedom), materialized in smaller dimensions following his assassination. Impoverished people were King's inspiration and metric for materialized spirituality. Radicalized factions within the talented tenth organized and executed political confrontations that made progress possible. Breaking Jim Crow (state and local laws mandating racial segregation in public facilities), civil disobedience determined the success of the civil rights movements. Activists understood that the 1954 *Brown v. Board of Education* Supreme Court ruling to desegregate required a movement led by Black children and their families, so families organized the 1957 Little Rock, Arkansas integration of schools. Diversity and integration became the official prize for those struggles. Diversity offers stability for a social order riddled by racism; it does not necessarily offer solidarity with the poor. Part of the mandate of talented tenths (in their multiracial, cross-class, and cross-sexuality pluralities) is that they epitomize responsible change: nothing to the "left," or independent of their extension of officialdom, should accrue political value. King began to condemn capitalism and imperialism, and, as had Du Bois, saw civil rights bridges to the mainstream being burned by liberals.[23] (They would be rebuilt after his death, and his voice of reason and passion extending civil rights into human rights and domestic into foreign policies was largely silenced.)

In 1963, Malcolm X publicly criticized an assassinated president who was cautiously moving towards civil rights. Malcolm outraged whites and alienated Blacks in mourning when he referred to John F. Kennedy's death as "chickens coming home to roost."[24] That utterance alluded to alleged CIA involvement in the coup assassination of the African independence leader Patrice Lumumba, who briefly served as the first prime minister of the Republic of Congo. Reserving his grief for the Black lives that mattered most to him, Malcolm's leadership was splintered off from the Nation of Islam. That painful event allowed Malcolm X to grow into Malik el-Shabazz. Malcolm was the master of traumatic reinvention. Before assassination, he had survived parental loss, dismemberment of family, foster care, criminality and pimping, incarceration, demagoguery, sexism, chauvinism. Even as a child, Malcolm seems to have been an old spirit, familiar with sorrow, tears, and blood. Like the other male leaders who fractionated the talented tenth, he was not a saint, but his risk-taking love for people transformed and inspired lives.

Decades ago, as a seminarian on a class trip to Puerto Rico, I met a Puerto Rican senator, blond, blue-eyed, seemingly "white," who spoke about how proud he, as a student, felt as a Black man when Malcolm X debated at Harvard University, militantly denouncing white supremacy.

The mystique of the Kennedy administration, often subsequently referred to as "Camelot" by mainstream press, grew after the 1963 assassination which would facilitate Kennedy's being culturally enshrined as a hero of civil rights.[25] President Lyndon Johnson had Martin Luther King Jr. as teacher and co-architect of the passage of the 1965 voting rights act. King was a *public critic* of Johnson's domestic and foreign policies. Their relationship went beyond theater. Mass movements kept it honest; suffering and morality demanded more. King's assassination in 1968 horrified a nation in which most elites had faded as he marched with sanitation workers and poor people. No counterparts to Martin and Malcolm exist today. That was then; this is now. Yet domestic and international human rights continue to demand opposition to police violence, drone killings of civilians, torture, and the funding of genocidal occupations while opposing Palestine's entry into the International Criminal Court. The space between Martin Luther King Jr. and Malcolm X, whose initially divergent politics converged to inspire freedom movements half a century after their assassinations, cannot be measured. There is a wealth of possibility in their distance from each other and the bridges that can be built between these two icons. To a

significant degree, these heroic insiders who became larg-
er-than-life outsiders are in constant conversation. Which
is a relief: it removes the burdensome fixation on the space
between President Barack Obama and Rev. Al Sharpton,
whose convergent politics privilege the movements they can
manage. Such movements do not possess the capacity for an
expansive concept for change.

Infinity in between the Fractions

With the chorus "Them regular trademark!," the Nigerian
musician-activist Fela Kuti's 1977 song "Sorrow Tears & Blood"
chronicles police-military violence against citizen artists and
government opposition. Fela was politicized by his mother,
Funmilayo Ransome-Kuti. An "aristocrat" by birth, Ransome-
Kuti led Nigerian reform movements in education, anti-pov-
erty initiatives, and women's rights, before her son became
internationally known. Embracing Yoruba marginalized her
from the politically assimilated culture, yet inspired Fela's
music or art as the weapon of the future. Arrested and beaten
scores of times, Fela Kuti lost his mother in 1978, fourteen
months after army troops beat and threw her out of a window
during a raid on her son's compound.[26] The Nigerian government violently repressed Fela and his family and loved
ones, along with other political victims. Still, Fela's cultural
and political movements against (neo)colonialism and state
corruption were influential. He qualified as an international
member of the "talented tenth" through his prestigious family and a London education at the Trinity College of Music,
but left himself vulnerable through radical advocacy.

Fela was also politicized by his African-American lover
Sandra Izsadore. As an artist-activist, Izsadore introduced him
to the writings of Malcolm X.[27] With lyrics that describe how
oppressed people focus on personal achievements—babies,
parties, new homes, wealth—Fela argues that this focus diverts

from or masks fears of fighting for justice and freedom-as-happiness; these fears are rooted in the potential loss of access, affluence, and safety stemming from resistance. Fela's video for "Sorrow Tears & Blood" opens with a golden portrait of the saxophone player standing under the banner "Black President," an unofficial executive presiding over an embattled people. It ends with his assertion: "Music is the weapon of the future."[28] A talented musician, Fela achieved celebrity status independent of political leadership roles, merging art with politics. When Fela fractionates the African and Nigerian talented tenths, as a radical member, he replaces missionary origins with Orisha, Afrobeat, and guerrilla theater. With no public image or ratings to maintain, he and his collaborators pursue convictions outside of conventional society, creating "The Movement of the People." Their failings, imperfections, contradictions, like those of W.E.B. Du Bois, Martin Luther King Jr., and Malcolm X, have been and will be subjected to critiques. It is important to note that given that they did not seek governmental powers, none of these leaders had to develop a plan for liberalism in an apartheid state—as did Nelson Mandela, whose last prison, a spacious home with a swimming pool and white servants (and guards), held regular meetings with Afrikaner leaders and capitalists that shaped the trajectory of poverty for Black South Africa.[29] Fela, as an unofficial president, belonged to the aberrational talented tenth, that fraction of elites that accepted political tutelage from "below," and was transformed into creativity. Leadership is fractionated by proximity to suffering. Departing from the chorus in harmony with liberal corporate-state sponsors, hearing the critiques of radical counterparts, refusing the disciplinary function of role models, allows a mass leadership of people struggling in crossfires (misogyny, homophobia, colorism, and classism) to resist conflating respectability politics with freedom, and resist appending the title of "best and the brightest" to those most disciplined and incentivized to conform to institutional instruction. Collectivism celebrates the brilliance of the wild card. The gifts of the "rabble" can fractionate elitism and flood the market with talents that cannot be easily sold.

Whatever factions or fractions we belong to, we can develop a keener understanding that, despite individual personal character, as a group, elite leadership by itself lacks the political will to self-divest of its economic and existential interests cultivated by the robber barons. The talented tenths are not designed to change, and so by themselves are incapable of altering the trajectory of a national economy based in concentrated capital, a proclivity for war for capital, and a rewriting of historical struggles of democracy that make elites the "natural" leaders of progress. Talented tenths need to be fractionated by collectivities that understand that the call for "jobs," if severed from radical economic justice, will mean more jobs guarding prisoners and borders, militarizing police, deploying troops. Without radical agency, employment remains linked to captivity and violence. Street rebellions cause us to pause and reflect; but in the absence of experiential knowledge about organizing they may become texts for leadership studies that reify or obscure radicalism.

In academia, politics may be overly textual. One can assign *Assata: An Autobiography*, by the former Black Panther leader Assata Shakur, a fugitive in Cuba who escaped from a US prison in the late 1970s and maintains that she was falsely accused of killing a trooper, and a target of the FBI's murderous COINTELPRO policing. At the same time, one might hesitate as faculty to organize a teach-in about the significance of the FBI placing Shakur on its terror list alongside members of al-Qaeda. That list presents as a drone kill list. Tragically, thousands of civilians have been killed by US drones in the Middle East, more than died by terrorism on 9/11.

History Is Instructive

Of the leaders cited here, only the middle-class ones with PhDs—Du Bois and King—had to re-educate themselves in order to increase their analysis and agency. For Wells and Malcolm, their personal and familial struggles with dispossession—both were impoverished, self-raised orphaned children—gave them experiential knowledge that expanded their perspective, flexibility, and passion. Unfiltered by family structure, money, or caste, the experiences of Black life are more traumatic. There is a version of the "talented tenth" in every ethnic and economic group. In a consumer society, multi-ethnic elites are alienated from traumatic suffering tied to poverty and racism. Reform seems reasonable to some due to their distance from daily denigration and violence. Practical politics and freedom reduced to personal achievement or idealism become attainable goals. "Inequality" thus becomes a euphemism for oppression. Profits from policing, captivity, warfare, and military technology go without critique in party-driven politics. Civilian deaths by drones and/or genocides are often under-reported in United States news and rarely discussed in classrooms and conventional media. Yet, when centuries-old phenomena crowd the present moment, suffering can fractionate any organized entity, even a "great power" Western democracy.

Fractionation happens because Black people are taxed in their desires to love: to love their children and their selves. Reform policies do not bring back dead babies, at home or abroad. So, the void between loss and justice is not spanned. Legislative regulations, or judicial interpretation, police enforcement, and managerial alleviation of some forms of stress while instituting forms of dependency and dishonor mean that Black families suffer for their children's futures and battle as they bury them. History is always instructive.

Ida B. Wells pioneered an anti-lynching movement in 1892 only after the father of her two-year old goddaughter was lynched. Professional, funded civil-rights leadership found Wells too difficult to deal with in combatting lynching, although they needed her militancy in order to be effective. Mamie Till-Mobley defied law and respectability by having an open-casket funeral at Roberts Temple Church of God in Christ, Chicago, for her mutilated teenage son Emmett, murdered by self-deputized whites. Mass attendance at Emmett's funeral on September 3, 1955 is now credited, coming months before Rosa Parks's refusal to give up her segregated seat on December 1, 1955, as a catalyst for the modern civil rights movement. The NAACP failed to manage Mamie Till-Mobley's grief and rage and channel it into legislative reforms. Suffering rebels resist: they write, sleep, watch screens, self-medicate, go to the streets. Resistance is spontaneous or organized, or alternates between the two. It is never bureaucratic. Bureaucracies do not grieve; they offer protocol and grief management. Tensions between autonomous activism and bureaucratic reforms are inevitable. Spaces between old and new advocates shrink or expand. Activism still cannot raise the dead. Humbled, it displays the discipline and autonomy to transcend multicultural "talented tenths."

There are endless possibilities within and between the talents of leaders who emerge, one after another, in our collective treks towards freedom. Some say that there are two types of infinity, a lesser and a greater one. The lesser is the sequential march of leaders. The greater infinity exists within the expanse between leaders. Those infinite spaces for freedom exist within the gaps between leaders, beyond the control of funders or the corporate state. That is where radicals work, fractionating the talented tenths, exploring the void, and fabricating armor for the future.

Notes to Chapter 2

1   Ralph Nader, acceptance speech, Green Party National Convention, UCLA Campus, August 19, 1996, https://www.cs.cmu.edu/afs/cs/user /jab/mosaic/pol/naccept.html.

2   See Joy James, "Radicalizing Black Feminism," *Race and Class* 40 (1999);

and Joy James, *Seeking the Beloved Community: A Feminist Race Reader* (Albany, NY: SUNY Press, 2013), 59.

3   Alfred Ng, "NYPD Supporters Wear 'I Can Breathe' Hoodies at City Hall, Sparking War with Opposing Demonstrators," *New York Daily News*, December 19, 2014, https://www.nydailynews.com/new-york/nyc-crime/suspect-arrested-assault-cops-brooklyn-bridge-article-1.2051361.

4   See Frances Fox Piven and Richard Cloward, *Regulating the Poor: The Functions of Public Welfare* (New York: Random House, 1971).

5   After being fatally shot by Ferguson Police Officer Darren Wilson at 12:02 p.m. on August 9, 2014, Michael Brown's body was left for approximately four hours at the crime scene: United States Department of Justice, "Memorandum: Department of Justice Report Regarding the Criminal Investigation into the Shooting Death of Michael Brown by Ferguson, Missouri Police Officer Darren Wilson," March 4, 2015, https://www.justice.gov/sites/default/files/opa/press-releases/attachments/2015/03/04/doj_report_on_shooting_of_michael_brown_1.pdf.

6   Tamir Rice was shot by Cleveland Police Officer Timothy Loehmann on November 22, 2014; Judge Ronald B. Adrine wrote in his judgment entry, "There appears to be little if any time reflected on the video for Rice to react or respond to any verbal or audible commands given from Loehmann and [Police Officer Frank] Garmback from their Zone Car between the time that they first arrived and the time that Rice was shot. Literally, the entire encounter is over in an instant": Cleveland Municipal Court, "Judgment Entry on the Tamir Rice Case," Cleveland, Ohio, June 11, 2015, https://www.scribd.com/document/268410100/Judgment-entry-on-Tamir-Rice-case. For critiques of the state's refusal to prosecute Loehmann, see Da'Shaun Harrison, Joy James, and Samaria Rice, "'Justifiable Police Homicide' and the Ruse of American Justice," *Scalawag*, March 8, 2022, https://scalawagmagazine.org/2022/03/doj-tamir-rice-civil-rights-investigation/.

7   Eric Garner was killed on July 17, 2014 after New York Police Office Daniel Pantaleo put him in a prohibited chokehold while arresting him on suspicion of selling single cigarettes. No charges were made.

8   John Crawford III was fatally shot by Police Officer Sean Williams on August 5, 2014, while shopping in Walmart in Beavercreek, Ohio: Jon Swaine, "Ohio Walmart Video Reveals Moments before Officer Killed John Crawford," *Guardian*, September 25, 2014, https://www.theguardian.com/world/2014/sep/24/surveillance-video-walmart-shooting-john-crawford-police.

9   See e.g. Innocence Project New Orleans, "Mass Incarceration and Racial Oppression," accessed September 29, 2022, https://ip-no.org/what-we-do/advocate-for-change/mass-incarceration-and-racial-oppression/.

10 See Federal Bureau of Prisons, "Inmate Race," September 24, 2022, https://www.bop.gov/about/statistics/statistics_inmate_race.jsp; and Wendy Sawyer and Peter Wagner, "Mass Incarceration: The Whole Pie 2022," *Prison Policy Initiative*, March 14, 2022, https://www.prisonpolicy.org/reports/pie2022.html.

11   US Attorney's Office, Southern District of New York, "Norman Seabrook, President of Correction Officers Benevolent Association, Sentenced to 58 Months in Prison for Accepting Bribes in Exchange for Investing Union Money in New York-Based Hedge Fund," Department of Justice, February 8, 2019, https://www.justice.gov/usao-sdny/pr /norman-seabrook-president-correction-officers-benevolent -association-sentenced-58.

12   David Howard King, "With 'Raise the Age,' Cuomo Continues Push to Reform Juvenile Justice," *Gotham Gazette*, February 19, 2015, https://www .gothamgazette.com/government/5583-with-raise-the-age-cuomo -continues-push-to-reform-juvenile-justice.

13   W.E.B. Du Bois, *Black Reconstruction in America: 1860–1880* (New York: Free Press, 1999; originally pub. 1935).

14   Jim Hightower, "J.P. Morgan: The Man and the Bank," *Progressive Magazine*, November 29, 2013.

15   Sean Braswell, "US Higher Education's Great Robber Barons," *OZY*, September 5, 2014.

16   See Evelyn Brooks Higginbotham, *Righteous Discontent: The Women's Movement in the Black Baptist Church, 1880–1920* (Cambridge, MA: Harvard University Press, 1994).

17   W.E.B. Du Bois, *The Souls of Black Folk*, ed. Brent Hayes Edwards (Oxford: Oxford World's Classics, 2008; originally pub. 1903).

18   See Joy James, *Transcending the Talented Tenth: Black Leaders and American Intellectualism* (New York: Routledge, 1996).

19   See W.E.B. Du Bois, *The Philadelphia Negro* (Philadelphia, PA: University of Pennsylvania Press, 1899).

20   Ida B. Wells, *Southern Horrors: Lynch Law in All Its Phases* (New York: New York Age, 1892).

21   Ida B. Wells, *Crusade for Justice: The Autobiography of Ida B. Wells*, ed. Alfreda M. Duster, 2nd edn (Chicago, IL: University of Chicago Press, 2020).

22   Jessie Kratz, "LBJ and MLK," *Pieces of History* blog, National Archives, February 28, 2018, https://prologue.blogs.archives.gov/2018/02/28 /lbj-and-mlk/.

23   Zaid Jilani, "Martin Luther King Jr. Celebrations Overlook His Critiques of Capitalism and Militarism," *The Intercept*, January 18, 2016, https:// theintercept.com/2016/01/18/martin-luther-king-jr-celebrations -overlook-his-critiques-of-capitalism-and-militarism/.

24   See Michael Kirkpatrick, "'Chickens Coming Home To Roost': Malcolm X," accessed October 17, 2022, YouTube video, https://www.youtube .com/watch?v=oD6aX3dHR2k.

25   Patricia Sullivan, "How Robert F. Kennedy Shaped His Brother's Response to Civil Rights," *TIME*, August 11, 2021, https://time .com/6089512/robert-kennedy-civil-rights-alabama/.

26   Editors of the *Encyclopaedia Britannica*, "Funmilayo Ransome-Kuti," *Encyclopaedia Britannica*, October 21, 2022, https://www.britannica.com /biography/Funmilayo-Ransome-Kuti.

27   See Anon., "Sandra Izsadore and Fela," *Fela*, accessed September 29,

2022, https://felakuti.com/us/news/sandra-izadore; and Black Power Media, "Sandra Izsadore the Woman Who Gave Fela Kuti His Politics and Shaped Afrobeat," accessed September 29, 2022, YouTube video, https://www.youtube.com/watch?v=kyw-LWA5FPk.

28   Fela Kuti, "Sorrow Tears & Blood (Original Extended Version)," accessed October 17, 2022, YouTube video, https://www.youtube.com /watch?v=tj1wpNuQRaM&ab.

29   Greg Myre, "Nelson Mandela's Prison Adventures," *NPR*, July 2, 2013, https://www.npr.org/sections/parallels/2013/07/01/197674511 /nelson-mandelas-prison-adventures.

3 Seven Lessons in One Abolitionist Notebook: On Airbrushing Revolution

When you kill a living being, you kill yourself and everyone else as well.
—Thich Nhat Hanh[1]

In a 1990s interview, the late Vietnamese Buddhist monk Thich Nhat Hanh, who convinced Rev. Martin Luther King Jr. to publicly denounce the US imperialist war in Vietnam, noted that it was essential to prepare to stop a war ten years before it began. To stop wars, one must anticipate them, discuss and strategize against them years before they manifest on the ground. The war to prepare for is not just the one external to our endeavors, it includes the conflicts and contradictions within our endeavors to stop war and captivity. I have learned from young Black doctoral students who study violence and organize in non-elite communities that "war is not a metaphor."

In his nineteenth-century treatise *On War*, the Prussian general Carl von Clausewitz describes war as "an act of violence intended to compel our opponent to fulfill our will." Black/African and Indigenous peoples were terrorized as enslaved and colonized *opponents to empire and war*. Conquest was war. Slavery was war. Convict leasing was war. Sharecropping was war.[2] COINTELPRO was war.[3] The "war on drugs" criminalized anti-war protestors as "pothead hippies" and Black radicals as "junkies" in a counter-insurrectionist war. Mass incarceration—where deaths classified as "suicide" or "natural" include police murders and medical neglect and life spans shortened and disfigured—is war. At a NYC library lecture, Black survivors of the 1971 Attica Prison rebellion described their bullet wounds and torture scars after the government waged war against a human rights uprising from captives. Their anguished narrative claimed that they took hostages, weeks after George Jackson's 1971 death in San Quentin, igniting a rebellion seen around the world, yet academics airbrushed them out of history.[4] Although alliances between abolitionists and rebels are essential, the airbrushing of revolutionary struggles continues to undermine coalitions and political convergence.

There are global political prisoners on every continent. Popularized US abolitionism, which is exported as progressivism around the world, tends to minimize the *agency* of US political prisoners. Those incarcerated and tortured for decades as prisoners of war should be released and supported. Their names—as noted on the website of the Jericho Movement (which campaigns for the "recognition of the fact that political prisoners and prisoners of war exist inside of the United States, despite the United States government's continued denial")[5]—are more familiar than those incarcerated from more recent rebellions or those killed by vigilantes or the state, or who largely remain anonymous.[6] Even in advocacy for freeing political prisoners, we are warned not to get "too political," i.e., not to raise the issue of COINTELPRO at hearings because the state mandates that there was and continues to be no legitimacy in rebellion against its violence and its exploitation and degradation of targeted communities. Concerns about alienating police/parole boards, funders, and a sympathetic public promote airbrushing as a "responsible" task as activists note the urgency of freeing *all* people given that the pandemic functions as a death sentence in prison.

Angela Davis introduced me to prison abolitionism in the 1990s when I was a postdoc Ford Foundation fellow at the history of consciousness program at the University of California, Santa Cruz, when she asked me to organize a 1998 prototype for Critical Resistance at the University of Colorado Boulder (CU-Boulder).[7] Alongside several thousand attendees at the "Unfinished Liberation" conference, I learned about the prison–industrial complex. Seven lessons studied then and in the years that followed are noted below.

#1. The parental ethos of academic bodies filters professionalism and conformity into activism, and veils inherent contradictions. When few pro-radical public platforms critique progressivism, little value is recognized left of the "left." Radical analyses are then dismissed as anti-progressive distractions aiding the repressive right. With public transparency, historical abolitionists debated strategies across the ideological spectrum; this likely enhanced their effectiveness.

#2. Black political prisoners received the anthology from the 1998 prison conference with thank-you notes remarking on the disappearance of their agency. They thus inspired future anthologies, shaped by students, of the writings of captive revolutionaries. Unlike the mass of the incarcerated, imprisoned radical activists cannot be easily portrayed (or led) as a purely victim caste. Influenced by decades of captivity and violent trauma, their intellectualism offers analyses assimilated into (and altered by) progressivism's multicultural reforms.

#3. On the political continuum, US conservative-centrist-progressive "advocacy democracy" works for reforms with an anti-Black racism that has structured democracy's evolution through: an *anti-abolitionist* revolutionary war that blocked the expansion of the 1772 *Somerset v. Stewart* ruling, which emancipated a Black slave brought to Britain from colonial America; an *anti-abolitionist* Thirteenth Amendment that codifies slavery to prison; an *anti-abolitionist* Fourteenth Amendment that transfers Black political personhood (and social standing) to corporations.

#4. On continuum, extreme political positions *appear* as essential differences. On-continuum reforms (such as decarceration) diversify elites in government, corporate, nonprofit, academic, and policing sectors; they do not decentralize power or custodial care. Leaning into privileged structures, which historically create, manage, tabulate, or ameliorate crises, requires leaning back from the control and radicalism of those most vulnerable to police and prison violence.

#5. Popularizing prison and police abuses through books and reports, television series and podcasts appears to deflect from off-continuum resistance and theories of "revolution," "rebellion," and "violence" in both resistance and repression.

#6. Off-continuum grief and suprarational demands to state authorities—"Resurrect the children you kill"—exceed the capacities of on-continuum politics.

#7. Expanding capacities for change, off-continuum "leaderless" maroons—policed or captive youth, Black-identified (maroon societies were often multi-ethnic or multiracial), queer, maternals calling out "Black Love"—save their own lives and enable those of others.

Academic Abolitionist Censorship

"Unfinished Liberation," the abolitionist conference at CU-Boulder, which Davis named after one of her 1969 lectures at the University of California, Los Angeles, was originally designed as a prototype for Critical Resistance held at the University of California, Berkeley that September. However, due to the presence of Black Panther Party veterans, CU-Boulder's largest, most expensive conference at the time became a zone of conflict between radical Panthers and the University of California (UC) leadership collective that accompanied Davis to Boulder. I invited the Black Panthers and former political prisoners K. Kim Holder, Safiya Bukhari, and Gabriel Torres; the Panther Lee Lew-Lee was invited to screen his documentary *All Power to the People! The Black Panther Party and Beyond*.[8] All Panther invitees were recommended by Holder, an academic and Panther trained in Harlem by Assata Shakur. UC academics had requested the conference in part as an organizing endeavor to prepare students and activists for the launch at UC-Berkeley. Their entourage was multiracial; no members of the Panther party were present. No Panthers or political prisoners had been named on the list of invitees sent by UC academics. Davis did not then identify as a member of the BPP, according to Dhoruba Bin Wahad.[9] Along with a small coalition of Black and white undergrads who dedicated unpaid labor, I too was exhausted by tasks and a demanding funder (faculty senate) commanding meetings to justify the budget, by the lack of discussion about incarceration, and by the sidelining of local activists, largely based in the working-class city of Denver and not the more expensive Boulder—as an assistant professor I did not fight vigorously to include their experience, analyses, and politics. The Asian-American woman chairing ethnic studies used the conference to raise the profile of her department, but vetoed invitations for academic spouses to the dinner held in Davis's honor. (Academics on the planning committee wanted their spouses to meet Davis, a popular and iconic persona. In protest, a number of academics boycotted the dinner given that their spouses or partners could not attend.) The noticeable empty seats did not deter Davis, who graciously spoke to those who attended the opening dinner.

The ethnic studies chair also rejected Elmer "Geronimo" Pratt, a veteran of Black Panther Party and the Black Liberation Army. Pratt led the LA chapter of the Panthers and became a political prisoner—a prisoner of war—after he was framed by the FBI and LAPD. His trial and Davis's took place at the same time. Incarcerated in jail for seventeen months on a conspiracy trial based on the use of weapons registered in her name by Jonathan Jackson in August 7, 1971 at the Marin County Courthouse raid (see below, pp. 154–5), Davis's 1971–72 trial dominated (inter)national news. Pratt's trial lacked significant coverage by investigative reporters. He would be imprisoned for twenty-seven years for a murder he did not commit. The FBI and police withheld exculpatory evidence. Pratt's attorneys—Johnnie Cochrane, Kathleen Cleaver, and Stuart Hanlon—litigated for his exoneration. For academics, Pratt lacked academic credentials and celebrity status, and although Pratt would have provided a valuable additional keynote, academics demurred. (The US government provided a financial settlement for Pratt as compensation for the government railroading him into prison.)[16]

Days before the conference, Davis warned me in a late-night call that the prison activist—and former Black Panther Party chairwoman—Elaine Brown would sue me if I did not withdraw Lew-Lee's documentary from the conference and essentially oust him from the forum. The nearly two-hour film, dominated by male voices but also featuring Safiya Bukhari, Kathleen Cleaver, Yuri Kochiyama, and Sarah McClendon, included a brief clip of a former male Panther political prisoner disparaging Elaine Brown's relationship with Jay Richard Kennedy, an author and screenwriter who was also an FBI spy. The threat to airbrush from "Unfinished Liberation" knowledge of the CIA's impressive reach into Black radical politics was rudely rebuffed (but later accepted for *The Angela Y. Davis Reader* when I agreed to delete any reference to Gloria Steinem's work with the CIA, as she was raising funds for Critical Resistance). FedEx delivered the legal cease-and-desist papers. I delivered and explained them to the vice provost's office, exiting as white male administrators received them with laughter. Safiya Bukhari, Lee Lew-Lee, Gabe Torres, and K. Kim Holder, all recognized members of the Black Panther Party, were not on the list of invitees sent by UC academics who requested the conference; as noted above, they had been suggested by Holder. In spite of the cease-and-desist papers, no litigation ultimately followed the screening of *All Power to the People!*, which was well received.

On the final day of "Unfinished Liberation," which drew some 2,000 participants, Angela Davis's closing keynote publicly chastised Lee Lew-Lee, without naming him: she denounced the "old trope" of blaming enslaved Black women for sleeping with white slave masters and betraying slave rebellions. The keynote inverted Davis's 1971 article "Reflections on the Black Woman's Role in a Community of Slaves,"[11] which is dedicated to the prison theorist, militarist, and Black Panther field marshal George Jackson (whom Davis considered her husband) following his *assassination* (Michel Foucault's terminology).[12] Repurposed, the article was no longer an analysis of how Black women fought alongside Black men for freedom *in community*. It became over the years known primarily as a Black feminist manifesto, castigating the 1965 Moynihan Report on "Black matriarchy"[13] and highlighting the centrality and indispensability of Black feminist leadership. (Both functions could have been simultaneously possible and highlighted.) Davis would state that the article was always about Black feminism but she did not realize this when she wrote it in her jail cell. Insurrection faded. Jackson maintained from the site of prison that the US was proto-fascist; from the site of the university, Davis asserted it was not. Struggle became conflict not war. The defense of Brown foreshadowed the future of disciplinarian endeavors or censorship to protect forms of leadership and political advocacy.

Elite politics are progressive-centrist, advocating civil and human rights mandates that are well funded and popular in networks built within academia and celebrity. Those politics include pragmatic compromises. In a 2014 interview with the SNCC civil rights leader Julian Bond, Davis asserted that President Barack Obama "identifies with" the "Black radical tradition"[14]—a tradition shaped by militantly principled and risk-taking leaders such as Martin Luther King Jr., Fannie Lou Hamer, Malcolm X, Ella Baker, Robert Williams, Rosa Parks, and Assata Shakur. Their radical tradition opposed capitalism and imperialism. As the US's first Black imperial president, who raised considerable corporate funds for his presidential campaign,[15] Obama, as POTUS 44, decreed that "Black success" under capitalism equals "Black Power" (akin to Nixon's "Black capitalism equals Black power"). As the Panthers noted, the betrayal of revolutionary struggle would come from within and without.

Airbrushing Revolution in Abolition

Two decades after the 1998 "Unfinished Liberation" conference, a generation of cultivated young scholars and rogue
young intellectual activists were shaping and leading abolition. Some accumulated "prestige and power," along with
wealth (becoming what I came to call "movement millionaires"), steeped in portfolio management from funds (at
times derived from finance capital) and powerful networks
intersecting state, corporation, and academia, all purport-
edly organizing against violence and captivity. For example, a prominent abolitionist known for his work in the Bay
Area and the Ella Baker Center, the abolitionist Van Jones,
accepted funding from the right-wing Koch Brothers; he also
provided stealth editing for the Trump presidency police
and prison reform policies promoted by the presidential
aide and son-in-law Jared Kushner. The "Sammy Davis Jr.
Conundrum" reflects a performer who can do benefits for
radical causes—Angela Davis's legal defense—and reactionary causes—Richard Nixon's re-election—while seeking progress. Dual relationships in abolition politics have existed
for centuries as "pragmatic compromises." The billionaire
Jeff Bezos, who leads Amazon's exploitation of workers and
denies their rights to decent working environments and
living wages, included Jones's nonprofit in a $100 million
award dispersed in the wake of the BLM protests.[16] Complex
critiques of current pragmatic compromises between abolitionists, corporations, and the state and reactionary political
personas exist; but they are rare.[17] The June 2020 Panther
letter[18] (see below, pp. 65–6) addressed some of the concerns
of an online organization called "Black Like Mao" (which
might have had links to the Black Revolutionary Guard
organization), which had asserted that academics/pundits
would inform on militant or radical activists to the state.[19]
Elite academics inherently are *not* a revolutionary cadre and
tend to function as anti-revolutionary (hostile to revolution,

but distinct from police/state forces that are counter-revo-lutionary, such as the FBI and CIA). Academics rarely per-sonally know revolutionaries except for political prisoners who have obtained high profiles or have been profiled in the research, writing, and conference-hosting done by aca-demics and the academy. Radical, on-the-ground activ-ists work with considerable risk and no wealth. Elites are given more protections (employment, legal connections, platform punditry) than they tend to share with or offer to under-resourced radicals; elites also tend to offer more peer-recognition to progressive (or conservative) associates than to working-class militants. The political economy of social justice produces employment, honoraria, royalties, and stellar salaries, generating personal wealth or portfolio management with low risk of surveillance and repression. Progressive academics performed for Obama the labor that Van Jones provided to Trump: airbrush to transform rev-olutionary demands for power and community-defense into "non-reformist reforms" or "revolutionary reforms" (oxymorons). Before abolitionism, there was revolution-ary struggle. Alliances exist between the two: Panther free breakfast programs—mutual aid—created a model that now serves public schools; yet water/food/housing/educa-tion security and scarcity continue to plague towns, com-munities, cities, families. The catalyst for change was always risk-taking organizers, artists, and teachers who challenged the status quo. COINTELPRO/police violence targeted *rev-olutionary* capacity and political independent thought. In their December 4, 1969, predawn Chicago raid, the FBI/Chicago Police Department assassinated the Panther lead-ers Fred Hampton and Mark Clark. Hampton gifted us with revolution as the Rainbow Coalition: white power to white people, brown power to brown people, yellow power to yel-low people, red power to red people, Black Power to Black people: *all power* to the people, none to police, or (petty-) bourgeois politicians and pundits aligned with the state.[20]

Elite or hegemonic forms of abolition could block these powers from accruing to working class and impoverished and captive militants, by siphoning the meanings of radicalism away from the analyses of the most vulnerable and militant and redirecting endeavors towards reform of political norms.

Notes to Chapter 3

1   Thich Nhat Hanh, *Teachings on Love*, Sounds True W560D, 2 x CD, disc 2.

2   See *Vice*, "Genealogist Who Tracks Down Modern-Day Slavery Practices," February 27, 2018, YouTube video, https://www.youtube.com/watch?v=6OXbJHsKB3I.

3   See Branko Marcetic, "The FBI's Secret War," *Jacobin*, August 31, 2016, https://jacobin.com/2016/08/fbi-cointelpro-new-left-panthers-muslim-surveillance/.

4   See e.g. Heather Ann Thompson and Khalil Gibran Muhammad, "Between the Lines: Heather Ann Thompson & Khalil Gibran Muhammad," Schomburg Center, September 9, 2016, https://livestream.com/schomburgcenter/events/6114428.

5   Jericho Movement, "About," accessed October 3, 2022, https://www.thejerichomovement.com/about.

6   See Amelia McDonell-Parry, "Ferguson Activist Claims Son Was 'Lynched' as Police Investigate His Death as Suicide," *Rolling Stone*, November 2, 2018, https://www.rollingstone.com/culture/culture-news/ferguson-danye-jones-death-lynching-suicide-melissa-mckinnies-751275/.

7   See http://criticalresistance.org/.

8   Lee Lew-Lee, dir., *All Power to the People! The Black Panther Party and Beyond* (1996), available online, https://www.youtube.com/watch?v=pKvE6_s0jy0, accessed October 26, 2022.

9   See Black Power Media, "Dhoruba Bin Wahad on Assata Shakur, Angela Davis and COINTELPRO," accessed December 5, 2022, YouTube video, https://www.youtube.com/watch?v=qwMISdg0JAs; see also Angela Davis's Foreword in Stephen Shames and Ericka Huggins, *Comrade Sisters: Women of the Black Panther Party* (Woodbrige: ACC Art Books, 2022), 19, where Davis writes she was a "rank-and-file member" of the Black Panther Party.

10 Eric Greve, "Geronimo Pratt (1947–2011)," *BlackPast*, April 1, 2012, https://www.blackpast.org/african-american-history/pratt-geronimo-1947-2011/.

11 Angela Davis, "Reflections on the Black Woman's Role in a Community of Slaves," *The Black Scholar* (December 1971).

12 See Michel Foucault, Catharine von Bülow, and Daniel Defert, "The

Masked Assassination," trans. Sirene Harb, in *Warfare in the American Homeland: Policing and Prison in a Penal Democracy*, ed. Joy James (Durham, NC: Duke University Press, 2007); available online, https:// abolitionjournal.org/wp-content/uploads/2020/06/Joy-James-ed. -Warfare-in-the-American-Homeland_-Policing-and-Prison-in-a -Penal-Democracy-Duke-University-Press-2007.pdf, accessed October 12, 2022.

13   Daniel Patrick Moynihan, *The Negro Family: The Case For National Action* (Washington, DC: Office of Planning and Research, United States Department of Labor, 1965).

14   Julian Bond and Angela Davis, "Reflections on Brown," UVA Arts and Sciences, accessed October 3, 2022, https://blackleadership.virginia .edu/transcript/davis-angela.

15   Angie Drobnic Holan, "Obama Campaign Financed by Large Donors, Too," *PolitiFact*, April 22, 2010, https://www.politifact.com/factchecks /2010/apr/22/barack-obama/obama-campaign-financed-large -donors-too/.

16   Oliver Darcy, "Bezos Donates $100 Million Each to CNN Contributor Van Jones and Chef Jose Andres," *CNN Business*, July 21, 2021, https:// www.cnn.com/2021/07/20/media/van-jones-bezos-100-million/index .html.

17   See Jane Meyer, "New Koch," *New Yorker*, January 25, 2016, https://www .newyorker.com/magazine/2016/01/25/new-koch.

18   Kathleen Cleaver, Sekou Odinga, Cleo Silvers, Jamal Joseph, Yasmeen Majid, Victor Houston, Paula Peebles, Bilal Sunni Ali, Jihad Abdulmumit, Dhoruba Bin Wahad, K. Kim Holder, Harold Welton, Harold Taylor, Arthur League, Rashad Byrdsong, Khalid Raheem, and Ashanti Alston, "An Open Letter from the Original Black Panther Party," June 26, 2020, https://abolitionjournal.org /an-open-letter-from-the-original-black-panther-party/.

19   Black Like Mao [formerly Black Revolutionary Guard], "Was Angela Davis a Panther," blogpost, July 8, 2020, https://blacklikemao.medium .com/was-angela-davis-a-panther-8b16c6269023.

20   See *History.com* editors, "This Day in History: December 04 1969— Police Kill Two Members of the Black Panther Party," *History*, November 13, 2009, https://www.history.com/this-day-in-history /police-kill-two-members-of-the-black-panther-party; and Jacqueline Serrato, "Fifty Years of Fred Hampton's Rainbow Coalition," *South Side Weekly*, September 27, 2019, https://southsideweekly.com/fifty-years -fred-hampton-rainbow-coalition-young-lords-black-panthers/.

4   Anti-Racist Algorithms in Abolition Alchemy

Slaveholders cited Black militancy as a justification for their brutality. In response, late-eighteenth-century abolitionists would rally around the image of a kneeling supplicant begging to be recognized as a man and a brother; as if the condemnation of evil required the meek innocence of its victims. That icon of abjection has shaped the prevailing understanding of bondage and race to this day.

—Vincent Brown, *Tacky's Revolt: The Story of an Atlantic Slave War*[1]

Hegemonic Algorithms

An algorithm can be as simple as a brownie or kombucha recipe. As a list of instructions, it permits the completion of a task. Yet, what if the task—social justice—requires rewriting the algorithms we have inherited in our struggles against US racism? In its June 19, 2020 campaign "calling on Facebook corporate advertisers to pause ads for July 2020," the nonprofit Color of Change argued for the multi-billionaire corporation "to do the right thing and make their platform safer for the millions of Black people that use it." From their "monetization of hate speech to discrimination in their algorithms to the proliferation of voter suppression to the silencing of Black voices, Facebook has refused to take responsibility for hate, bias, and discrimination growing on their platforms." Corporate investment allowed the platform to accumulate "$70B of revenue from corporations every year," according to Color of Change, which argued that these investors could have "their businesses featured on Facebook's platforms side-by-side with racist attacks on Black people"[2]—an incendiary association following the public's growing awareness of the police/vigilante murders of George Floyd, Ahmaud Arbery, and Breonna Taylor; a boycott to demand Facebook to monitor and remove hate speech was thus reasonable. The demand to dismantle Facebook as a monopoly that violated public interest and (antiquated) anti-trust legislation was not made. (In July 2020, the US Congress held hearings on the tech titans Facebook, Google, Apple, and Amazon, with conservatives decrying "censorship" and liberals seeking to reinvigorate anti-trust laws.)[3] The important call to hold Facebook accountable—as a platform that boosts revenues by promoting social and political violence—threatened to "shame" Facebook into progressive neutrality by diminishing its stock value. Just as Facebook has an algorithm of racism, an algorithm of anti-racism is deployed to correct it. However, the progressive algorithm of *anti-racism* aligns with—rather than disrupts—the reactionary algorithm of Facebook's racism. Both are structured to the same metric or metaparadigm. Both monetize their endeavors, amplify influential platforms to please funders, and reassure the general public of a stable (democratic) structure that can accommodate the "common good" without the need for revolutionary struggle. It is not just the corporate ethos or deference to capitalism that structures the two antagonists. It is the selective memory of the history of anti-racism that joins the two to define the parameters of popularized anti-racist struggle.

The dominant algorithm for anti-racism and contemporary abolitionism are traceable to eighteenth-century abolitionism. The insurgence of liberation is traced to the abolitionism encircling the Civil War, in which some 200,000 Black Americans fought. The dominant algorithm rejects analyses of slavery as actual war (as opposed to a metaphor for war). Analyses of white supremacy and captivity as war extend to postbellum lynching, the convict leasing system, sharecropping, COINTELPRO, and mass incarceration. Terror is a technique of warfare and functions within asymmetrical war (e.g., US-funded Contras).[4] The dominant algorithm of anti-racism airbrushes war; rebellions thus become "protests" that can be resolved in the dominate algorithm, rather than revolutionary struggles that require the rewriting of the algorithm of anti-racism.

The popularized algorithm elevates passive Black suffering over Black militancy and resistance and has thus stymied the development of an algorithm of community defense against the violence of civilians or police. Prominent abolitionists lived among and fought alongside the Black working class and laboring poor—those most vulnerable to poverty, captivity, and violent death. Today, the wealth of Black elites and the concept of Black success under capitalism as "Black Power" skew solidarity struggles as liberal hegemony and investment portfolios shape anti-racist politics and policies. The activist and anthropologist Archie Mafeje has argued that general hegemony is "opposed to any real change in *power relations*" because in Southern Africa powerful progressives were "prepared to be ruled by" others yet "reserve[d] the right to *reign*".[5] Derrick Bell's "interest convergence" theory likewise argues that US civil rights gains progressed when compatible to the needs of elites.[6] The ban on the African National Congress (ANC) party was lifted in 1990, the year that Nelson Mandela was formally released from prison. In 1993, Chris Hani, the general secretary of the South African Communist Party and the chief of staff of uMkhonto we Sizwe, the ANC's paramilitary wing (founded by Nelson Mandela), was assassinated in his driveway. Hani's popularity equaled that of Mandela's among the Black electorate. Six months after Hani's death, Nelson Mandela and F.W. de Klerk shared the Nobel Peace Prize. Most Americans remember 1993 as the year that Toni Morrison received the Nobel Prize in Literature; the symbolism of Black success as a victory over anti-racism overshadowed Hani's murder and the lack of redistribution of land and resources to the South African masses. *The dominant algorithm minimizes wars against dissidents and their disappearances.* Against the proliferation of conservative (in fact, reactionary) prosecutors, attorneys general, and judges (Trump appointed over 200 to the bench)[7] that protect police violence, tools designated for horizontal or communal/family violence—education and therapeutic intervention—do not seem effective. The nonprofit investigative journalism organization ProPublica's use of declassified NYPD substantiated abuses reveals predatory behavior rewarded with promotions and pay increases.[8] The rise in gun violence and civilian homicides in New York City is accompanied by the NYPD's 68 percent decrease in arrests in Black/brown neighborhoods, those most afflicted by civilian and cop violence. The FBI's "IRON FIST" program uses counterintelligence to conduct surveillance and persecution of dissidents, focusing on the FBI's fabricated "Black identity extremists."[9]

The Alchemy of Abolitionisms

Spiritual, metaphysical, and material components of abolitionism suggest the merger of art, science, and political will in the "alchemy"—understood here as a significant transformation in political agency for freedom—that originated in ancient Egypt, where "mummification procedures . . . gave rise to rudimentary chemical knowledge and a goal of immortality."[10] Logically, the abolitionist is alchemist. In the rational world of unabated loss and terror, it is only natural that the liberator would be a magical thinker and radical doer. Trying to better understand the roles of political prisoners as intellectuals and political agents in global abolitionist struggles, I reflect here on the spiritual and political drive of activists; their labors suggest a force of nature that calls upon the ancestral in order to design a future beyond captivity.

A fluid, multi-layered abolitionism, one aligned with dedicated activists experimenting as "alchemists," shares leadership with imprisoned intellectuals. Radical alliances forge a golden norm for addressing crises. Susceptible to glossy reforms endorsed by the privileged and police and policy wonks, abolitionism without alchemy cannot meet the demands from captives, particularly the differently abled, the impoverished, women, children, and LGBTQ+ radicals for dignity, autonomy, and care.

During the 2020 "Black August" Black Is Black virtual conference on US political prisoners (such as the recently released MOVE 9),[11] activist intellectuals referenced the Hadith's adage to thrive in transforming predatory violence: first, one must feel in their heart the injustice; next, one must politically act; finally, one must raise their fist against injustice. This sequence or process to challenge repression through abolitionism deploys emotional intelligence, political analytics, and physical engagement for justice.

"Abolitionism" always existed for those with wealth and power: existential whiteness,[12] money, or capital, and connections with governing elites. Elite "offenders," *if* prosecuted and convicted, are largely redirected to therapy, counseling, drug treatment, and expensive residential treatment centers. Internationally (and nationally), they can also engage in crimes against humanity or human rights violations yet still accumulate wealth and prestige and remain in governance. The quest for alchemists is how to obtain *abolitionism for all* and instill justice as a universal norm when "caught between a rock and a hard place"—with predatory opportunistic civilian violence on one side, predatory police violence on the other, and prisons run as organized zones of trauma and terror (the US leads the world in both mass incarceration, with over 2 million captives, and pandemic deaths). The quest to control organized violence is highly politicized on all sides. Hence, abolitionists seek strategies in radical traditions.

The "Imprisoned Black
Radical Intellectual Tradition"

Academic abolitionists often speak of the "Black Radical Tradition" (BRT), tracing it to anti-slavery abolitionism, the civil rights and Black liberation movements, and analyses of "racial capitalism" in texts by Black academics. I first read the term "*Imprisoned* Black Radical Intellectual Tradition" (IBRT) while working with abolitionist academics responding to queries posed by the imprisoned Black queer educator and abolitionist Stephen "Stevie" Wilson.[13] Wilson raised the IBRT as related to the aforementioned BRT of the civil rights and Black Power movements (as distinct from the Black liberation movement waged by organized radicals). The latter is often tethered to academic texts. Differences in ideologies and strategies can be ill-defined if both phenomena—IBRT and BRT—are referenced in the singular, not in the plural (e.g., "Black feminism" as opposed to "Black feminisms"). It is easier for a hegemonic (Black) left—if such an entity exists[14]— to shape definitional norms if IBRT is presented as a unitary formation. Using the standard nonplural, I see IBRT as fluid, multi-layered, and aligned with BRT as they co-exist and overlap. Prisons mirror and magnify state and social ills. One query Wilson posed to the group of academics was: "If free world scholars are not willing to engage [with] the work of imprisoned intellectuals, from where will they get their information, the factual basis, of their work?"[15]

Eighteenth-century abolitionisms depended upon an anti-racism algorithm that depicted enslaved Blacks/Africans as primarily sufferers imploring the assistance of white elites and ethicists. The Black/African captives also included intellectuals, theorists, activists, rebels, and warriors—but the optics for autonomous Black agency proved disturbing to many conventional abolitionists. An eighteenth-century algorithm favored by elites might be operational in the twenty-first century; yet should it be the norm? Is the "practical" effective for transformational change? Given that civilians, judges, attorneys, police, and prison guards dehumanize the incarcerated, the legacy of political prisoners or rebels is key for understanding the longevity of US policing and imprisonment as reiterations of the atrocities of chattel slavery, convict leasing, Jim Crow, COINTELPRO, the fabricated "war on drugs,"[16] mass incarceration, medical (pandemic) neglect, and experimentation in prisons.

IBRT's legacy spans centuries from the first kidnapping/ purchase and cargo shipment and rebellion to the present moment of mass protests. Its leaders, captives, combatants, and casualties are both historically known and anonymous. The better-known nineteenth-century abolitionists include David Walker, Nat Turner, Harriet Tubman, Sojourner Truth, and Frederick Douglass. IBRT history also includes forgotten or less well-known insurrectionists imprisoned and killed for their abolitionism. Osborne Perry Anderson, Shields Green, Lewis Sheridan Leary, John Anthony Copeland Jr., and Dangerfield Newby, for example, were Black men who accompanied and fought with John Brown during the 1859 raid on Harpers Ferry that some argue precipitated the Civil War. Some were killed during the raid, others imprisoned and hanged. Brown's body was given a ceremonial burial in New York. Yet, the bodies of the named Black men, who fought to free their families and communities, were dissected in the streets or "donated" to a local medical college for experimentation.[17]

During the twentieth-century civil rights movements (the Southern Christian Leadership Conference referred to the civil rights movement as the "second Reconstruction," while SNCC activist youths referred to it as the "second civil war"), IBRT intellectuals and activists—such as Fannie Lou Hamer, Stokely Carmichael, and W.L. Nolen (who mentored George Jackson)— were caged in jails or prisons and beaten and tortured with "surplus" punishment to discourage or destroy their political commitments. Contemporary abolitionists lead collectives such as New York City's Release Aging People in Prison (RAPP); Chicago's Campaign to Free Incarcerated Survivors of Police Torture (CFIST); and the Jericho Movement for the release of the political prisoners Jalil Muntaqim, Russell Maroon Shoatz, Mumia Abu-Jamal, and Rev. Joy Powell.[18] Jericho and other abolitionist organizations mobilized for 2021 tribunals on the seventieth anniversary of the aforementioned *We Charge Genocide* petition, which called attention to state violence against Black Americans and which was presented to the UN and the globe by the Civil Rights Congress in 1951.[19] Internationalist organizing was always central to abolitionists, from the anti-lynching crusader Ida B. Wells through the Black Panther Party to the Black Is Black Coalition. Black abolitionists as internationalists were jailed and/or imprisoned yet still informed and inspired the world. As ancestors and "psychopomps," alongside international political prisoners who took risks to build communities and nations—Patrice Lumumba, Tom Mboya, Nelson Mandela, Chris Hani, and Dulcie September (incarcerated for six years, she later worked for the ANC in Paris, where she was assassinated in 1988)[20]—they continue to influence international struggles.

Abolitionist Educators

When academics dominate abolitionist print culture, it is easier to forget the alchemical lineage of radical street and prison movements. Books on incarceration and abolitionism written by academics are at times more popular and celebrated than the memoirs and analyses of incarcerated radicals. The under-acknowledged schism between the world views of abolitionist academics and radical imprisoned abolitionists creates a blind spot that obscures radical agency from within prisons and jails.

The administrators of prisons and jails remain the greatest obstacles to studies deemed "too" political. The intellectual and personal property of imprisoned IBRT educators are routinely confiscated.[21] Abolitionist advocacy helps to recover and prevent prison admin theft and wreckage. Yet, for decades, solitary confinement disrupted movements inside and outside as educators were and are removed from their communities. (In addition to expensive books, Stephen Wilson notes that Pennsylvania imprisoned workers earn 19 cents per hour while prisons promote distractions from the study and development of IBRT with entertainment and digital devices.)[22] JPay email can be costly to users and families. Digital culture creates isolation between abolitions. Speaking for incarcerated intellectuals, Wilson reflects: "We are not part of the conversations. We are afterthoughts."[23] Noting that (sometimes inaccessible) abolitionist texts often lack writings by the incarcerated, Wilson poses challenges to academic and pundit abolitionists: "Too often, in discourses on prisons and policing, a totalizing definition of prisoner or defendant, usually Black or brown, able-bodied, cis-het male, is used, thereby invisibilizing the lived experiences of so many other people behind the walls. There is no monolithic prison experience. Marginalized populations often find themselves erased from the conversation. I see my work as an intervention, a correction."[24]

Imprisoned journalists covering the pandemic face more life-threatening violence than that endured by journalists attacked by federal and local police during the recent unrests for racial justice. (The Thirteenth Amendment legalizes slavery in US prisons and thus essentially nullifies most constitutional rights, including First Amendment rights.) Incarcerated educators who labor to inform the public of the pandemic devastating US prisons are punished for their courageous exposés in health and safety reporting. Many US prisons have been woefully incompetent or indifferent in providing adequate safety protocols and sanitation for those forced to live under COVID-19 as a potential death sentence. US prisons "contain" the virus with lockdowns and solitary confinement; they also limit health programs and services.

The Pennsylvania Department of Corrections retaliated against Wilson for reporting on COVID conditions in prison; using "vague, shifting, and contradictory accusations of misconduct," it silenced him, putting him in solitary confinement. Wilson began a hunger strike on April 7, 2020, which lasted more than a week; he has asserted: "Now I am truly a political prisoner."[25]

Radical Solidarity
amid Political Repression

In August 2020, US media reported that some 21 million people had participated in marches or protests since the May 2020 police lynching of George Floyd. Hundreds if not thousands of those protestors have been or will be arrested. This suggests that social justice protests will extend the IBRT legacy with new political prisoners. Within prisons, forming bonds and study groups among intergenerational radicals is often undermined by prison administrations seeking to destabilize networks among politicized intellectuals.

Among political prisoners, even if abolitionists lack ideological agreement given the different levels of threat, fear, depression, and repression, they continue to build zones for study, engagement, critique, and constructive work to leverage civil and human rights through a multi-realm compressor: from the mechanisms of policing and imprisonment within an imperial democracy through the realm of social justice movements to the maroon sites of study collectives built from repurposed time and labor, to more engagement with changing the quality and duration of life for our community members.

Maroons escaped enslavement or indentured servitude and fought for their freedom by fleeing plantations and towns to embed in forests and mountains. IBRT's literary and theoretical legacy spans centuries of testimonials, speeches, and writings by abolitionists from the antebellum to the contemporary era. Its breadcrumb trail and navigation include: David Walker's 1829 *Appeal*; Haywood Patterson's 1950 *Scottsboro Boy*; Rev. Martin Luther King Jr.'s 1963 "Letter from a Birmingham Jail"; Malcolm X's 1965 *The Autobiography of Malcolm X* (shaped by Alex Haley); Anne Moody's 1968 *Coming of Age in Mississippi*; George Jackson's 1970 *Soledad Brother*; the 1971 "Attica Manifesto"; Assata Shakur's 1987 autobiography; Safiya Bukhari's 2010 *The War Before*;[26] and former and current political prisoners who serve as journalists: The Real News Network's Eddie Conway, and Prison Radio's Mumia Abu-Jamal.[27] The intellectual, political, emotional-psychological contributions of IBRT are stabilized by "coming-of-age stories" that brilliantly reveal doubt, desire, determination, and sacrifice. The narratives, dominated by male authors, are not pretty or always reassuring. They are powerful, disturbing, and quieting. Neither pessimistic nor optimistic, their realism dominates. The IBRT past manifests in the present. IBRT authors and actors as Captive Maternals have labored in confinement through centuries.

Victories exist but not as "successes." Without the inclusion of the Imprisoned Black Radical Tradition, Black intellectualism becomes less clear and more likely to be polished with a glossy preservative that appeals to the privileged and reassures with palliative rather than "curative" politics. We the people have not transcended captivity, social violence, exploitation, poverty, trafficking, femicide and infanticide, transphobia, and the devastation of the natural world. Yet we have a legacy. Not all of it is written down. Not all existing IBRT writings are evenly distributed and read. Still, we continue to learn from IBRT oral and written contributions.

What then is the nature of the relationship(s) between white-collar abolitionists and enslaved rebel abolitionists? What structures our encounters with each other? The open heart, vocal advocacy, the raised fist? When do the imaginaries of incarcerated maroons meld with those of the professionalized educators? Do we even share the same "freedom dreams"[28] from our disparate sites—from pen pals or visitors of captives to being entombed by governmental/ corporate capture? Global struggles encompass pandemic deaths and health precarity; recessions and increased poverty; climate devastations and forced migration; regional wars and execution; police and paramilitary repression of dissenters and authoritarian rule. Fighting for and with those battling within the bowels of prisons and jails—the "disposables" from the waste generated by prison regimes, profiteers, and politicians—continues the traditions of ancient experimentations in transmutation as we imperfectly measure but determinedly perform how radical traditions enlighten and transpose trauma into freedom.

Notes to Chapter 4

1   Vincent Brown, *Tacky's Revolt: The Story of an Atlantic Slave War* (Cambridge, MA: Harvard University Press, 2020), 17–18.

2   Color of Change, "Stop Hate for Profit," accessed July 20, 2022, https:// colorofchange.org/stop-hate-for-profit/.

3   Tony Romm, "Amazon, Apple, Facebook and Google Grilled on Capitol Hill over Their Market Power," *Washington Post*, July 29, 2020, https://www.washingtonpost.com/technology/2020/07/29 /apple-google-facebook-amazon-congress-hearing/.

4   See Jonathan M. Katz, "Who Was Naive about Bernie Sanders Meeting the Sandinistas?," *Mother Jones*, May 30, 2019, https:// www.motherjones.com/politics/2019/05/who-was-naive-about -bernie-sanders-meeting-the-sandinistas/.

5   Archie Mafeje, "White Liberals and Black Nationalists: Strange Bedfellows," *Southern Africa Political and Economic Monthly* 11, no. 13 (December 1998), 45.

6   Alexis Hoag, "Derrick Bell's Interest Convergence and the Permanence of Racism: A Reflection on Resistance," *Harvard Law Review Blog*, August 24, 2020, https://blog.harvardlawreview.org/derrick-bells -interest-convergence-and-the-permanence-of-racism-a-reflection -on-resistance/.

7   John Gramlich, "How Trump Compares with other Recent Presidents in Appointing Federal Judges," *Pew Research Center*, January 13, 2021, https://www.pewresearch.org/fact-tank/2021/01/13/how-trump

-compares-with-other-recent-presidents-in-appointing-federal
-judges/.

8   See ProPublica, "The NYPD Files: Investigating America's Largest
     Police Force," accessed October 3, 2022, https://www.propublica.org
     /series/the-nypd-files.

9   See Rights and Dissent, "Leaked FBI Documents Show FBI Developed
     'IRON FIST' to Counter 'Black Identity Extremists,'" accessed October
     3, 2022, https://www.rightsanddissent.org/news/leaked-fbi-documents
     -show-fbi-developed-iron-fist-to-counter-black-identity-extremists/;
     and ACLU, "Leaked FBI Documents Raise Concerns about Targeting
     Black People under 'Black Identity Extremist' and Newer Labels," August
     9, 2019, https://www.aclu.org/press-releases/leaked-fbi-documents
     -raise-concerns-about-targeting-black-people-under-black-identi-1.

10   Anon., "A Brief History of Alchemy," University of Bristol School of
     Chemistry, accessed October 26, 2022, http://www.chm.bris.ac.uk
     /webprojects2002/crabb/history.html.

11   See Marpessa Kupendua, "Who Are the MOVE 9?," December 7, 1997,
     https://theanarchistlibrary.org/library/marpessa-kupendua-who-are
     -the-move-9.

12   See Cheryl Harris, "Whiteness as Property," *Harvard Law Review* 106,
     no. 8 (June 1993).

13   See Stephen Wilson, Orisanmi Burton, Toussaint Losier, et al., "The
     Lasting Influence of the 'Imprisoned Black Radical Tradition,'" *Black
     Perspectives* blog, AAIHS, August 28, 2020, https://www.aaihs.org
     /the-lasting-influence-of-the-imprisoned-black-radical-tradition/.

14   See Mafeje, "White Liberals and Black Nationalists."

15   Garrett Felber and Stephen Wilson, "The Makings of a Forum:
     'Imprisoned Black Radical Tradition,'" *Black Perspectives* blog,
     AAIHS, August 24, 2020, https://www.aaihs.org/the-makings-of-a
     -forum-imprisoned-black-radical-tradition/.

16   See Dan Baum, "Legalize It All: How to Win the War on Drugs,"
     Harper's Magazine, April 2016, https://harpers.org/archive/2016/04
     /legalize-it-all/.

17   Eugene L. Meyer, "Five Black Men Raided Harpers Ferry with John
     Brown. They've Been Forgotten," *Washington Post*, October 13, 2019,
     https://www.washingtonpost.com/history/2019/10/13/five-black
     -men-raided-harpers-ferry-with-john-brown-theyve-been-forgotten/.

18   See Linda G. Ford, "Black Women Political Prisoners of the Police State,"
     Counterpunch, May 3, 2019, https://www.counterpunch.org/2019/05
     /03/black-women-political-prisoners-of-the-police-state/.

19   Civil Rights Congress, *We Charge Genocide*.

20   Rasmus Bitsch and Kelly-Eve Koopman, "The Erasure of
     Dulcie September," *Africa Is a Country*, August 20, 2019, https://
     africasacountry.com/2019/08/the-erasure-of-dulcie-september.

21   See Stephen Wilson, "Help," *Dreaming Freedom Practicing Abolition* blog,
     April 20, 2022, https://abolitioniststudy.wordpress.com/2022/04/20
     /help/.

22   Twenty-twenty email correspondence with faculty responding to

Wilson's queries for the AAIHS was shared by the former University of Mississippi professor Garrett Felber, who was fired for his public criticisms of the university's ties to the private prison industry: see Ashton Pittman, "Emails Show UM Officials' Concern over Fired Historian Criticizing Private Prison Ties," *Mississippi Free Press*, July 30, 2021, https://www.mississippifreepress.org/14250/emails-show-um-officials-concern-over-fired-historian-criticizing-private-prison-ties.

23   Author's email exchange with Wilson for AAIHS, 2020. For publications of Wilson's analyses, see Dan Berger, "'Imagining a New World without Cages': An Interview with Stephen Wilson," *Black Perspectives* blog, AAIHS, August 28, 2020, https://www.aaihs.org/imagining-a-new-world-without-cages-an-interview-with-stephen-wilson/; and Felber and Wilson, "The Makings of a Forum."

24   Ibid.

25   Ian Alexander, "Incarcerated Abolitionist Stephen Wilson on Hunger Strike against Retaliation for Speaking Out about COVID-19," *ShadowProof*, April 14, 2020, https://shadowproof.com/2020/04/14/incarcerated-abolitionist-stephen-wilson-on-hunger-strike-against-retaliation-for-speaking-out-about-covid-19/.

26   David Walker, *Walker's Appeal, in Four Articles; Together with a Preamble, to the Coloured Citizens of the World, but in Particular, and Very Expressly, to Those of the United States of America, Written in Boston, State of Massachusetts, September 28, 1829* (Boston, MA: self-published, 1830); available online, https://docsouth.unc.edu/nc/walker/menu.html, accessed July 22, 2022; Martin Luther King Jr., "Letter from a Birmingham Jail," April 16, 1963; available online, https://www.africa.upenn.edu/Articles_Gen/Letter_Birmingham.html, accessed July 22, 2022; Malcolm X with Alex Haley, *The Autobiography of Malcolm X* (New York: Grove Press, 1965); Anne Moody, *Coming of Age in Mississippi* (New York: Bantam, 1968); George Jackson, *Soledad Brother: The Prison Letters of George Jackson* (New York: Bantam, 1970); available online, https://www.historyisaweapon.com/defcon1/soledadbro.html, accessed July 22, 2022; Attica Prison Liberation Faction, "Manifesto of Demands" (1971); available online, https://libcom.org/article/attica-prison-liberation-faction-manifesto-demands-1971, accessed July 22, 2022; Assata Shakur, *Assata: An Autobiography* (Westport, CT: L. Hill, 1987); Safiya Bukhari, *The War Before: The True Life Story of Becoming a Black Panther, Keeping Faith in Prison, and Fighting for Those Left Behind* (New York: Feminist Press, 2010).

27   See https://therealnews.com/author/eddie-conway and https://www.prisonradio.org/correspondent/mumia-abu-jamal/.

28   This is a reference to the name of Stephen Wilson's blog, *Dreaming Freedom Practicing Abolition*: see https://abolitioniststudy.wordpress.com/.

5   The Limitations of Black Studies

With K. Kim Holder

Reconciling Liberation
with Repressive Education

Liberation pedagogies tied to Black studies stem from well-known political thinkers and activists who created a popularized form of political education originally rooted in community struggles for civil and human rights. Those struggles and studies emerged from an era of battles against repression in which traumatized and grieving students, educators, and communities sought to build and fortify a more equitable and just world.

Activists were central to political education that would eventually return to the classroom after tracing the contributions to communities made by students such as Howard University's Stokely Carmichael or Barnard's Kathleen Cleaver, both of whom worked with the SNCC (Kathleen Cleaver relocated to Oakland to join the Black Panther Party). Social justice activists developed community-based methods of learning and teaching political theory, civic engagement, and community protection. Mid- to late-twentieth-century teachers and organizers created oral and literary texts. Bayard Rustin and Ella Baker, with the attorney Stanley Levine, were members of the New York City-based organization In Friendship. Rustin and Baker travelled south to assist the Montgomery Bus Boycott in Montgomery, Alabama. As the Southern Christian Leadership Council (SCLC) emerged, it promoted the leadership of male clergy and Rev. Martin Luther King Jr. Miss Baker left the SCLC in 1960: the male ministers were not ready for radical female leadership, particularly from a socialist. In 1960, Baker, alongside the historian Howard Zinn, became a mentor to the SNCC, formed by college and university students who wanted what King would later describe as the "beloved community" in which equity and dignity—and the cessation of terror and captivity—became the norm and not the exception.[1]

Baker, who originally attended a Black college in the South, moved from Southern communities to meet other community learners and teachers in Harlem. Years before the Southern civil rights movement, she organized with domestic workers and unemployed Black women during the Depression. Eventually she and Rosa Parks met, heard of and learned from the Black Muslim revolutionary and (inter)nationalist educator Malcolm X (later Malik el-Shabazz).[2] The 1960s informed and inspired an oral tradition of speeches that reflected the precarity and power of communal-based experience, suffering, and resistance in a matrix of education. Emotionally and politically reeling in the aftermath of the spring 2020 police/vigilante killings of Breonna Taylor, Ahmaud Arbery, and George Floyd, one can find instruction and emotional intelligence—if not always comfort—in the bracing (and abrasive) lectures of Malcolm X. His 1962 speech in Los Angeles on police brutality and the killings of unarmed Blacks reflects this present moment and calls upon us to investigate more deeply the repetitions of violence and disposability that we face and the difficulty in teaching about it to others who do not share the same levels of vulnerability nor desire an intensity of resistance.[3] Now the Smithsonian Channel can post such a speech by Malcolm X, but years ago he was considered a hate-filled "bigot." It is odd but familiar that things change but stay the same. We struggle to build community-based liberatory education to offset mass-produced factory- and corporate-based instruction that denies the possibility of transformational wisdom based not only in suffering but also in resistance against suffering and degradation. According to Malcolm X, "Truth is on the side of

the oppressed." Yet, in the classrooms where community-focused teaching grapples with the specificity of the violence
enacted through white supremacy and predatory capitalism,
the "truth" seems to be taught based on what is conventional
and agreeable to the institution and the publisher.

This struggle of building community out of activist (not
professionalized) culture is an international struggle. Here,
we can draw upon the Brazilian educator and philosopher
Paulo Freire. According to Freire, "'Washing one's hands' of
the conflicts between the powerful and the powerless means
to side with the powerful."[4] He emphasizes the non-hierar-
chical ways in which communities teach each other and with
each other without professionalizing the sharing of knowledge and ethical action. Countless unnamed activists and
students functioned as pedagogues as well, boldly creating
theories of social justice in tandem with their communities,
often marginalized from the elite or from the academy. Baker
organized with the SNCC to counter racism and economic
exploitation and war. Malcolm spoke to the people about freedom, and lectured on university campuses (often elite institutions). Freire demonstrates how to speak in systematic ways
about the poor and oppressed, about the various forms of
education that would work in their interests. Baker's strategic
brilliance, Malcom's cultural eloquence, and Freire's educational academic-communal frameworks are expressed in various ways by student activists who engineered Black studies in
the academy to reflect liberation movements. Anniversaries
celebrating Black studies recall on-campus activism that created academic programs decades ago. Yet the repression—
which went beyond rhetorical slights and racial slurs, which
sought to kill Black intellectual and political autonomy—is
not often referred to in these celebrations of ethnic studies
and Black studies programs that grew out of militant movements. That activism is sometimes distanced from radicalism
traceable to the Black Panther Party (BPP) and student organizers. Liberation pedagogy is traceable to the theologies of

Nat Turner, Harriet Tubman, Sojourner Truth, Vernon Johns, Martin Luther King Jr., Fannie Lou Hamer, James Baldwin, and Malcolm X. Their pedagogies reflect theories emanating not from academic research or textual studies but from within mass mobilizations to change oppressive material conditions and political disenfranchisement. Violence and intimidation against those movements have been a constant threat to critical pedagogies and theories that seek to deepen public understanding of liberation movements and the academy. There are key things to remember as we go forward to building or setting a legacy for future communities. In the era of resistance for a better world, the academy, pundits, and texts were not the center of leadership, analysis, or ethics. In student mobilizations and transformative theory, students' relationships to their communities, not their relationships to faculty or administrators, were the driving forces behind the development of Black studies. What inspired the students to learn and teach were the political responsibilities that they shouldered alongside their communities and leaders that risked their lives for freedom and justice.

Those educated included those who were imprisoned and who wrote from their cells, or who wrote after their release or escape from those cells. The intellectual foundations of Black studies remain founded in the writings of former prisoners such as Malcolm X, George Jackson, Angela Davis, Assata Shakur, and Safiya Bukhari. Prison resistance shaped the consciousness of campus radicals and liberation pedagogies. Inhuman conditions which existed beyond the view of the public were exposed in print and oratory as the "dregs of society" expressed themselves in university culture after having spoken to their communities of origin. During the movement era in the mid-1960s, the imprisoned demanded human rights as Black students organized alongside Mexican Americans, Puerto Ricans, Native Americans, and Asian Americans for social justice and an end to US wars in Southeast Asia and repressive policies administered through national, state,

and local governments.⁵ In the 1960s, militant groups challenged the legitimacy and authority of US institutions. In Los
Angeles, Newark, and Detroit, Black and other youths vented
frustration and rage by confronting or attacking—through
protests, boycotts, and street battles—the most visible symbols of oppressive conditions: white businesses and police.
As young Blacks took to the streets in hundreds of rebellions
(which included the rage of destruction and the opportunism
of looting), colleges increased enrollment of Black and "Third
World" students. Those students brought to campuses the
ideological, philosophical, and ethical rebellions and desires
of their communities. They also sought out campus cultural
centers as an extension of demands for community control
for working-class people. At San Francisco State University
(SFSU), Cornell University, Harvard University, and Jackson
State University, student organizing aligned with the political
demands of their home communities. Unfortunately, repression, at times violent, was the general response. When these
protests or rebellions subsided, "community building" inevitably became more structured and managed by the educational institutions, which not only hired personnel to manage
"community engagement" but also steered students to focus
militancy into policy negotiations and platforms for advocacy. The purpose of the university as educational site was not
to empower working-class militancy or expand autonomous
educational zones that could critique capitalism and imperialism. State universities and private universities, respectively
government and corporate entities, were to create (lower)
middle classes to stabilize governmental administration.⁶
Managerial duties obscured the origins of Black studies and
the sacrifices that birthed communal education dedicated to
the freedom of exploited communities. That often obscured
history is codified not just on May 4, 1970 at Kent State, when
trust in community, university, and state was shattered as the
university president requested the Ohio National Guard to
suppress student protests against police violence and the war

in Vietnam, specifically the US invasion of Cambodia. Four middle-class white students were shot and killed during protests by the National Guard. White students and protesters who carried no weapons would be imprisoned for "inciting" those deaths.[7] Two years prior, in February 1968, Orangeburg police shot at South Carolina State University student protestors, killing Samuel Hammond Jr., Henry Smith, and the high school student Delano Middleton, and injuring at least thirty students, who were largely shot in their backs, sides, or soles of their feet as they fled police and National Guard. All police were exonerated at trial.[8] The trajectory of outrage and injustice that has driven so many to protest and struggle for community-based education and political demands in 2020 and after is a reflection of our past. Just as protestors, often young people, are targeted for their protests for a just society today, in the aftermath of the Orangeburg massacre, only the SNCC field organizer Cleveland Sellers was convicted—of inciting a riot. Sellers, who would later become the director of the African-American studies program at the University of South Carolina, maintained that he was attempting to shield and save students by moving them to safety and away from a bonfire they had lit.

Black/Africana studies is not merely the study of Black Americans through the traditional disciplines or the cultural productions, acquisitions, and contributions of Africa and the diaspora. Black studies began in 1968 at SFSU. In ethnic studies, George Mason Murray, a graduate student in English and the first minister of education of the BPP, was hired to teach special-admittance students from low-income neighborhoods. The professor of sociology Nathan Hare was charged with creating a Black studies department in February 1968. Murray taught the first course on Black studies at SFSU in September 1968. When the board of trustees fired Murray for controversial political statements concerning anti-racism, the Black Student Union and the Third World Liberation Front protested. Hare was allegedly targeted for his role in the protests. When the SFSU president Robert Smith resigned based on his refusal to fire Murray, S.I. Hiyakawa was named president and called in police to repress students; police did so with considerable violence.[9]

Panther Clashes on Campuses, Panther Clashes on Ideology

Huey P. Newton and Bobby Seale were enrolled in Merritt College when they co-founded the Black Panther Party for Self-Defense in 1966 in part as a response to police violence in Black urban neighborhoods. The upheaval of the era included the vertical violence of local and federal police and the National Guard as well as the horizontal violence among community members. University campuses were not spared tragedies. The Panthers John Huggins and Alprentice "Bunchy" Carter were killed on the campus of the University of California, Los Angeles (UCLA), allegedly by members of the Black-nationalist US Organization (and COINTELPRO) as they contested a rival group's control of the Black Cultural Center as indifferent to the needs of poor people. (James Baldwin and Kathleen Cleaver attended Bunchy Carter's funeral.)[10] Revolutionary not cultural nationalists, Panthers asserted class struggle as key to liberation pedagogy and Black studies. Huggins and Carter, along with Geronimo Pratt and Elaine Brown, were party members enrolled at UCLA. These nontraditional students were acquaintances of Angela Davis, UCLA's first Black female instructor in philosophy, a more "traditional" student and a member of the Communist Party USA (CPUSA) who faced death threats due to her party affiliation and anti-racism. Panthers provided Davis with off-campus security.

Whereas in the South, student activists had to contend with racist vigilantes and police, in California—where prisons and police departments recruited whites from the Deep South because they "knew how to handle" Blacks—Southern

vigilantes merged into the ranks of state and city employees. Still, students demanded educational programs relevant
and beneficial to their communities, despite vulnerability
to police violence. (The historical role of campus police as
repressive enforcers to contain Black and anti-racist student organizing is understudied.) Campuses familiar with
the fiery rhetoric of H. Rap Brown (now the political prisoner Jamil Abdullah al-Amin)[11] and Stokely Carmichael
(Kwame Ture) saw the civil rights movement decline as the
movement for Black studies surged. In 1965 Malcolm X was
assassinated—before his Organization of African American
Unity could develop a Black liberation pedagogy that mobilized Blacks for self-determination and human rights rather
than civil rights and integration. Malcolm had politicized
unemployed urban youth. Martin Luther King Jr.'s assassination three years later forced a spotlight onto a democratic dystopia that students brought to campus. The BPP
attracted these students as universities and colleges (cautiously) recruited them. Using Malcolm's preaching, SNCC
tactics, and the Nation of Islam's 1965 Ten-Point Program,[12]
the 1966 Black Panther Party program was built. Born on
the streets of Oakland in October 1966 in response to the
police killing of a Black teen, the BPP sought educational
and pedagogical channels to militancy among youth who
could create concrete programs beneficial to communities. Organizing to meet medical, food, housing, and safety
needs, the BPP developed survival programs serving hundreds of thousands within a form of liberation pedagogy. Its
motto—"Serve the People"—was emblematic of philosophy
and pedagogy committed through action to alleviate the suffering of the poor. Sovereign Black communities and socialism would be difficult to attain without an intellectual base
on campuses. While Blacks were protesting in the streets,
Mexican-American agricultural workers were protesting in
the fields, and students and people of faith marched against
the Vietnam War.

Unlike the fading of the SNCC, the SCLC, the Congress of Racial Equality (CORE),[13] and the NAACP—whose leadership largely sought integration—the BPP's demise directly impacted radical campus culture. The civil rights movement sought access to elite institutions; hence student recruitment. The BPP or Black Power movement sought to transform society. *Ideological* transformation that met the needs of the poor, not inclusivity or intersectionality, was the goal of a liberation pedagogy that was confrontational and justice-focused. A liberation pedagogy developed in children's free breakfast programs, junior high and high school walkouts, and college and university mobilizations.

Focusing on historical figures as superheroes/heroines or supervillains obscures the theory that historical Black studies nurtured as a reflection of mass or collective engagement. The New York Panther veteran and scholar Kwando Kinshasa notes the dilemmas in documenting historical struggles by over-emphasizing the heroic: "While historical 'characters' do act, their actions occur not in a vacuum, but as a response to perceptions of reality."[14] Reality as a social phenomenon is created by community within social orders that are contested or obeyed. Theory as a verb does not emerge in isolation from community or as an individual attribute.[15] Teachers who have worked in movements for radical change are likely the best informants for critical thinking. Without a pedagogy of the oppressed or a non-elite community to structure analyses, generalities might dominate and hegemonic progressivism displace critical thinking. After weeks of protests following the 2020 murder of George Floyd in Minneapolis, Minnesota, a June open letter from Panther veterans addressed to Black hip-hop artists was released to the public through organizing networks and platforms.[16] Among the signatories were the names of the academic professors Kathleen Cleaver (Emory University), Jamal Joseph (Columbia University), and K. Kim Holder (Rowan University) who encouraged "the next generation of freedom fighters, cultural workers and activists" to learn from—rather than mystify or intellectualize—past revolutionary struggles: "an oppressed people can resist domination from one generation to the next without reinventing failures, pitfalls, or the mistakes of the previous generation. It is our enemy's job to . . . isolate one generation from the other . . . to denigrate the history of militant and radical traditions and burnish the history of integrationist[s] who think we can simply vote our way out of this problem."[17]

The Panther veterans write that they "have stepped forward at this neo-fascist moment in history driven by the current crisis of capitalist culture, an ongoing pandemic and the now renewed attention and massive demonstrations brought on by ongoing police murders in our community."[18] They describe combatants in the revolutionary Black underground responding to a murderous COINTELPRO war waged by the FBI, CIA, and local police; they assert that the Black Liberation Army (BLA)[19] is part of the "history in our people's struggle [that] has been kept away from you and [is] seemingly unavailable to your generation as you reinvent what was done in the past." The educators maintain that although "circumstances and conditions" change, the "enemies" of Black communities remain poverty and police violence.[20]

Recalibrating Black Studies

Passively receptive "students" for whom knowledge is textual and an acquisition have little resemblance to the militant students who created Black/ethnic and women's/LGBTQ+ studies decades ago. Those activists as learner-participants encountered and created theoretical content through their collective powers to implement programs to counter violence and injustice. Students, community members, rank-and-file Panthers, imprisoned activists, and grassroots organizers constructed the basic structures and tools for theory that were later (re)articulated in scholarship. During Black studies militancy, theory was active not passive. Its content and goals were directed by the material and emotional needs of communities deprived of security and dignity who continuously rebuilt themselves, only to be continuously attacked.

Half a century ago, tied to activism, strikes, boycotts, and battling police violence, Black studies sought an intellectual base inside the academy as a strategic site to grapple with the political and cultural realities of communities. Catalyzed by liberation pedagogy, it rejected the notion of a political or neutral education. Political objectives guided the emergence of Black studies; just as political objectives to stabilize or expand or rationalize capitalism guides other disciplines—ditto for imperialism. The academic Harold Cruse described Black studies as "a school of interdisciplinary approaches to the understanding of a living experience."[21] Black lived experiences against racist violence, poverty, and dishonor created Black studies as a radical innovation. Crafted by largely anonymous intellectuals whose names would not be recorded on syllabi, such theory is reflected in the liberation pedagogy promoted by the civil rights leader Ella Baker: "You didn't see me on television, you didn't see news stories about me. The kind of role that I tried to play was to pick up pieces or put together pieces out of which I hoped organization might come. My theory is, strong people don't need strong leaders."

Notes to Chapter 5

1   Howard Zinn, "Ella Baker: 'One of the Most Consequential and Yet One of the Least Honored People in America,'" April 24, 1968; available online, https://www.howardzinn.org/collection/ella-baker -consequential-people/, accessed October 26, 2022.

2   See Jeanne Theoharis, "Mrs. Parks and Black Power," *The Rebellious Life of Mrs. Rosa Parks,* accessed October 3, 2022, https:// rosaparksbiography.org/bio/mrs-parks-and-black-power/.

3   See Smithsonian Channel, "Malcolm X's Fiery Speech Addressing Police Brutality," February 16, 2018, YouTube video, https://www .youtube.com/watch?v=6_uYWDyYNUg.

4   Paolo Freire, *The Politics of Education: Culture, Power, and Liberation,*

trans. Donaldo Macedo (Westport, CT: Bergin & Garvey, 1985), 122.

5   See Joy James, ed., *Imprisoned Intellectuals: America's Political Prisoners Write on Life, Liberation, and Rebellion* (Lanham, MD: Rowman & Littlefield, 2003); available online, https://repositories.lib.utexas.edu /handle/2152/7098, accessed October 6, 2022.

6   See K. Kim Holder, "The History of the Black Panther Party, 1966–1971: A Curriculum Tool for Afrikan-American Studies" (PhD dissertation, University of Massachusetts Amherst, 1990).

7   Zinn Education Project, "This Day in History—May 4, 1970: Kent State Massacre," accessed October 6, 2022, https://www.zinnedproject.org /news/tdih/kent-state-massacre/.

8   Zinn Education Project, "This Day in History—Feb. 8, 1968: Orangeburg Massacre," accessed October 6, 2022, https://www.zinnedproject.org /news/tdih/orangeburg-massacre/.

9   See Holder, "History of the Black Panther Party."

10 Abhishek Shetty, "Throwback Thursday: Fifty-Year Anniversary of 'Bunchy' Carter, John Huggins Shooting," *Daily Bruin*, January 17, 2019, https://dailybruin.com/2019/01/17/throwback-thursday-fifty-year -anniversary-of-bunchy-carter-john-huggins-shooting/.

11 See https://hrapbrown.blogspot.com/.

12 See Nation of Islam, "What the Muslims Want," accessed October 6, 2022, https://noi.org/muslim-program/.

13 See Editors of the *King Encyclopedia*, "Congress of Racial Equality (CORE)," *Martin Luther King Jr. Encyclopedia*, accessed October 6, 2022, https://kinginstitute.stanford.edu/encyclopedia/congress -racial-equality-core.

14 See Holder, "History of the Black Panther Party."

15 For a discussion of Black feminist theory's use of the term "theorizing," see Barbara Christian, "The Race for Theory," *Cultural Critique* 6 (spring 1987).

16 Cleaver et al., "Open Letter."

17 Ibid.

18 Ibid.

19 See Jared Ball and Dhoruba Bin Wahad, "The Story of Kamau Sadiki, Assata Shakur and the Black Liberation Army," Black Power Media, accessed October 17, 2022, YouTube video, https://www.youtube.com /watch?v=UK0Onr8gDSU.

20 Cleaver et al., "Open Letter."

21 See Harold Cruse's *The Crisis of the Negro Intellectual* (New York: Morrow, 1967) and his *Rebellion or Revolution?* (New York: Morrow, 1968).

6   Power and the Contradictions of Communal Socialism

With K. Kim Holder

You have to go back and reach out to your neighbors who don't speak to you! And you have to reach out to your friends . . . get them to understand that they, as well as you and I, cannot be free in America, or anywhere else, where there is capitalism . . .
—Ella Baker[1]

We live in strange times. We have a Black president using race-neutral framing for social justice, alongside a Black Lives Matter movement using structural racism framing for participatory democracy. Killer Mike, a Southern rapper best known for his work with the Grammy Award-winning superduo Outkast, has endorsed a sitting US senator and self-described socialist, Bernie Sanders. Some Black preachers, apparently, are tripping over themselves to cozy up to Donald Trump or reposition themselves within the arc of Hillary Clinton's historic candidacy. Strange times indeed.
—Rev. Andrew J. Wilkes[2]

The state targeted the Panthers because we were socialists, not because we were armed.
—Eddie Conway[3]

Introduction:
Defining "Democratic Socialism"

In the US, progressives rarely agree on the meaning of "democratic socialism" (DS). DS is a concept for politics used by progressives, workers, academics, anti-racists, feminists, LGBTQ+

activists, and elected officials, increasingly so following Bernie
Sanders's 2016 primarying of Hillary Clinton and the emergence of COVID-19, which revealed the lack of medical care,
housing, and food for working-class and poor communities.
In 2016, using the New Deal language of President Franklin
Delano Roosevelt (FDR), the presidential candidate Sanders, an
independent senator from Vermont, asserted that democratic
socialism is not the belief that "government should own the
means of production," nor is it tied to any Marxist belief about
the abolition of capitalism. Rather, Sanders argued, democratic
socialism is based in the belief that "the middle class and the
working families who produce the wealth of America deserve
a fair deal."[4] Unsurprisingly in the United States, Marxism is
disavowed with progressive concern that the benefits of capitalism be directed to the laboring, working, and middle classes.
Sanders campaigned on the dignity and wellbeing of the (US)
worker, not the abolition of capitalism.

The Democratic congresswoman Alexandria Ocasio-
Cortez (AOC), who evolved into a political celebrity for the left,
advocated for the Green New Deal built upon FDR's New Deal.
AOC stated that the "ideology of capital" and the "concentra-
tion of capital" require "that we seek and prioritize profit and
the accumulation of money above all else, and we seek it at any
human and environmental cost . . . [D]emocratic socialism . . .
means putting democracy and society first."[5] Here, capitalism
exists as subordinate to democracy and society. (Ocasio-Cortez's
family comes from Puerto Rico, one of the last remaining US
colonial possessions, a country with a radical tradition of resisting racial capitalism and imperialism.)[6]

A key campaigner for Sanders's 2015–16 presidential bid,
and a supporter of AOC, the activist scholar Cornel West views
DS as pursuing a transformative goal:

> the fundamental commitment is to the dignity of ordinary
> people and to make sure they can live lives of decency . . .
> it's about the accountability of the powerful vis-à-vis those

who have less power at the workplace, women dealing with a household, gays, lesbians, trans, Black people, Indigenous peoples, immigrants. How do we ensure that they are treated decently and that the powerful don't in any way manipulate, subjugate and exploit them?[7]

Subtle differences exist between Sanders, Ocasio-Cortez, and West. West acknowledges multiple forms of DS. The most popularized versions of DS, as articulated by left political celebrities, shows that its progressive potential was realized in the past and is entwined with the origins of the Black Panther Party, a radical, if not always revolutionary, anti-racist international party seeking the end of colonial rule across the globe and anti-Black repression (internal colonies) at home, which made significant contributions to socialism—contributions that remain relevant to the contemporary democratic socialism pursued in the US—and which analyzed responses to communal socialism in Black communities in which conflicts or antagonisms were shaped by class and/or social economic status.

Given the amount of state violence arrayed to destroy the BPP, it is logical to scrutinize its ideological threat to racial capital. This very small, young, bold organization inspired national and international communities to rebel against imperialism, racism, and classism. First organized in 1966 as the Black Panther Party for Self-Defense, the BPP monitored and deterred urban police aggression, and sought to meet communal material needs—for food, clothing, shelter, medicine, and education. Criminalizing radical politics and militant Blackness, local, state, and federal police decimated an organization whose membership, several hundred max, was mostly under twenty-five years of age. (Members of the organization believed in self-defense and armed struggle, and contesting state militarism and COINTELPRO; internal party failings concerning self-defense and violence are well documented.)[8] The BPP wielded both pragmatic and visionary politics.

Pragmatic Analyses

BPP programs functioned as the realization of a Black communal society, one embedded within captivity shaped by anti-Black imperial democracy. US segregation, labor exploitation, sexual violence, police forces, and prisons required engagement from key theorists within the Panther Party. Those theorists included women: Kathleen Cleaver became a key strategist and formidable theorist in a freedom struggle. Cleaver, the first woman to sit on the BPP's Central Committee, was an internationalist. Her father had worked in the foreign services, so she had traveled extensively as a child. When the BPP split following Huey P. Newton's denouncing of armed self-defense and paranoia that led to Oakland "death squads" seeking to disappear "rogue" Panthers on the east coast, Kathleen Cleaver and her husband Eldridge Cleaver, the author of *Soul on Ice* (1968), fled the US, first to Cuba and then were transported to Algiers. Co-founders of an Algerian internationalist wing, fleeing from Huey, a cadre of Black Panthers separated from Oakland's hierarchy and criminality that had begun redefining Black Power as Black capitalism and electoral politics. However, the international wing was unstable or destabilized by Newton. Cleaver became a mother while in Algiers. Being a product of the Black petty bourgeoisie, and an analyst of international socialism and underground militarism, Cleaver's critiques of anti-revolutionary animus among Black Americans remain essential.[9]

In a 1997 PBS interview with the Harvard scholar Henry Louis Gates, Cleaver describes nuanced ways in which a revolutionary movement rose, faltered, and fell. Class and ideological divisions among Black Americans shaped Black middle-class or Black bourgeois disparagements of radical or revolutionary struggle, according to Cleaver, as a caste of affluent Blacks held paternalistic relationships with Black poor and working-class communities and ideological animus toward Black radicals and revolutionaries. For Cleaver, the romantic search for "Black unity" required ignoring class divisions and led to superficial agreements that publicly presented a Black united front despite the fact that confrontations with state and capital would disproportionately benefit those best positioned for personal gains: "many of the goals of the Civil Rights Movement were essentially goals for easier assimilation for middle class people . . . working class people and poor people weren't going to get too much out of [the civil rights movement]."[10] The BPP were different from other civil rights organizations that "succumbed to red-baiting": they studied the revolutionaries Malcolm X, the Ghanaian Kwame Nkrumah, and the Martinican psychiatrist Frantz Fanon to forge a (neo-)Marxist party.[11]

According to Cleaver, revolutionaries believed that if "Third World" international movements challenged global capital and empire they could prevail as an "international revolutionary vanguard that would have restructured the economy, restructured the educational system, taken the United States out of the role of world policeman, and made it the American people's revolutionary United States." For the majority of the world's "liberation" movements to be successful would require more than that they "seize power," given that conventional "independence" left the IMF, the World Bank, and global colonizing corporate capital with control of national resources in Africa and in South America.[12]

In the 1960s, pragmatic revolutionaries presciently organized against extreme concentrations of wealth and poverty. In the 1990s, Cleaver reminded public television audiences that government-by-corporation would be dominated by those who controlled resources and "15- and 20-year plans." Waging a rebellion against the emergence of a governing corporate–state partnership with "billions and billions of dollars to get rid of us," Cleaver's Panthers were imperfect visionaries in struggle who did not anticipate material wins in their lifetime, but rather wished to leave a model for liberation struggles: "we had ideals, and we had commitment, and we had this glorious belief that the spirit of the people was greater than man's technology."[13]

Today, politicians and reformers work for white nationalist and anti-racist struggles to be denuded of class analysis. In the absence of a critique of capitalism, the workings of national economies within international predatory capital remain obscured. Cleaver notes that:

> the colonial power creates a middle class, usually to control the colony for itself . . . the creation in black American communities of a class of physicians and managers and lawyers and judges [means that] their education takes them away from the communities that created these people. These are not like my parents' generation, people who are trained in the black schools and whose talents are confined to the black community through a regime of segregation. These are people who are trained in the major institutions and are able to use their talents in the corporate and business structures of the larger society. Therefore, they're not available to the poorer black communities.[14]

BPP Survival Programs

During the revolutionary era, the BPP created "survival programs" to build socialist institutions within local communities; in their intent they channeled the theories of love espoused by Ernesto "Che" Guevara, killed in 1967 by CIA-aided Bolivian military forces.[15] Following the Southern civil rights movement of the 1950s to mid-1960s, the BPP grew out of the radical and militant atmosphere of the 1960s. Many, particularly students and young radicals—radicalized by racism or the war in Vietnam—studied "Third World" liberation struggles in Africa, Asia, and Latin America, as well as alternative economic systems. Blacks questioned the economic realities and promises of capitalism, under which they were the last hired—often working for the lowest wages—and first fired. Along with poverty, police violence and white vigilantism were the most heinous or offensive of crimes against Black humanity. Black solidarity with Puerto Ricans (including Afro-Puerto Ricans) and Native Americans (including Afro-Indigenous), as well as Chicanos and Asians, was based on a need to collectively address racism, poverty, and economic exploitation. The political climate of the 1960s was conducive to an embrace of socialism viewed as closely aligned to liberalism (similar to what Sanders et al. advocated for during the 2016 presidential election). Unlike the CPUSA's Du Bois Clubs, and other socialist-oriented organizations of the time, which were integrated, or even its all-Black Che-Lumumba Club, which Angela Davis joined in 1968, the BPP was rooted in Black communities, in which Panthers lived and worked.

The BPP's socialist stance appeared to be more practical than intellectual. Rather than theorize, it focused on the practical aspects of distributing wealth. One of the Panthers' mottos—"All Power to the People!"—was concretized in socialist economics. Through socialist politics the BPP advocated for its goal of community control—over policing, housing, education, healthcare, and food distribution. The BPP introduced socialism to the community in practical ways. For example, the lieutenant of health of Corona (Queens, NY), Dianne Jenkins, echoes the civil rights leader Ella Baker, breaking down and sharing the knowledge that mutual aid is communalism: "Sisters, you practice socialism. If you needed a cup of sugar, all you had to do was go next door . . . socialism, or the idea of socialism, is no big phenomenon . . . the BPP will continue to develop these programs to serve the people and constantly raise the political level of the masses."[16]

Elmer Dixon, the coordinator of the BPP's Seattle free breakfast program, discussed the party's socialist goals: "Serving the basic needs of the people is the primary task of the BPP. Implementing socialism within the community is one way of serving the people."[17] The survival programs were designed to serve and educate the Black community. Attempting to be responsive to the needs of the people, staffed by non-elite rank-and-file members, survival programs developed institutions that met the material and emotional needs of disenfranchised people who were also dispossessed by capitalism: "The conditions of living in a nation that can send a man to the moon . . . and burn excess wheat at harvest time while small children suffer year round from malnutrition . . . is too depressing to be allowed to continue without taking some positive action . . ."[18] Developing programs that would lay the foundation for a new alternative, Dhoruba Bin Wahad (formerly known as Richard Moore) of the Panther 21 trial noted: "it is definitely in the laboring masses best interest to institute through survival programs . . . an alternative to inferior high-priced foods . . . where people of the community collectively own, support and run cooperative stores . . . In order to reach this level, we must . . . [work] in a manner that necessarily involves the community because it relates to their survival."[19]

The BPP understood that survival programs were neither revolutionary nor capable of solving the material conditions of Black impoverishment. The programs sought to educate about the relevancy of socialism to daily life. Abstract theory is not always relevant to communities' needs; hence survival programs became a form of theory-in-practice. Key also in survival programs were material needs for security or safety from police aggression, imprisonment, mass incarceration, and police homicide. All too often, however, security strategies are left out in conventional narratives on the BPP.

Community Control

Black Lives Matter and diverse forms of activism have popularized if not shaped concepts of community, racial-profiling, and militarized policing within democracy. That advocacy shapes debates about the relevance of democratic socialism. The BPP's first police-watch program in 1967—following the party's original name, "Black Panther Party *for Self-Defense*"— sought to monitor and diminish police misconduct. It did so in ways distinct from but similar to cell-phone footage today (although there is no consensus outside of high-profile police murders that there have been substantial gains in control over predatory policing through cell phones). As Panthers became the focus of police harassment and conflict, effective monitoring of police misconduct diminished. By 1968, programs became more broadly political. For example, the BPP assisted tenants with landlord and tenant disputes. The Panthers were asked by residents to provide protection from gangs, given their distrust of or alienation from the police departments that targeted low-income communities of color. In 1969, in New York's Lower East Side, members of the organized-crime-syndicate motorcycle gang, the Hells Angels, lived in a building as tenants; they terrorized Black tenants in an attempt to evict them from the apartment building, in order to make it an all-white residence or all-"motorcycle club" building. They might have been able to segregate the building had not a Black tenant called the BPP for assistance. NYC Panthers accompanied National Field Marshal Don Cox to investigate the situation, speaking to both white gang-member and Black tenants. The Panthers then guarded the building until harassment from the Hells Angels ceased, according to K. Kim Holder, a Panther vet who provided overnight protection for harassed Black tenants.[20]

Regular party members participated in community programs. They often lived in a collective manner, and took turns cooking, cleaning, and providing for household needs; the basic need centered on food and health. Transitioning from the domestic communal to the public political, the most popular BPP program became the free breakfast program (FBP). The FBP developed because of the numerous hungry children who attended school without proper meals or food security. Each BPP chapter had at least one FBP that highlighted the importance of nutritional assistance within communities. Feeding children before they went to school also exposed the economic inequities within US racial capital: underemployment and exploited labor led to low wages that could not adequately sustain families particularly if they were Black, Indigenous, or brown.[21] Exposing the fact that government and corporations had the resources but not the desire or the will to provide the basic human right of a nutritional meal, especially for children, highlighted the need for an alternative to the capitalist economy: "[It] is not enough to publish 2,000-page reports containing facts and statistics on hunger in Babylon because we cannot feed a report to a hungry child . . . the Party has put its theory of serving the people into practice," by providing free breakfast for children throughout the US.[22] Showing by example that communities had the power to control hunger among their children through organizing and alternative models of care increased the possibilities for creating a more just social order.

Malika Adams of the New York FBP expressed the feeling of working with the program: "I was doing something concrete and I could understand it . . . I could clearly see that if I get up at 4:00 in the morning and feed children . . . I know these children were hungry because I'd have to go get them and I could see they were hungry."[23] All children were welcomed. According to the Philadelphia FBP coordinator Sam Coley: "We feed any and all children who come to us hungry."[24] Programs included white, Latinx, and Black children. In New York, Berkeley, Seattle, Washington, and Chicago, multicultural and multiracial children and staff populated the building. Many centers lacked formal interaction between staff and children due to the shortage of staff and the volume of meals served. At other centers, staff members conducted informal discussions or classes on Black and Latinx history and political education discussions about the need for the FBP. The Des Moines Panther Clive De Patten saw that the FBP wove socialist thinking into care and food: "We would say like there are five kids here, and one of these individuals has five pieces of candy. If you give each one of the others a piece of candy that would be socialism. Socialism was simply sharing, an equal distribution of whatever somebody had. This is the way we broke it down."[25]

The FBP was a tremendous source of support for communities served by and contributing cash or food donations to the FBP. Organizations such as the Puerto Rican Young Lords, the Chicano Brown Berets, the Asian I Wor Kuen, and the white Young Patriots began their own independent FBPs and also jointly ran breakfast programs with other groups. Food was obtained either by cash donations from individuals and/or food and material donations from businesses and organizations. This model of communal socialism was autonomous: until 1971, the BPP did not accept government funding. Governmental agencies attempted to demonize and vilify the organization for attending to human needs neglected by corporate-capitalist government. The BPP's position was oppositional to capitalism, but party rules prohibited intimidation or theft to provide for the FBP. The BPP also initiated boycotts of specific stores that would not support the FBP.[26]

By 1970, the FBP had become a model for other survival programs such as free health clinics and food and clothing distribution programs. The focus on socialism was a constant. At Corona, New York, the Panther Carlton Yearwood noted of a free clothing rally: "Solidarity among the masses is becoming an objective reality through bringing the masses together so that they can see the contradiction of this capitalist society and weigh these findings with the ideology of Socialism 'Serving the People.' The reality of socialism overthrowing capitalism is because through their practice this will be the will of the people."[27] All programs, including the FBP, were models for the community to initiate and run: "People in the communities where our programs are in operation have come forth to cook and donate their money and time as they see that the program is for their benefit. Also, they see it as a bright example of them using their resources and energies, without the burden of a bureaucratic program . . . We honor the people who care about our youth."[28] At many FBP sites, there were more non-Panthers working than Panthers. This was consistent with the Panthers' view of serving the people. The BPP was more interested in initiating rather than controlling the programs. The Party welcomed non-members who wanted to be involved in communal care programs.

During 1970, the federal government provided 51,380 "free or reduced" breakfasts daily to school children. The average cost per meal was 25 cents. A 1972 Department of Agriculture report stated that this amount covered the cost of one piece of white bread and a half a glass of milk.[29] In contrast, BPP-initiated programs fed well over 3,200 children daily: thirty-two branches serving one hundred children each. The BPP's FBP and similar endeavors were thus perhaps the most comprehensive free-food program within a communal socialist context of its time. Constant opposition to communal socialism included San Diego FBI agents lobbying the Catholic hierarchy to transfer a priest hosting a FBP in his New Mexico church.[30]

The BPP liberation schools were modeled after the SNCC freedom schools, established during the 1964 "Freedom Summer" in Mississippi and offering progressive curriculum for African-American students to "examine their personal experiences with racial discrimination."[31] Attached to FBPs, conservatives and the government accused such sites of conducting ideological indoctrination of youths. Despite the opposition, community and communal care continued. Children and families required not only food or material sustenance, but also critical educational tools to evaluate the politics, ethics, and economics shaping their lives. Workers' families with small children, the un(der)employed, and elders desperately needed quality care. In 1970, the BPP began to expand daycare centers for the public; originally childcare centers had been organized to care for the infants of Panther members (in Philadelphia, Los Angeles, and Algiers). Centers began to expand to include community members. One mother of five, whose children made satisfactory grades in school, was impressed by the instruction at the liberation school coupled with the FBP. Noting her children voluntarily writing and giving oral reports on global news, she observed that, "Their work shows that they can relate to what is happening to them and other poor people in the world." Encouraged to contribute to community, young students devoted more time to learning to read and write in order to offer effective support to Black communities.[32]

Medical Programs

There is much discussion and organizing today around single-payer healthcare (aka "Medicare for All").[33] The BPP sought free and universal healthcare for all communities, including grassroots programs that developed free medical clinics and healthcare programs. In 1969, various chapters of the party collaborated with health professionals and medical students to offer medical check-ups in local neighborhoods.[34]

Conditions and problems such as high-blood pressure, sickle-cell anemia, lead poisoning, and drug abuse were major concerns for the early BPP medical programs and teams which offered blood and blood-pressure testing, nutritional counseling, general checkups, and drug counseling. Most medical teams were trained by medical volunteers: medical students or professional nurses and physicians. Initially, BPP members concentrated on first-aid skills as branches conducted first-aid classes for medical cadres who were responsible for Panther medical and dental appointments, teaching basic emergency first aid. On street-corner tables, the Panther medics provided free tuberculosis tests and information on sickle-cell anemia. The BPP launched a national campaign to raise public consciousness of sickle-cell anemia in 1971, and was a leading participant in establishing a research foundation on the condition. Black medical students and doctors assisted in Harlem's free clinic. Weekly meetings were held for the medical cadres of the Bronx, Brooklyn, Harlem, Jamaica, and Corona (Queens). Panthers worked with progressive white and Puerto Rican medical corps in Manhattan's Lower East Side clinic while Brooklyn saw the emergence of the New York 21 Community Health Clinic. Health education and preventive medicine were routinely taught to Panthers and members of the community.[35]

In Rockford, Illinois a branch clinic opened, while in Chicago, the Spurgeon Jake Winters Free People's Medical Care Center, staffed by gynecologists, obstetricians, dentists, pediatricians, optometrists, general practitioners, registered nurses, lab technicians, and public advocates, served over 2,000 people within the first two months of its opening. Organized volunteers and medical students canvassed communities, testing for lead poisoning, sickle-cell anemia, and diabetes.[36] Chicago's health authorities repeatedly attempted to close the clinic despite the fact that it was staffed by qualified medical staff and had adequate equipment. In 1970, a medical clinic was housed in a trailer on land seized by the Boston Black United Front in an attempt to stop the city from building a highway through the African-American community. In addition to holding public health classes, the Boston center also trained lab technicians, nursing assistants, and medical secretaries. The BPP used the death of an African-American patient, who had been shot by Boston police at Boston General Hospital, to mobilize support for community control of medical care and the emergence of the Boston Peoples Health Centers. At the opening ceremony, Julia Mack, the mother of the slain man, donated a portrait of her son to the clinic. On the clinic's first anniversary, over one hundred community people attended a dinner honoring Mack's support.[37]

Conclusion

The journalist and former BPP political prisoner Eddie Conway asserts that it was the party's rejection of capitalism that made it a target of police repression. However, a combination of factors—including the BPP's own missteps and violence, along with its insistence on the right to self-defense, its anti-racist analyses, internationalist frameworks, and demands for community and police control—led to its demonization and rejection.

The BPP was anti-capitalist. Racism and (hetero)patriarchy are major forms of oppression, but they cannot be eradicated until the capitalist system and imperialism disintegrate. The petty bourgeoisie and Blacks who found careers in government, military, and corporations did not share the same class status or deprivation of the unemployed and working poor, nor did they share the same vulnerability to police violence.

By demonstrating socialism through material support via free breakfast, housing, and medical programs, Panthers believed that they could harness a perceived historical tendency and mandate among Black communities, and address individual financial oppression through collective means. Half a century has passed since COINTELPRO targeted Panthers for elimination or "neutralization" through intimidation, false imprisonment, and assassinations.[38] Individualism, consumerism, digitized addictive entertainment, movement millionaires, celebrities-as-influencers and political leaders, the search for "Black faces in high places" serving the state and capital, COVID-19, rising unemployment, diminishing affordable housing, insufficient quality healthcare, and education—all are also key factors in the rise of alienation and mental and physical distress. Academics and mainstream journalists as the authorities on (radical) politics has meant revisionism from sectors that rarely fought in the streets or within working communities, but instead largely perched within the academy, nonprofit think tanks, or publishing houses, to view mass struggle and then disseminate and distribute interpretations that become dominant ideological frameworks that resist substantive change from below.

Conventional campaign cycles of electoral politics are shaped by the US Supreme Court's 2010 *Citizens United* decision, which allowed wealthy donors and corporations to skew electoral power away from the mass,[39] and other court rulings that permit voter suppression, gerrymandering, and felon disenfranchisement. The Electoral College nullifies the popular vote in presidential elections, and the Democratic and Republican parties cater to billionaires and oppose progressive grassroots activists. The BPP had opposed centrist politics at the height of its militant opposition to state violence and in its search for socialism (or communism, which is not discussed here). The environmental activist Kali Akuno, a member of Black Socialists in America, offers an assessment of Black socialism's role, reflecting the refrain of half a century past—"All power to the people":

> the working class remains a divided subject, fractured by language, nationality, culture, religion, race, sex, and gender. The proletariat is also under constant assault by the bourgeoisie, as well as the reactionary state institutions and social forces that it controls and marshals to execute its will. Despite its present fragmentation and the never-ending assaults that it is forced to endure, the proletariat is objectively growing in size and strength throughout the world as a result of being subjected to ever-intensifying processes of accumulation, dispossession, communication, and enculturation by the capitalist-imperialist system.[40]

Notes to Chapter 6

1   Baker speaking at Puerto Rico solidarity rally, 1974; available online, https://www.writingcities.com/2017/12/15/ella-baker-puerto-rico -solidarity-rally-1974/, accessed October 6, 2022.

2   Andrew J. Wilkes, "Socialism in Black America?," *religioussocialism.org*, January 14, 2016, https://www.religioussocialism.org /socialism_in_black_america.

3   Eddie Conway, "'The State Targeted the Panthers Because We Were Socialists, Not Because We Were Armed'—Eddie Conway on Reality Asserts Itself (4/12)," The Real News Network, September 14, 2014, https://therealnews.com/econway140904raipt4.

4   Sam Frizell, "Here's How Bernie Sanders Explained Democratic Socialism," *Time*, November 19, 2015, https://time.com/4121126 /bernie-sanders-democratic-socialism/.

5   Ocasio-Cortez quoted in Annalisa Merelli, "Alexandria Ocasio-Cortez Explained Democratic Socialism and Capitalism at SXSW," *Quartz*, March 20, 2019, https://qz.com/1569538 /sxsw-watch-the-alexandria-ocasio-cortez-interview/.

6   See Naomi Klein, "The Battle for Paradise: Naomi Klein Reports from Puerto Rico," *The Intercept*, April 7, 2018, YouTube video, https://www .youtube.com/watch?v=pTiZtYaB3Zo.

7   West speaking in Tucker Carlson, "Tucker Takes On Cornel West over Democratic Socialism," Fox News, accessed October 17, 2022, YouTube video, https://www.youtube.com/watch?v=kuc6C2_Txmw.

8   See e.g. PBS *Frontline*, "Interview: Kathleen Cleaver," accessed October 6, 2022,https://www.pbs.org/wgbh/pages/frontline/shows/race /interviews/kcleaver.html; and Kathleen Cleaver and George Katsiaficas, eds, *Liberation, Imagination and the Black Panther Party: A New Look at the Black Panthers and Their Legacy* (New York: Routledge, 2001).

9   PBS *Frontline*, "Interview: Kathleen Cleaver."

10   Ibid.

11   Ibid.

12   Ibid.

13   Ibid.

14   Ibid.

15   Peter Kornbluh, "The Death of Che Guevara: Declassified," National Security Archive, George Washington University, accessed October 6, 2022, https://nsarchive2.gwu.edu/NSAEBB/NSAEBB5/

16   *The Black Panther,* November 1, 1969, 19.

17   *The Black Panther*, November 15, 1969.

18   *The Black Panther*, February 28, 1970, 18.

19   *The Black Panther*, November 28, 1970, 9.

20   Author's interview with K. Kim Holder, 2021.

21   Anon., "New Child Poverty Data Illustrate the Powerful Impact of America's Safety Net Programs," Annie E. Casey Foundation blog, September 20, 2021, https://www.aecf.org/blog/new-child

-poverty-data-illustrates-the-powerful-impact-of-americas-safety-net
-programs.

22   *The Black Panther*, February 28, 1970.

23   Adams quoted in Holder, "History of the Black Panther Party," 87.

24   Coley quoted in ibid., 88.

25   De Patten quoted in House of Representatives Committee on Internal
Security, *Black Panther Party Part 4: National Office Operations and
Investigation of Activities in Des Moines, Iowa, and Omaha, Nebr. (Hearings
before the Committee on Internal Security, House of Representatives, Ninety-
first Congress, Second Session, October 6, 7, 8, 13, 14, 15, and November 17,
1970)* (Washington, DC: US Government Printing Office, 1971), 4,812.

26   Holder, "History of the Black Panther Party," 90–92.

27   *The Black Panther*, November 1, 1969, 19.

28   *The Black Panther*, March 28, 1970, 8.

29   Select Committee on Nutrition and Human Needs, *Nutrition and Human
Needs—1972: Hearings Before the Select Committee on Nutrition and Human
Needs of the United States Senate, Ninety-second Congress, Second Session,
on Nutrition and Human Needs . . .* (Washington, DC: US Government
Printing Office, 1972), part 1.

30   Kenneth O'Reilly, *Racial Matters: The FBI's Secret File on Black America,
1960–1972* (New York: Free Press, 1989), 316.

31   See SNCC Digital Gateway, "Freedom Schools," accessed October
6, 2022, https://snccdigital.org/inside-sncc/culture-education
/freedom-schools/; and Deborah Menkart and Jenice L. View, "Exploring
the History of Freedom Schools," *Civil Rights Teaching*, accessed
October 6, 2022, https://www.civilrightsteaching.org/exploring
-history-freedom-schools.

32   Philip S. Foner, ed., *The Black Panthers Speak* (Philadelphia, PA:
Lippincott, 1970), 172.

33   Single-payer healthcare: "a system in which a single public or qua-
si-public agency organizes health care financing, but the delivery of
care remains largely in private hands. Under a single-payer system, all
residents of the US would be covered for all medically necessary services, including doctor, hospital, preventive, long-term care, mental
health, reproductive health care, dental, vision, prescription drug and
medical supply costs": https://pnhp.org/what-is-single-payer/.

34   Holder, "History of the Black Panther Party," 110–14.

35   *The Black Panther*, February 28, 1969, 17.

36   *The Black Panther*, January 29, 1970, and April 3, 1971, 3.

37   *The Black Panther*, June 12, 1971, 15.

38   See Zinn Education Project, "This Day in History—March 8, 1971:
FBI's COINTELPRO Exposed," accessed October 6, 2022, https://www
.zinnedproject.org/news/tdih/cointelpro-exposed/.

39   See Tim Lau, "Citizens United Explained," Brennan Center for
Justice, December 12, 2019, https://www.brennancenter.org/our-work
/research-reports/citizens-united-explained.

40   Kali Akuno, "Joining BSA: Kali Akuno," Black Socialists in America,
March 28, 2019, https://blacksocialists.us/news/joining-bsa-kali-akuno.

Part II
Power in Structures

Reaching beyond
"Black Faces in High Places"

With George Yancy and *Truthout*, 2021

George Yancy Black suffering is pervasive; its arc long. As a scholar-activist who takes seriously such themes as radical politics and abolitionism, when will Black suffering "bend"? Or is it the case that Blackness is always already a site of "permanent" suffering or oppression? To put this metaphorically, are we still in the holds of slave ships? When I ask this question, COVID-19, and Black vulnerability to it, feels almost normative vis-à-vis the death of Black people.

Joy James Your first question relates to an existential theme that we discussed years ago about "misery" following the publicly displayed police executions of Eric Garner in Staten Island and Michael Brown in Ferguson. I do not think that Blackness as a permanent site of suffering and oppression is the defining marker of who we are. I would say that white supremacy and its violent iterations are clearly historically documented. Think here of enslavement, the convict leasing system, Black Codes,[1] Jim Crow, voter disenfranchisement, redlining,[2] and spectacular war and violence (as reflected in Tulsa, Oklahoma's "Black Wall Street" 1921 bombing, burning, and mass murders of Black residents, in which white police looted and lynched, re-enacted decades later by Philadelphia police in the 1985 bombing of the MOVE house and city employees deciding to burn down an entire Black neighborhood).[3] White-supremacist culture is a permanent site of predatory consumption, extraction, and violation. Its aggressions seek to distract from the dystopia depicted in T.S. Eliot's *The Waste Land*.

Oppression and devastation preceded and engineered the creation of the "Black"; we are just in a long dirge in which resistance and rebellion follows repression and adds shouts, prayers, and expletives. How do we resist? We do so in innumerable ways through arts and activism, betrayal and code switching as "shape shifting".[4]

We are in the "hold": slave ships, dungeons, prisons, jails, Immigration and Customs Enforcement (ICE) "family centers" (in Texas, Haitian families form 40 percent of the detained population)[5] and "womb collector" hysterectomies that seem to "favor" Black women/mothers. Yet the rebellion by whistleblowing was done by a sister, the nurse Dawn Wooten, who reported both medical violations and medical neglect concerning COVID-19.[6] From the hold of a slave ship to solitary confinement in prison or psych wards, our people fight for life in the presence of death by caring for ourselves and others.

GY   When I think about the theme of Black leadership and hope, I think that there were many who may have conceptualized Barack Obama's presidency as the panacea for anti-Black racism, that he might help the arc of the moral universe to bend. I think that such an expectation was unreasonable for many reasons, one being that he was commander-in-chief, head of the American empire. My question has to do with radical political change and its possible realization from within the space of state power. I'm thinking here of Kamala Harris but trying to do so beyond her symbolic significance as the first Black and South-Asian-American woman to hold such political power. What can she do that might be identified as politically radical? After all, as you have argued elsewhere, hegemonic structures exist alongside a diversity of Black faces. As with Obama, her allegiance is to the American empire first. What would it take for "insiders" to bring about radical change, counter-hegemonic change, or is the instigation for genuine radical change only possible as "outsiders"?

JJ   We both work for private corporations defined as non-profit educational institutions. We have no romantic illusions about the nature of our jobs. We were hired to affirm and stabilize the elite university/college. We can demand accountability for white-supremacist/(hetero)sexist eruptions and ask for security (which can be denied or curtailed), but we do not pretend that these institutions exist to bring justice to the world or function in the interests of the oppressed (particularly if such institutions are gentrifying neighborhoods, and taking donor money from the right-wing oil and gas mogul Charles Koch, for example). If you don't have illusions about your day job and its functions to stabilize (while admonishing excessive violence from) racial capitalism, why would you have illusions about the government/state investment in racial capital?

No one forced Barack Obama to be the first Black *imperial* president for a nation whose democracy was built on racial conquest and rape. He wanted the gig. Black people, the working-class, laboring poor, or those dispossessed of paid labor, did not draw up petitions to draft Obama to primary Hillary Clinton (whose policies were more neoliberal-progressive than Obama's in the 2007–8 primary). White wealthy donors seemed to be his early backers along with a slice of the Black elite that had not yet peeled off from the Clintons. Anti-Black racism was furthered by Clinton policies and never seriously challenged by Obama policies. If the big ask now is to "see Black faces in high places," then enjoy the Biden–Harris administration. It is definitely better to not be taxed to pay for violent white nationalists and the salaries and pardons of white-collar and war criminals. However, no longer being taxed to pay for predatory rogues, rot, and incompetence is not the definition of transformative justice. Empires thrive on violence and racial capitalism.

Harris campaigned on "Joe." Not just for the president-elect's policies but for his persona as the caring white leader who can bargain with those who empowered white nationalism and the devastation of the health and wellbeing of the laboring poor and working class.

Biden's revolving door of the Obama administration attempts to re-center Washington, DC into a romanticized past. There should be more money for jobs and social welfare programs—as much money as corporations and bureaucrats deem "prudent" from those exploited and abandoned by the corporate state and its racial/sexual/religious anima. With the return of the (neo)liberals, expect less autonomy for independent thinking, as everybody will be charged to "get on board" with the elite-driven programs that never adequately addressed white supremacy, poverty, and violence against women, children, and LGBTQ+ people, and are not designed by those most negatively impacted by racial-colonial capitalism.

Black masses are consistently told by the Black elite pundits, academics, nonprofit leaders, or movement specialists to stay in line and follow. But follow whom? What is the possibility that Obama and Harris have been sold to Black people by corporate-state elites as responsive to the needs of the Black mass and the impoverished and denigrated? Biden's only strong competitor was Bernie Sanders, who campaigned on "Medicare for All"[7]—until Black civil rights icons merged in the political machine with the Obama/Clinton Democratic National Committee (DNC) to warn folks not to go "too left" and to stop asking for "free stuff." How much misery from 20 million COVID-19 cases and over 400,000 deaths in the US could have been mitigated or prevented if universal healthcare existed? Where Black politicians and advocacy Democrats share the same donor base and think tanks—and propaganda networks—with the DNC, it is illogical to expect transformative justice. There are possibilities with congresswomen and men such as Cori Bush and Jamaal Bowman, and the sort of rogue Democratic Socialists of America (DSA), if their roles as productive disruptors and creators for the (Black) masses are not cannibalized by the party machine.

GY   How do we engage in "free discourse," that is, a discourse that challenges how liberals have defined freedom and liberty? What does a political vision of freedom look like outside of logics that maintain the status quo, that imprison not just our discourse but our political imaginative capacities? 〕〕 Free discourse is the ability to be radical in service to the disenfranchised and imprisoned without being attacked. Obama instituted the most repressive laws against whistleblowers and investigative journalists. To stop the white-(Black?-)washing of the Obama legacy and acquiescence to its heirs apparent, radicals would have to negotiate the terms of struggle and sacrifice, and face insults for attempting to illuminate contradictions, hegemonic betrayals, and performative politics within celebrity activism and education masking ideology and accumulation from the monetization of Black suffering. There is razor-like irony at play in performative politics inching towards the Achilles heels of radicals. Black radicals are lectured to stop being so "lefty" by Joe and Barack (and others who castigate as "purity politics" analyses which decades ago would have been described as principled rather than opportunistic). Millions protested against the police murders of George Floyd and Breonna Taylor, and the police and white-supremacist killings and dishonoring of community members, such as Anjanette Young in Chicago;[8] in addition there are the deaths due to medical neglect and racism, such as that of Dr. Susan Moore; yet rarely if at all are officials held accountable for those homicides or deaths. Dr. Moore's last testimony offers a clear warning: "Being Black up in here, this is what happens."[9]

Historically, anti-Black violence was used to enslave and accumulate wealth for non-Blacks, including Indigenous tribes granted "civilized nations" status if they trafficked and enslaved Black people. Some doubt the New Mexico congresswoman Deb Haaland, named the first Indigenous secretary of the interior by Biden, will positively respond to the Choctaw–Chickasaw Freedmen/Black Indian petition to seek tribal recognition and monetary and land support.[10] Anti-Black violence was also embedded in Biden's choice of new secretary of agriculture, Tom Vilsack, the former agriculture guy in the Obama administration who expedited Black farmers' loss of their lands and livelihoods due to denial of civil rights protections.[11] Violence from historical slave ships to contemporary administrators enabled accumulation through Black loss. One can monetize Black suffering and raise revenue through private prisons, repressive charter schools, Wells Fargo Bank loan fraud targeting Black homeowners.[12] Those opposed to anti-Black violence and dispossession can also monetize Black suffering by refashioning narratives and traumas into marketable writing and lecturing, fashion wear, public relations, voter registration drives, nonprofit sector jobs, punditry and podcasts. Black misery is profitable for racists and anti-racists alike. Yet, Black street-activists or imprisoned activists—whose heads are most likely to be cracked open by violent cops, guards, and white supremacists—take the greatest risks for transformative justice and reap the smallest percentage of monetary gains from "advocacy democracy."[13] Explaining Black people or anti-Black terror to non-Blacks, reassuring Blacks that there is a way to evolve out of predatory anti-Blackness without revolutionary struggle, is lucrative. Those funds garnered from the narratives of those who engage in radical risk rarely go back into Black institutions, community centers, houses of worship, food banks, freedom schools, and, most importantly, *transformative political education*, what the Panther Fred Hampton defined as the only real weapon against oppression.

GY   The Black Lives Matter movement is crucial as a dynamic process of bringing attention to various forms of anti-Blackness. Meanwhile, Indigenous struggles are often erased even in the middle of racial justice movements. Speak to the theme of solidarity here. I'm thinking of Martin Luther King Jr., where he says that "Injustice anywhere is a threat to justice everywhere."[14] It seems to me that marginalized people can't claim liberation until Native Americans are also liberated. In fact, Native American suffering, or so I would argue, is often elided.

⅃⅃   There were debates before an abolitionist platform changed its motto statement from a quote by a Black academic to a declaration for sovereign rights by the Indigenous South Dakota leader Harold Frazier seeking to secure the roads into the reservation, despite the Trumpist governor Kristi Noem attempting to claim that she had jurisdiction over highways running through Indigenous lands and thus would keep those roads open to random truckers.[15] The attempts of a collective of radical Black women abolitionists to highlight Article 16 of the Fort Laramie Treaty (1868) as "abolitionism" was permitted as a *momentary* intervention. Radical Black women and allies for Indigenous autonomy could only temporarily refocus the abolitionist motto. We later circulated a statement asserting that Indigenous nations and elders—not Black, white, or people of color (POC) academics—determine the status of those who claim to belong to Indigenous communities (and build careers as representatives of said communities); we opposed the assertion by non-Indigenous people (Black and white) that we were engaged in "narrow identity politics" for not recognizing a white person who claimed indigeneity because they were a privileged academic.

In the US, we grapple with white supremacy, "POC" ethnic chauvinism toward Indigenous people, and anti-Black racism among Indigenous people. We lack consensus on how progressive multiracial "coalitions" should respect the desires of Black working-/laboring-class people and Indigenous reservation communities to define their needs and assert autonomy. Revolutionary acts respect global Indigenous autonomy and culture, including Indigenous peoples in Africa, Australia, the Americas, and beyond.

The lawyer and civil rights activist Derrick Bell analyzed "interest convergence," in which the strongest party steers the coalition and so betrays the needs of the less empowered by the racial state and capital.[16] Alliances with hegemonic wealthy white liberals tilt the balance of the scales. If Indigenous elites are white-wealth-identified, they will not align with Black people unless they are also white-wealth-identified. Either way, Black masses are marginalized.

I am curious about why Afropessimism is so vilified for its contributions not just its limitations. Its contributions are to cut through the smoke and mirrors of banal coalitions that castigate Black people for being "too Black," that is, for addressing the need to be free from anti-Blackness/white supremacy through a political project that forecloses compromise (the "virtue" of coalitions that are not dominated by radical Black masses). Perhaps we could focus on what we have in common as Indigenous, Black Indigenous and Black people: rebellion. Hence the need to free our political prisoners, such as Leonard Peltier, Mutulu Shakur, Mumia Abu-Jamal, Joy Powell, Russell Maroon Shoatz, Sundiata Acoli, Veronza Bowers, Ruchell Cinque Magee, and others who rebelled against conquest and genocide.

We need each other as allies in struggle, but as Black people our struggles remain distinct; it is not a hierarchy in oppression, it is a *specificity* in combating it that we as radicals demand. Let's see if we can form an alliance around the recognition of the rights of Black Indigenous people alongside the recognition of non-Black Indigenous rights to land and autonomy. Also, let's see if we can discuss reparations with specificity, not generalizations; that this is an imperial democracy built on stolen Indigenous land and with stolen Black labor. Let's see if we can collectively mourn the mass rapes of Black women baked into the "Three-fifths Compromise" of the US Constitution[17] by which former slavery-bond states (Southern "red states") deployed terror for reproduction to accumulate political power and pro-plantation presidencies. Let's see if we can fight the murders and disappearances of cis and trans Black women and girls interlocking with the battles to stop the murders and disappearance of cis and trans Indigenous women, girls, and two-spirit people.[18]

GY   You have written about spirituality and Black feminist thought. As an approach to healing so much human suffering, speak to the importance of a specifically *spiritual* awakening that is necessary for this country. In what ways does your understanding of spirituality overlap with Black feminist thought in terms of rethinking relationality, community, and humanity?

JJ   Spirituality and trauma forced me to recognize the limited capacity of bourgeois Black feminist thought and reflect on how the ideological markers of Black feminism were blended into hegemonic discourse and "progressive" marketing.

We have passed the fiftieth anniversary of the 1971 Attica Prison rebellion. Think about how those in Attica maintained the structures of their captivity under pain of torture or death, until they chose to risk life to defeat a living death. Trustees and imprisoned nurtured and nursed each other and performed the labor under penal slavery (the Thirteenth Amendment to the US Constitution codifies enslavement to incarceration) that allowed the massive prison to exist. Rejecting the first or early stage of contradiction and caretaking and collaboration, the captives decided to organize a prison strike for human rights and dignity. They allowed spirit to lead them into mass movement and rebellion (some were inspired by the assassination of George Jackson).[19]

After taking over the massive prison, they had to rebuild community as a maroon camp within a prison, setting up a food delivery system, waste removal, political education, a medic site, security, spokespersons to address the press and public about their 1971 Liberation Manifesto.[20] Spirit formed community out of chaos; amid precarity and extreme vulnerability they were able to forge unity and purpose for transformative justice.

There are spirit-filled stages—conflicted caretaker, movement activist, maroon, war resistor—where those who risk their lives to achieve life outside of the fetid hold see "losses" transformed into victories. Attica captives were moved to the fourth and final stage of war resistor when the racial state born with a lust for slavery treated the rebellion for human and civil rights as an act of war and responded with Vietnam military surplus (imperial wars amplify domestic supremacist violence). The National Guard were called in by the New York governor Nelson Rockefeller (backed by President Nixon) and killed Black and brown resistors, maroons, community builders, and defenders; later guards would torture and murder rebels once the prison was retaken.

Rebellion creates origin stories and birth-making. Any moment of freedom means that the world is reborn sweeter: exhilarating hope laced with fear and despair.

Notes to Chapter 7

1   Black Codes: restrictive laws intended to curtail the freedom of Black Americans and to ensure their availability as cheap labor after the abolishment of slavery during the Civil War.
2   Redlining: in the US, the illegal and discriminatory practice of denying financial services (loans, insurance, etc.), often because of the racial characteristics of the applicant's neighbourhood.
3   See Jeremy Cook and Jason Long, "How the Tulsa Race Massacre Caused Decades of Harm," *The Atlantic*, May 24, 2021, https://www.theatlantic.com/ideas/archive/2021/05/1921-tulsa-race-massacre-economic-census-survivors/618968/; and Pilkington, "The Day Police Bombed a City Street."
4   As noted by a brilliant webinar, "Octavia E. Butler: Slow Read-A-Long," led by young Black feminist intellectuals and artists: https://njeridamalicampbell.wordpress.com/2020/06/22/octavia-e-butler-slow-read/, accessed October 7, 2022.
5   See RAICES, "Black Immigrant Lives Are under Attack," accessed October 7, 2022, https://www.raicestexas.org/2020/07/22/black-immigrant-lives-are-under-attack/.
6   José Olivares and John Washington, "'A Silent Pandemic': Nurse at ICE Facility Blows the Whistle on Coronavirus Dangers," *The Intercept*, September 14, 2020, https://theintercept.com/2020/09/14/ice-detention-center-nurse-whistleblower/; Miranda Bryant, "'I'm Back on Food Stamps': Nurse Who Exposed 'Uterus Collector' Still Faces Consequences," *Guardian*, October 17, 2022, https://www.theguardian.com/us-news/2022oct/17whistleblower-uterus-collector-repercussions-ice-detained-immigrant-women.
7   See Jonathan Michels, "The Fight for Medicare for All Made Some Important Progress in 2020," *Jacobin*, December 30, 2020, https://

jacobin.com/2020/12/medicare-for-all-2020-coronavirus-progress.

8   Gregory Pratt, "Mayor Lori Lightfoot Was Told by Staff in November 2019 that Anjanette Young Raid Was 'Pretty Bad,'" *Chicago Tribune*, December 31, 2020, https://www.chicagotribune.com/politics /ct-lightfoot-anjanette-young-raid-emails-20201230 -dhnc67ikorawdhm5a2xw7s4x7u-story.html.

9   See Democracy Now!, "'This Is How Black People Get Killed': Dr. Susan Moore Dies of COVID after Decrying Racist Care," December 30, 2020, YouTube video, https://www.youtube.com/watch?v=7vlOyp_bBGk.

10 Choctaw-Chickasaw Freedmen, "Deb Haaland: Stand against Modern-Day Jim Crow in Indian Country," change.org petition, accessed October 7, 2022, https://www.change.org/p/debra-haaland-deb-haaland-stand-against-modern-day-jim-crow-in-indian-country; see also the work of Keziah Anderson, "'On the Forty Acres That the Government Give Me': Independent Freedpeople of the Five Slaveholding Tribes as Landholders, Indigenous Land Allotment Policy, and the Disruption of Racial, Gender, and Class Hierarchies in Jim Crow Oklahoma" (undergraduate senior thesis, Columbia University, 2020); available online, https://history.columbia.edu/wp-content/uploads/sites/20/2020/05 /Anderson-Keziah_SNR-Thesis_web.pdf, accessed October 26, 2022.

11 Bill Siegel, "Why Black Farmers Don't Trust Tom Vilsack," *Agriculture*, February 2021, https://www.agriculture.com/news /why-black-farmers-dont-trust-tom-vilsack.

12 Derek Seidman and Gin Armstrong, "Scandal-Ridden Wells Fargo Rips Off Customers while Funding the Gun Industry and Carceral State," *Truthout*, March 30, 2018, https://truthout.org/articles /scandal-ridden-wells-fargo-rips-off-customers-while-funding-the -gun-industry-and-carceral-state/.

13 This is a term theorized by Marina Sokolova: see e.g. her "Advocacy Democracy Modes: Benefits and Limitations," *e-belarus.org*, accessed October 10, 2022, https://www.e-belarus.org/article /advocacydemocracy.html.

14 King Jr., "Letter from a Birmingham Jail."

15 Harold Frazier, "Chairman Harold Frazier Statement on Governor Kristi Noem Letter Regarding Health Checkpoints on Reservation," *indianz.com*, May 8, 2020, https://www.indianz.com/covid19 /2020/05/08/chairman-harold-frazier-cheyenne-river-sioux-tribe-2/.

16 Hoag, "Derrick Bell's Interest Convergence and the Permanence of Racism."

17 Three-fifths Compromise: "Although the Constitution did not refer directly to slaves, it did not ignore them entirely. Article one, section two of the Constitution of the United States declared that any person who was not free would be counted as three-fifths of a free individual for the purposes of determining congressional representation. The 'Three-Fifths Clause' thus increased the political power of slaveholding states": https:// www.thirteen.org/wnet/slavery/experience/legal/docs2.html.

18 See Carolyn Smith-Morris, "Addressing the Epidemic of Missing & Murdered Indigenous Women and Girls," *Cultural Survival*,

March 6, 2020, https://www.culturalsurvival.org/news/addressing
-epidemic-missing-murdered-indigenous-women-and-girls.

19   See Joy James, "George Jackson: Dragon Philosopher and
Revolutionary Abolitionist," *Black Perspectives* blog, AAIHS, August 21,
2018, https://www.aaihs.org/george-jackson-dragon-philosopher-and
-revolutionary-abolitionist/.

20   Attica Prison Liberation Faction, "Manifesto of Demands."

8   Political Theory in the Academy

With Carlotta Hartmann of People for Womxn* in Philosophy, 2021

Joy James Political theory is to do with engaging or thinking about the world as a political place, as the contestation of power. This starts in childhood. You know, you want to do something, your parents say, "No." Or school, the teachers have authority, and you do not. Your agency gets limited or is mitigated by the demands of others. That's great when you're in line with them in terms of ethics and desires, it's not great when they express power in authoritarian ways and you become the subject-object of their decrees or their rules and their policies.

I grew up in a military family, always confronted with the issue of power and control, the role of the state as an employer, the backdrop of warfare. My father was in Vietnam with the 101st Airborne Division, and he was probably deployed to quell the uprising—some people would call them riots—in Detroit. He was probably in a number of invasions. Even though you don't actually talk about power over the dinner table, or ask, "Where's Dad? What's he doing right now?," there's an understanding of policing as ingrained in the fabric of social life. Social life then becomes personal life, which is, by extension, political life and militarized.

By the time I was a preteen, I was interested in rebellion. I was eleven when I started to read my father's books, like E. Franklin Frazier's *Black Bourgeoisie*.[1] Frazier wrote this when he was working for UNESCO in the 1950s, as an African-American intellectual who understood the contradictions around power and hegemonic political theory coming from the right schools. He taught at the University of Chicago, and then went to teach at Howard University, the alma mater of

Vice President Kamala Harris. In his books he questions how the Black bourgeoisie, or the Black middle class, is an imitation of the white bourgeoisie. We don't have their money, but we have the same aspirations. He points to the contradictions: You come from a people who were enslaved for centuries, and then after that subject to the convict leasing system where you died at faster rates than you had on the plantations, jointly owned by corporations and the state. Then you faced Jim Crow legislation, prohibition to voting, voting at the cost of your life, at times sharecropping. You just go on up the stages to George Floyd and Breonna Taylor. The contradictions of being in the Black middle class are all about politics, compliance, or occasionally rebellion. At eleven, I'm reading this book, which shapes my feminism in the future and my suspicion of the Black bourgeoisie or the Black middle class of academic elites. That turned me into the political thinker that I am. I start with the family because it's the site of contradictions. If you work for the state, either private corporation or corporate state . . . you literally work for the government or the military.

I've always been a reader, trying to understand the world through books, and not usually the books that people my age were reading. So, you're reading about power that you do not have because you're not allowed to possess it. As a dark-skinned Black girl in the South, you're being groomed to be an intellectual outsider. Do you want in or do you want to break out? It seems like a contradiction; you're technically not in, but you're governed by those who set the program, the teachers, the parents, the principals, the university professors, the dissertation director, etc. How much do you want in, to the extent that your thinking is just conformity, and how much do you want out, to the extent that your thinking becomes a rebellion against conformity? These are the questions I was struggling with in my early years, along with the general sexism, racism, patriarchy, colorism, and anti-Black aggression.

Carlotta Hartmann You've just mentioned all sorts of obstacles. How did you deal with them?

JJ I'm not quite sure I can tell you. You know I hold this Ebenezer Fitch Professor of the Humanities chair. I'm sure Fitch was not an anti-racist feminist. For me it's a bit ironic and conflicted, all these titles that say, "You're a real intellectual," "You're a real professor," and, "You teach at a real school." Who gets to define what is "real," and why does it always look like another manifestation of elitism? My whole intellectual development was a constant struggle. Even now that I'm looking at retirement, I don't think it's been resolved. To what extent do you just give in and go with the program, even if you believe it to be unethical? It feels like a Ponzi scheme, the smartest people are not in academia, academics are just smart people who got the job. There are smart people in all economic classes and stations. The ones who are allowed to have the leisure time to write then have access to the most prestigious presses to publish and disseminate their thought, which usually seems to align itself with prevailing norms. This comes back to E. Franklin Frazier, and W.E.B. Du Bois before him: the notion of the talented tenth, that elite among African Americans who are going to lead the other 90 percent. That whole notion came from the American Baptist Home Mission Society, which were white philanthropists, during the era of the Civil War. After the war was won, after 200,000 formerly enslaved people fought in that war and helped the North to win, we have the resurgence of white supremacy as a norm in the United States. After the war is won, what do you do with an "emancipated" people? As white philanthropists, what they wanted was an educated cadre that would steer a Black mass that was impoverished, terrorized by the Klan, that gained rights that were then stripped away by these new Jim Crow laws. They wanted a kind of obedience and adherence to the rule of law, even if the law was corrupt and anti-Black.

To be educated, to attain these degrees was for me problematic. If you can't have a rebellion for your rights, if the point of having educated elites is to school them in a certain kind of civility and decorum that is compatible with existing democracy, I don't see how you get the other 90 percent free. In a way, it's almost like if you don't criminalize political rebellion, then you see it as a lack of civility and a lack of sophisticated politics. This was manifest in the promotion of the Democratic Party in the last election, too. Of course, Joe Biden is preferable to Donald Trump. But if you look at the specific policies that the Democrats have enacted, they have not, in large part, been beneficial and definitely not liberatory to impoverished or working-class African Americans and Native Americans. The Democratic Party shares the same kind of obedience mandate to corporate power that the Republican Party does. This comes back to the issue of political theory. Do you just accept that democracy is the Holy Grail for the liberation of LGBTQ+ folk, and for treating the natural environment as if it had real value other than that based on the extraction of coal, oil, and gas? Or do you want to use political theory to unthink the norms? I don't think it's enough, in an environment in which conformity in thinking is rarely challenged without being punished, to be a feminist theorist, or a critical race theorist, or a democratic socialist theorist, unless you're willing to understand the value of resistance and rebellion.

CH You've mentioned now, and elsewhere, how academia can be very limiting. How have you dealt with the limits of how far your theorizing within the academy can go, and how you would like to go beyond that?

JJ I don't know if I've achieved anything, only that I've tried. There's a form of loneliness in the academy. If the intent of our labor is to question authority, to call out what we think is racist, sexist, or homophobic—that's not welcomed, that wasn't in the job description. I've met so many students, mostly women, who wanted to articulate what they saw in terms of power, but who simply stayed mute. I've heard things like, "I need a letter to get a job," or, "I need to get published." People are disciplined to be disciplined. I'm not faulting them for that, I see all of this as the zone of compromise. The question becomes, how compromised you want to be in order to attain economic security, or see yourself as a white-collar worker, so that the next time there's a pandemic, you can stay home.

There's a lot of abuse in the academy, and it's gendered and it's shaped by race and ethnicity. What's often not talked about is that if you conform to a sort of corporate state norm, then your ethnicity and gender can be used to discipline those who refuse. The academy is the intellectual wing of the state. If you have a state that is progressive and doesn't believe in empires and has a critique of monopoly capitalism, then I don't think it's a bad thing to be the intellectual wing of that kind of state. My position is that the United States is not that kind of state.

CH   So far in academia, have there been any positive surprises about how far your studies and your theorizing can go that you didn't expect when you started out?

JJ   Let me not use me as an example, but some colleagues of mine. When I went to Brown University as a full professor, I brought former political prisoners to campus. On a panel discussion, I had invited graduate students who became the architects of Afropessimism, Jared Sexton and Frank B. Wilderson III. Years later I was surprised by what they were able to do in the academy, in codifying a school of thought that rejected the norms. I don't have the same politics as Afropessimism, but I have the same appreciation for rebellion against what I see to be predatory cultures, and the same sensitivity to deception, to people telling you they're not harming you while they are harming you, and getting you to believe that. The surprise there is that we're still employed, because we teach not to be popular, but to be relevant in a country full of crises, and that because of its military and its budget can create crises in other countries.

The beautiful thing that I see in the academy is when students ask you questions that sound like they're struggling. Not with grasping material so that they can "master" it and move up the ranks and get their gig or additional degrees, but struggling because they really want to comprehend how nothing fits the way they were told it would fit. We can think about the university as a replacement for parental authority; while you're there, they're supposed to be raising and polishing you. But then you realize that a lot of what you were told wasn't necessarily an accurate description of how much violence and corruption there is, and how hard we would have to work to care about the world which we weren't always the center of. The beauty, to come back to this, is when people realize they don't have superpowers, but they do have an intellectual capacity that can express not just compassion, but a certain kind of concern tied to a steely determination to do something. I think once you see people become more awake to the fact that they have the capacity to be political actors, but that in order to do so, they have to have political philosophy and political theory, the conversations shift from being the zone of consumption or mastery to being intimate. Afropessimism created a vocabulary to talk about this.

CH You've mentioned the sort of compromises that students and also academics have to face constantly. Do you have any advice to undergraduate students—or any student of political theory—in dealing with those compromises?

JJ I'll be honest, don't take advice from me. I wrote my dissertation on Hannah Arendt, a feminist critique of her analysis of communication. I was trying to talk about apartheid in South Africa during my dissertation defense, and I was so offended by the questions that came to me and the way I was challenged, not just for my "intellectual performance," but also for my ethics. I found these challenges unethical and racist. I was like, "Okay, when this is done, I'm done." I passed, because I knew what I was talking about, but I was so offended that I walked away with the PhD degree and never asked for a letter or recommendation to get hired in academia. I don't even have the words for it; I'm surprised I'm still really upset by this. But that's why you don't take advice from me. Eventually I did get a job, working for UN Women in Manhattan. I taught in seminaries part time and then went to seminary after a trip to Nairobi, and reflection on international politics (see below, p. 194). After seminary I tried again, and got my first academic job in women's studies at the University of Massachusetts Amherst. I'm not the only one who did something like that, there are a number of people who were disgusted and just quit the academy. That's the word I was looking for: disgust. I've read everything Arendt ever wrote, and then the dissertation where I'm, just in a sideline, just trying to say apartheid's bad, becomes problematic. And I was like, "I don't want your letter." Other people said, "I don't even want this job." The academy has probably lost some brilliant and passionate thinkers just because they couldn't stomach the environment.

CH   Is there anything that you deliberately do as a professor to break out of this environment?

JJ   I've always done it in different ways. When I was teaching women's studies at the University of Massachusetts Amherst, the predominantly white students complained about reading all this literature by women of color, as if they were not women. I was teaching a lot of memoirs by Native American women, Latinas, Asian women, African-American women, particularly political ones such as those by Angela Davis and Assata Shakur, but also by white women. The complaints kept coming, so I told them I'd give everyone an A, and they could show up, or leave. Not everyone returned, but the students who did were amazing because they weren't there for the grade.

I remember one white woman who was near tears saying that she was learning so much, she dreaded going home for the holidays—because if she actually said what she believed in terms of how white supremacy and misogyny operated, she would no longer have a family. At the time, I honestly did not know how to comfort people who evolved into more conscious and ethical beings . . . I don't believe you can evolve into a more ethical-political being without having losses.

Interacting outside of the classroom with some of the Black women who were at the university was amazing, too, because I was also learning from them. At the University of Colorado Boulder, I wrote about doing a prototype for Critical Resistance at the request of Angela Davis (see above, pp. 34–7). I organized this with the undergraduate students there, Black students who found the mostly elite campus quite problematic because of its racism. We were determined that this conference was going to go off well. It was the largest one that CU-Boulder had done at the time. A cadre of white, affluent students who were organizing and donating their labor, came to me and said they were going to miss class. And I was like, "What's the problem?," thinking that white affluent people don't have problems. They explained that the FBI wanted to interview them, because they had known people who were doing environmental liberation activism. I believe the United States put the Earth Liberation Front on some kind of terrorist list, the way they've been trying to do with Black Lives Matter. I get blinded this way sometimes; I don't see as clearly that white, affluent students are engaged in struggle as well. These were all educational moments for me.

Coming out of that conference I did an anthology, *States of Confinement*,[2] with works by a number of those who attended, and I got fifty copies to mail to incarcerated people. I got a letter back from a Black Panther, a Black Liberation Army political prisoner (who actually got out in October 2021 after serving forty-nine years in prison), saying that the academic work I thought I was being very helpful in producing was not that relevant. When I left CU-Boulder to go to Brown University, I was determined to write about and anthologize the most vulnerable of the radicals. Those people who were disappeared into prisons, who were being tortured, and who presumably were going to die there. I don't agree with all their choices, but I understood they saw themselves in a war. So, at Brown I took the greatest risk: I decided to invite people who had been in the Black Panther Party, people who had been in the Republic of New Afrika,[3] people aligned with the American Indian Movement, people who had been in the Puerto Rican independence movement. I used my personal research funds to do this, and my students helped organize that event. The three anthologies[4] that came out of the years that I stayed at Brown were driven in part by student intellect and student agency. That would be the height of teaching in which students taught me. I think that students are aware of the contradictions and the betrayals, from climate devastation and ongoing wars, to differential death rates around COVID-19 and new forms of authoritarianism. They actually know what's going on. The question becomes whether or not they feel somebody needs to give them permission or advice to act on the knowledge they already have. I don't give advice because I only know smart people, including people who never went to college. The best I can do is listen and maybe echo back to them some of the things that they've expressed, which are of concern to them or some of the things that they're willing to challenge. I don't think advice is useful, I think *solidarity* is.

CH   At this point of the COVID-19 pandemic, what are your hopes for the future?

JJ   I know that when I'm talking it's all really grim. In an interesting way, I am hopeful now. I am confident that we will respond to the crises, whether or not it's as many people as we would hope in solidarity. The certainty is that we, in different sectors, understand the threats. Affluent students are working on environmental issues because they understand the existential threat of that. Other students are working on police killings of civilians because they understand the existential threat of that. We're all laboring, on both the intellectual and the physical level, to stabilize the world that we have to live in and to allow it to be a more beautiful one. I see that happening all around.

As much as I have a critique of the academy, it has allowed me the leisure time, the extra time. I do have a roof over my head, I can buy my groceries and have a stable economic cushion, which has allowed me to use my time for social justice. That is the most beautiful thing about the academy, that whatever skills you acquire, you can redirect some to help people in ways that do not reproduce the cage. Having this job for decades has allowed me to practice my beliefs without being consumed by a machine. I've met beautiful people inside the Black Internationalist Unions, mostly Black women, academics. Since the pandemic started, we've been organizing and writing and trying to amplify the voices of the most vulnerable. Those sisters are fierce and they're much younger than I am. I can't help smiling because it's a good time to recede, when the young people and the young women, the young Black women who are stepping up, are very principled. They don't compromise just because they've been intimidated, they compromise because it's a necessity as a political strategy in the moment.

Notes to Chapter 8

1   E. Franklin Frazier, *Black Bourgeoisie* (New York: Free Press, 1957).
2   Joy James, ed., *States of Confinement: Policing, Detention, and Prisons* (New York: Palgrave, 2002).
3   See Dan Berger, "'Free the Land!': Fifty Years of the Republic of New Afrika," *Black Perspectives* blog, AAIHS, April 10, 2018, https://www.aaihs.org/free-the-land-fifty-years-of-the-republic-of-new-afrika/.
4   James, ed., *Imprisoned Intellectuals*; Joy James, ed., *The New Abolitionists: (Neo)Slave Narratives and Contemporary Prison Writings* (New York: SUNY Press, 2005); James, ed., *Warfare in the American Homeland*.

9 Captive Maternals, the Exonerated Central Park Five, and Abolition

With Chris Time Steele of *Time Talks*, 2019

Chris Time Steele I was wondering if you could speak about teaching counternarratives, how you approach combating propaganda? As you mentioned before, liberals don't like talking about violence. Often the academy will speak about how groups were repressed instead of also speaking about agency, such as the legacy of slave revolts leading to actual abolition—supposed "abolition," until you get to the Thirteenth Amendment—or academia not holding up Africana history but holding up Greek philosophy as a pillar of knowledge.

Joy James You can study the issue of violence as a concept and, in my perspective, you're permitted to do so if it's quite abstract. If you concretize it to contemporary violence, or the ways in which deprivation and disenfranchisement are tied to a long legacy of violence, it's perceived as controversial. For example, when I was recruited to Brown University, I was hired as a full professor, and provided with $10,000 for research. Most academics do individual research to produce new publications or whatever they choose to do with that kind of research funding. I decided to do a conference on political imprisonment. This was also at the time in which George W. Bush was preparing for his so called "shock and awe" invasion of Iraq under false pretenses of weapons of mass destruction being created there by Saddam Hussein. So, in doing this endeavor, I found all kinds of obstacles in opposition, some subtle, some not so subtle, to the fact that the political prisoners invited to campus were not just people who were incarcerated, but people who *fought* in Black liberation and other movements.

Speakers included Puerto Rican *independentistas*, white anti-racists from the anti-apartheid movements, people who represented the American Indian Movement. The state had used repressive violence against organizations that originally did not seek militaristic means to remedy or to protect themselves against state violence. War resistors against state violence became political prisoners. This discourse appeared to be not just novel to the university, but also controversial. Thus, it became a discourse that needed to be reprimanded and censored, if not completely shut down. This conference led to the anthologies *Imprisoned Intellectuals, The New Abolitionists* and *Warfare in the American Homeland*.[1] I found that if you treated the history of liberation movements not as an abstraction but as a living testimony to the will and desire of people to be freed from repression through refusal to succumb to state terror—which would include, to quote Malcolm X, "any means necessary"—that was considered a taboo. So, when I'm called into the president's office, I'm told that I can "teach anything" but "advocate nothing." Essentially: Don't advocate anything. Obviously, I'm not advocating any particular kind of day-to-day struggle, because people in their communities figure out their day-to-day struggles organically on the ground. As a theorist and an academic, I am pointing to the tangible material conditions under which a racist-capitalist democracy reproduces itself, through caging or terrorizing populations that it feels it needs to corral or disappear. Pointing to state violence not just as something we mourn, but as realities that have been consistently fought through various means, was prohibited. For me, it was not a prohibition against advocacy, even though it was couched in those terms. It was a prohibition against critical thinking.

CTS The theory that you produce, the seeds that that produces, you never know where that can go or how that will influence people. This is one of the most important things about theory.

JJ   The scariest thing about theory is that if people start thinking critically you have no idea what they will produce—amazing art, amazing culture, amazing resistance movements. I'm not talking merely about textual theory. In the academy you find one of the architects and then you become a specialist or scholar in their way of thinking and so you reproduce the norms tied to a particular kind of genealogy of thought. I'm not opposed to that. I mean, that is scholarship. I'm talking though about the kind of scholarship as critical theory that you can't put in the box because what it starts to reproduce is something that you've never seen before, and this seems like an anomaly or a contradiction in the university. The university is supposed to seek the most innovative, transformative means of thought and creation of critical thinking in order to create new knowledge or epistemologies. That's more like the marketing for it. The university, under capitalism, under racial capitalism, reproduces the norm, but expands its base in order to accumulate. You end up with the accumulation of other people's cultures, other people's thinking, as artifacts in some kind of museum, and that actually becomes one of the vulnerabilities of our movement. It's what some scholars, such as the Black Brazilian scholar João H. Costa Vargas, have called the "museum effect." Civil rights or Black Power movements become artifacts of the past. The national holiday "commemorating" Martin Luther King Jr. is sanitized of the violence (no or little discussion of political assassinations and imprisonment) that remains arrayed against Blacks/Africans. Radicals are portrayed in the "museum effect" as infantile if they cannot be reduced to pragmatism or alliance with state/nonprofit industries. But radicals are grounded in the needs of exploited communities. The university is not grounded in the needs of any community in struggle. If it's a state university, it is, technically and legally, a government entity. If it is a private university, it is a corporation. So, whether it's state capital, or private capital, which have been married in various ways—private corporations have dictated policies for

the state, the state has policed and protected private capital—
new thinking for freedom does not come from the university.
It comes from communities in struggle. New theories about
genes and about black holes, technical science using the
wealth of the state in the corporation, create new moments.
But those new moments of technology, of medicine, of engineering, while impressive, don't necessarily deliver freedom
or equity to people. People have to deliver that to themselves
and it is not the university's role to democratize and amplify
cultures through political struggle

CTS   That should be up to the self-determination of communities that decide to do whatever forms of liberation
they're seeking.

JJ   Some people believe that you can reform the state,
so that it actually will quell the levels of violence against disenfranchised peoples and communities, Indigenous people,
Black people, Puerto Ricans, people coming across the border, actually into territories that the US technically stole from
Mexico, south of the current US border through the Treaty of
Guadalupe Hidalgo.[2] Those people include a twenty-year-old
Guatemalan woman found shot in the head and killed by a
Border Patrol agent.[3] Other tragedies and outrages include a
twenty-year-old woman with two infants and a toddler found
dead in a desert. People live terror. Not because they inflicted
it on themselves. All communities have to deal with violence.
However, *structured* terror is delivered and organized through
the state. Those communities are the ones who face that reality and those communities are likely the ones who have the
experiential knowledge to address that. If you're looking for
purely legalistic reform, or reform through electoral politics,
as important as those endeavors are, if they do not directly
confront violence from the state apparatus, and its ability to
inflict harm on all people, of all ages, of all genders, or ungendered, then we haven't addressed the full capacity of our
thoughts. We haven't addressed the full capacity of our will to
be free of terror, which technically we pay for as taxpayers.

CTS This ties into your powerful essay, "The Womb of Western Theory: Trauma, Time Theft, and the Captive Maternal."[4] You write that Captive Maternals are "those most vulnerable to violence, war, poverty, police, and captivity; those whose very existence enables the possessive empire that claims and dispossesses them." You speak about how Western democracy, based in American exceptionalism, merged Enlightenment ideologies to create this white-supremacist background that you say "fed on Black frames," and you call Western democracy an "anti-soulmate of freedom." Could you talk about how, as you write, "the absent dialectic between master and Captive Maternal is a missed opportunity for the evolution of revolutionary theory"?[5]

JJ   Yeah [*laughs*]. You just said a lot . . . I totally abide by this fact of collective theory or as the UC-Berkeley professor of African-American literature and feminism Barbara Christian would say, "theorizing as a verb."[6] And the collective wisdom of the material world and the immaterial world, the spirituality of the people and of our ancestors guides me. We have conversations all the time, not always with fully physically embodied people.

The Captive Maternal as a concept came about after I started dealing with the state's treatment of children in its systems. It wasn't purely research. I was meeting mothers—I always met mothers from organizing—mostly I just organized with women and not on these high-profile levels or platforms. The academic profile is higher than the activist profile, but the activist profile is what I adore. It's not a profile, per se, it's a practice of humility, and also—to the best I can muster—courage.

When I was organizing alongside Black women at Medgar Evers College in Brooklyn, NY, I was in another political formation, a multiracial women's group that had ties with the Communist Party, Women for Racial and Economic Equality, which I joined (though I decided not to join the CPUSA). I saw the way in which Black radical women critique the world and their critique was dismissed because they were read as working-class Black mothers from a non-elite institution of higher education. They were not credited with critical savvy. Yet, they're the ones who predicted the fall of the Berlin Wall in 1989 and the rapprochement between—you could joke about Putin and Trump right now—Eastern Europe and Western Europe. That rapprochement would cement capital so that Black and Indigenous people and people of color would still be left out in the cold and still be treated as detritus or raw resources, not just their land and minerals per se, but the people themselves and their labor and cultures.

The Black women internationalists from Brooklyn offered that first critique, which led me to develop a critique of Michel Foucault that I first wrote about and published in 1996 in *Resisting State Violence.*[7] I took a postdoc with Angela Davis at the University of California, Santa Cruz. We were reading Foucault's *Discipline and Punish* in Davis's graduate seminar at the history of consciousness department. I gave a closing talk at the end of my Ford Foundation postdoctoral fellowship. My critique of Foucault would later be used by Davis in her own (less critical) critique of Foucault. A couple of years later, other critiques on Foucault's erasure of anti-Blackness followed. My views came from the framework of Black maternal activism, because the Medgar Evers Black women activists cared for their children, they cared for their communities. They cared for the elder and child. Yes, electoral politics were and are important. But so is the day-to-day reality of making sure your kids have enough food, have quality medical care, have a safe school environment, don't get harassed by cops, put in prisons, or shot, or brutalized. Through function I saw that our captivity stemmed not just from an oppression or the repression of the state. It was also this entanglement and love for families and communities, not just one's biological children, or particular grandmothers or grandfathers or grand-aunts, grand-uncles. There is this huge embrace. What kept you disciplined was not just the state's animus against you, which you were happy to return in varied forms. Discipline enabled your capacity to love the most vulnerable and to resist the most predatory. How we were and are positioned in struggle, radiated beyond any kind of linear or unitary animus. Intersecting those targets for aggressions was not sufficient for political analysis or strategic struggle. Violence is arrayed against me because I'm Black, or female, or queer, undocumented, etc. You could do an additive approach, like a vulnerability index, but that still could not deal with a multi-dimensional reality of people who literally kept communities alive, and are keeping them alive. This wasn't just about physical issues, medical issues, or not being brutalized in the street or in the home. Keeping folks alive was also about intellectual and spiritual issues. I started to watch more closely after I got involved with trying to figure out what is our relationship with children. Our relationships are always flawed because we didn't grow up in pristine or healthy environments. We're complicated with contradictions. We fail all the time. We keep trying. Within the matrix or framework of those attempts, I saw the concept of the Captive Maternal start to gel.

I wrote a piece in 2013 titled "Afrarealism and the Black Matrix" in *The Black Scholar*;[8] it was partly about the Captive Maternal, and an acknowledgement of how Afropessimism as a school of thought had contributed to critical thinking, particularly in its willingness to deal with violence not as an abstraction, or some kind of museum effect or artifact. I was also trying to locate the feminized persona nurturing and reproducing the social world with the knowledge that it was going to be used as raw resource to be exploited. In effect, their labor was keeping everybody alive so that they could become edible negroes or negresses—see Vincent Woodard's *The Delectable Negro*[9]—or to be consumed by or tossed away by the state. I was trying to figure out the dynamics at play here; and how do we track our struggles? Not just by recovering heroic women as role models or inspirational symbols.

As you know, the Captive Maternal is an ungendered phenomenon or persona. Assata Shakur was kept alive as JoAnne Deborah Byron, a child runaway, as a young teen, because she was taken underwing by another kind of maternal. It wasn't her biological mother; she left home and her mother behind. It wasn't necessarily her aunt Evelyn Williams, who defended Assata admirably in court after she'd been captured, tortured by police, and hunted by the FBI's COINTELPRO. She became a Black Panther in Harlem who worked in community care only to be forced into the underground of the Black Liberation Army because of the state's violent machinations to destroy radical organizations. In *Assata: An Autobiography* she describes her time as an unhoused young teen in Harlem, when she was befriended by a Black queer/trans woman who took her in and rescued, nurtured, and mentored her, so that the child could grow up past the age of twenty-one. These moving dynamics structure care.

The article begins with Shakur but dates back in history to Elizabeth Key, one of the first people of African descent to sue for their freedom in the American colonies in the 1600s.[10] The Captive Maternal is not purely a subjugated female in the household or the workplace, but is actually a nurturer who can have varied ideological expressions, ranging from conservative through liberal to radical or revolutionary. It's central to the reproduction of the world. Without this form of caretaking, without this form of sacrifice, without this kind of glue to the social order—which is tied to the economic order and the political order, and the very notion of what is familial and familiar in the world—we see that things do not function. The Captive Maternal that I find the most intriguing would be the one that embraces revolutionary politics. I've written about the Captive Maternal in these various aspects and stages; I hope I continue to explore, to figure out what this concept is, as a reality that is haunting me.

In the essay "Killmonger's Captive Maternal is MIA," I explore the Hollywood blockbuster *Black Panther* (2018).[11] I discuss how the one persona, a villain, who seems most likely to manifest as a US Black revolutionary, embodies the contradictions of a dispossessed person, is the antithesis of imagined Black royalty presiding over pristine environments. How the absence of their mother in the film's narrative is a huge hole, a vacuum. There is no mother for Erik Killmonger, the Black villain who represents the afterlife of Black enslavement and the "Black savage." The absence becomes significant in real ways. I think of the Captive Maternal not as an intersectionality persona, because the Captive Maternal comes with ideology. With intersectionality, you have this intersection, but you don't ask once you hit the corner, or arrive at the intersection, "Are we talking about *liberal* intersectionality, *radical* intersectionality, *neo-radical* intersectionality?" I'm pretty much interested in the function, not the identity marker of a Captive Maternal. I think of function as a form of activism, as a form of labor—sometimes forced and coerced, often given voluntarily, sometimes to the point of exhaustion and despair. At some juncture, that is an under-analyzed reality in our struggles, there might actually be a key foundation or platform that takes struggles to another level.

CTS You've written before that "the majority of social change agents continue to be women working in triple shifts for depressed wages, unpaid child-rearing and housework, and volunteer community building black women's pivotal role struggles that often go undocumented and unnoticed."[12] I thought that tied right into what you're speaking on now. I feel that this really connects to the Central Park Five trial.[13]

JJ   In 1989, I went to the Central Park trial, because I belonged to an all-women's dojo. It was this interesting dojo in Park Slope, Brooklyn, where the white woman who headed it, the sensei, to the best of my memory, had been trained by a former member of the Black Panther Party in Harlem. After we practiced one day, the sensei tells us about the Central Park Five trial, which we already know about because it's haunting New York City. The case appears around the time of the murder of Yusuf Hawkins, the sixteen-year-old who was murdered by a mob of white youths in Brooklyn. It's the moment of the anti-apartheid movement and the fights against police brutality. It becomes a lightning rod, not just because of the rape and the attack against the white victim, Trisha Meili, but because, in a way, the city needs a white victim in order to exonerate it for its white-supremacist violence against Blacks, and brown and Latinx, Puerto Rican, and Dominican people.

There's a very interesting miniseries based on the case that Ava DuVernay directed, *When They See Us* (2019), it's really emotionally rich. Before that, there was Ken Burns's documentary *The Central Park Five* (2012), but DuVernay really brings a resonance of Black cultural perspective on victimization that isn't present in Burns's documentary, maybe because it's a documentary or maybe because the stories of Black communities and Black families are not gone into that deeply.

Departing from the white-supremacist feminist hysteria, our sensei asked six or seven of us, Black, Latinx, white, to consider investigating the Central Park case. But when we go to the trial, the defendant Yusef Salaam is the only one to testify; he's the only one who did not do a taped or written confession. The actress who plays Sharon Salaam, his mother, in the miniseries interrupts the police interrogation where confession might have happened and she represents this incredible powerful persona of a Captive Maternal. Before organizing in Texas and New York City around what happens to our children in the system, I saw what happens to them when I was a grad student organizing around the Central Park Five case.

We were there when Yusef Salaam testified to his innocence. We stood for over an hour outside the courthouse to get inside. There were very few seats for the public. It was one of the smaller courtrooms and most of the seats were reserved for the mainstream press. The *New York Times* and the major papers had already shaped the narrative of the guilt of the teens. A little bit of that comes out in *When They See Us*, but not really how vicious the liberal media was. I watched as Salaam defended himself, the only youth to testify in court to his innocence. I watched the jury basically ignore him with yawns. Some jurors read the newspapers. I don't know if you can do that when you're in the jury box but the assigned judge was Thomas B. Galligan, known for his racism and harsh sentences. The jurors, who were multiracial, projected indifference; the attitude was, "We already know you guys are guilty," "We're just here because we answered the call," "When is this going to be over?" That was my sense of the trial. When I walked out, I followed up by going to other organizing events. One spokesperson was Suzanne Ross, a white radical woman, who actually used Angela Davis's article, "The Myth of a Black Rapist," and organized a forum at 1199, the labor union for healthcare workers, which had been very supportive of Martin Luther King Jr., and which was predominately Black. I had gone with a friend of mine who is white, we'd been together at Union Theological Seminary. I watched again how the press, this time a white feminist writer from *The Village Voice*, completely mischaracterized that gathering. There had been one or two negative voices about the survivor of the attack, Trisha Meili. But most of it was critical analysis. What is this rush to judgment? What does a legal lynching look like? What is the history of accusations of rape against Black men that's focused only on white women as victims?

I remember—but we don't remember—the names of women and girls and, yes, men and boys, sexually assaulted in NYC. The public narrative for being sexually assaulted in NYC did not include them. There was a woman of color who was thrown off the roof of an apartment building after she was raped. She died. There were horrific sex crimes. Violence against women. Violence against trans women, even though we didn't have a public discourse for that then. Violence against children. What made the news was the Central Park case, because the victim was white and affluent. This was newsworthy, not just because she was white, but because she worked for Wall Street, for Salomon Brothers, a high-level brokerage firm. It was whiteness and capital, it was blondness. It was everything within the category that Ida B. Wells wrote about as being this iconic formation of white chivalry and white victimization that was facing an existential predator codified in Blacks.[14] It was the mothers who I watched organize against a legal lynching. I went up to Harlem from Brooklyn in order to meet the Black internationalists and organizers Nomsa and Elombe Brath. Until I met the Braths, I could not be cleared to meet Yusef Salaam's mother Sharon Salaam. Once they gave me the green light, I met Sharon Salaam at the Schomburg Center for Research in Black Culture in Harlem. I was able to interview her and later do a bit of writing and secure an honorarium for her to speak at Hamilton College in New York, where I was a visiting professor. I had been gathering knowledge from community leaders and impacted mothers. I had seen the white feminist journalist from *The Village Voice* mischaracterize the organizing event at 1199 as another assault or crime against white females. That forum was a serious endeavor to understand what was going on in that moment, in which the city had a lynch mob mentality. And you see some of that in this miniseries when the youth—they were not even men, they were boys—say, "Everybody hates us." In the miniseries you see the placards, you see the support for them. You don't see the hatred. For those of us who were living in the city at the time, we not only saw it, we felt it as a form of collective trauma.

When I read the piece in *The Village Voice*, I decided to write a response, a letter to the editor. My white friend, who had been there with me at the forum, was partnered with a Black man: he was fearful, so she could not have her name attached to the letter to the editor; also, the *Voice* said it did not take co-authored op eds. I was partnered at the time with a Jamaican man: he was fearful and harangued me each day for not being a "feminist." I ended up signing only my name after being on the phone with the editor multiple times. This was before cell phones. I was basically using payphones on the street to talk with the editors at *The Village Voice*. They made me verify everything in that short letter to the editor; double-check verified; I jumped through multiple hoops. All the facts were correct. To the best of my understanding, they let go the white feminist writer who wrote the slanderous piece against the gathering. There was a need to prove not only that we were innocent until proven guilty, which was unprovable. There was also this need to prove that we weren't malicious liars, that we could actually tell the truth about reality. I was furious. Why? Two paragraphs took days to be vetted, because the white editors and writers couldn't understand that this wasn't about the rape itself—none of us defended it. This was about a gathering at the 1199 union hall. The white press could not comprehend, could not understand that a multiracial group of men and women could come together and have a critique of *racism and rape*, and *denounce both simultaneously*. After the trial and convictions, my first job was in women's studies in Massachusetts. So, I wrote another piece that was longer; stressed out, I submitted a poorly written article that the white feminist editor refused to edit. I was told by my white senior colleagues that my writing on the Central Park case in defense of the teens could jeopardize my job, because I was in women's studies. But I wrote about the facts; and the facts in this case made no sense, the case made no sense. Still, prominent Black men and women (such as bell hooks and Michael Eric Dyson), who were largely academics and not community organizers, publicly denounced the youths as guilty even before the conclusion of both trials—I wrote about this in "Searching for a Tradition: African-American Women, Writers, and Interracial Rape Cases."[15] Academics and pundits still appear in print and castigate the communities as protectors of rapists.

I'm trained as a political scientist, which probably means nothing to most. Politics have a material base. When police and district attorneys and white (liberal) media say that "the teens got the location of the crime wrong," and police had to bring one of the youths to the actual scene of the crime so that he could "put himself in it" with the correct details, then you know the police prosecution case is not built on facts or science. If there's no DNA, how could you have this rush to judgment? There was a segment of the Black community that didn't want to be associated with these views, because they represented all the stereotypes of Black depravity, then that meant they didn't want to be associated with the sex crime either. Facts would have told you that this was not exactly the Scottsboro Boys case,[16] because there had been a horrific assault, because it was done by Matias Reyes, individually. Not the Scottsboro case per se, but this was another miscarriage of justice that could be seen as a collective legal lynching that was just being enforced by juvenile prison and adult prison. I watched the four parts of the miniseries, I had to keep stopping at the last part in terms of the torture, the serial torture, of Korey Wise. As they point out, there's no way you can monetarily compensate for torture. Psychological, physical factors, there's no, "How big you want the check to be?" It's never, never going to reconstitute the whole person. There is just some kind of fee: "Sorry to disembody you." There is no real compensation. Captive Maternals, the mothers in a non-gendered phenomenon, the supportive fathers and pastors, the community activists, realize that righteous rage doesn't always focus on the state. Yet, some people did pay for this "legal lynching" that led to the torture of Black and Latino youths. The prosecutor Elizabeth Lederer resigned from Columbia University. The prosecutor Linda Fairstein lost her publisher after Ava DuVernay and Oprah Winfrey's *When They See Us* aired, but this restitution of sorts happens thirty years after the abuse of Black and Latino youths.[17] There were financial settlements and apologies but still it feels like our demands are low and our memory curtailed. We don't have a critique of how our own communities participated by not rebelling against a legal lynching. I never could have created what DuVernay did. I'm grateful for her gift. Still, our political critique is going to have to become much sharper, more focused beyond trauma and become more embodied in strategies. If we want to prevent these types of atrocities reoccurring on a regular basis, we cannot allow the sentiment of Hollywood films to determine the narratives of struggle.

Celebrityhood has allowed imitation to supplant the real because our culture is celebrity culture. When celebrities become a leadership cadre, they don't live the conditions of scarcity, but they become the advocates for the freedoms of the people who endure such conditions. Abolitionism now includes Kim Kardashian West. I'm not bashing. The notion of an "abolitionist" is so open, that it links to reactionaries such as Donald Trump and his presidential advisor son-in-law, Jared Kushner (e.g., the prison reform initiatives developed with Van Jones), and as well is connected to the billionaire Koch brothers.[18] According to the journalist Jane Mayer's *Dark Money*, the Kochs wanted to reform penal codes because they wanted to lessen the prosecutions of white-collar crimes and environmental crimes; their wealth is built on oil and gas industries. Mayer notes that the origins of Koch Industries' wealth came from the father and patriarch Fred Koch providing oil and gas drilling for the Third Reich.[19]

CTS Abolitionism and critique of racial capitalism are knotted together.

JJ   They are. But one of them may be the driving engine. I don't believe mass incarceration is the driving engine to this phenomenon of poverty, dispossession, over-policing, violent policing, incarceration detention centers. The driving engine would be racial capitalism: the accumulation of people's culture, their labor, their disposability through gratuitous violence. Being able to terrorize people because psychologically you have a badge and a gun or belong to ICE and have letters on your jacket. You have a battering ram; you can knock in somebody's door. You can grab their two-year-old and throw them in a cage. The animus that permits systemic violence exceeds the container of mass incarceration and exceeds the definitional norm of abolitionism as a remedy to violence. Your imaginary vision of the future will likely not be concretized unless you have a program that challenges the very notion that a state built on racial capitalism will ever deliver concrete gains that benefit the masses of people. People held captive have needs that exceed the political process. To meet those needs, logically, one will end up in a confrontation with racial capitalism.

CTS   When people have fought back, such as in Ferguson, "Black identity extremists" came up as a term to continue COINTELPRO. There was the death of Ferguson protesters and the surveillance keeps growing, and then you're shown the juxtaposition: it's okay for celebrities to do this but when you organize, or communities organize, it turns into extreme state repression.

JJ   I don't think people consider celebrities to be much of a threat, particularly if they reiterate the norm. The only thing that is threatening is radical deviation. I talk to students about the "wild card." People always struggle in different ways. Elites don't live in those communities of struggle.

There is no rescue team coming for us. With that knowledge, we need a different operational base to recreate the world. It is not going to be a celebrity savior. Never was, never will be celebrity saviors. If you're in a religious tradition that is millennia-old, consider how the last savior went out. It was always going to be bloody. It was always going to be traumatic. But there's a beauty to facing the reality of our lives. Not our lives as they're broken apart, written about, and then sold back to us in academic or celebrity discourse. But our lives as we understand them, because we continually fight for ourselves and communities and get up the next day to still be in community. The most important thing is showing up, and not on the platform, stage, or screen. Showing up and learning how to live by and with others, learning how to reinvent ourselves in this increasing wasteland. That's the good life.

Being present to the struggle without trying to reduce the struggle into containable objects means understanding that all of this is wild. Most of this is going to be violent. Even if we're pacifist, this state is not. Any opposition or threat to it will be disciplined in some way. Celebrities might lose gigs. Other people might lose their lives. Remembering political prisoners honors the fact that in revolutionary struggles people died or were disappeared into cages for decades. Because they (we) fought, the state had to adapt. Because it had to adapt, we got some modicum of resources and accommodations that never would have happened without a fight.

Go back to the political prisoners, incorporate ourselves within a community that incorporates them. That's the fuller story. The real narratives are always in the communities of struggle. The non-celebrity captives know the stories written in the grittiest form. It's that grit that enlightens.

Notes to Chapter 9

1   James, ed., *Imprisoned Intellectuals*; James, ed., *The New Abolitionists*; James, ed., *Warfare in the American Homeland.*
2   US National Archives, "The Treaty of Guadalupe Hidalgo," accessed October 11, 2022, https://www.archives.gov/education/lessons /guadalupe-hidalgo.
3   Samantha Schmidt, "'Why Did You Kill My Child?' Border Patrol Shooting of Guatemalan Woman Stirs Protests," *Chicago Tribune*, May 29, 2018, https://www.chicagotribune.com/nation-world /ct-guatemala-immigrant-killed-border-patrol-20180529-story.html.
4   James, "The Womb of Western Theory."
5   Ibid. 255–66
6   Christian, "The Race for Theory."
7   Joy James, *Resisting State Violence: Radicalism, Gender, and Race in US Culture* (Minneapolis, MN: University of Minnesota Press, 1996).
8   Joy James, "Afrarealism and the Black Matrix: Maroon Philosophy at Democracy's Border," *The Black Scholar* 43, no. 4 (2013).
9   Vincent Woodard, *The Delectable Negro: Human Consumption and Homoeroticism within US Slave Culture* (New York: New York University Press, 2014).
10   Slavery and Remembrance, "Elizabeth Key (Kaye)," accessed October 26,

2022, https://slaveryandremembrance.org/people/person/?id=PP031.

11   See Joy James, "Killmonger's Captive Maternal Is M.I.A: *Black Panther*'s Family Drama, Imperial Masters and Portraits of Freedom," *Reading Wakanda: Reconciling Black Radical Imaginations with Hollywood Fantasies*, Southern California Library, May 1, 2019; available online, https://sites.williams.edu/jjames/files/2019/05/WakandaCaptiveMaternal2019.pdf, accessed October 11, 2022.

12   James, *Seeking the Beloved Community*, 30

13   See Nicole Ortiz, "The Central Park Five: How the Truth Set Them Free," *StMU Research Scholars*, November 8, 2019, https://stmuscholars.org/the-central-park-five-how-the-truth-set-them-free/.

14   Wells, *Southern Horrors*.

15   See Joy James "Searching for a Tradition: African-American Women Writers, Activists, and Interracial Rape Cases," in *Black Women in America*, ed. Kim Marie Vaz, 131–55 (Thousand Oaks, CA: SAGE, 1995); available online, https://sites.williams.edu/jjames/files/2019/05/Black-Women-in-America.pdf, accessed October 26, 2022.

16   See *History.com* editors, "Scottsboro Boys," *History*, February 22, 2018, https://www.history.com/topics/great-depression/scottsboro-boys.

17   Eli Rosenberg, "A Law Professor Resigns as Netflix Drama about Central Park Five Continues to Dredge Up Anger," *Washington Post*, June 12, 2019, https://www.washingtonpost.com/nation/2019/06/13/law-professor-resigns-netflix-drama-about-central-park-five-continues-dredge-up-anger/; Elizabeth A. Harris and Julia Jacobs, "Linda Fairstein Dropped by Her Publisher after TV Series on the Central Park 5," *New York Times*, June 7, 2019, https://www.nytimes.com/2019/06/07/arts/linda-fairstein-when-they-see-us.html.

18   Jordan Fabian, "White House Meets with Koch Officials on Criminal Justice Reform," *The Hill*, December 10, 2015, https://thehill.com/homenews/administration/262895-white-house-meets-with-koch-officials-on-criminal-justice-reform/.

19   Jane Mayer, *Dark Money: The Hidden History of the Billionaires Behind the Rise of the Radical Right* (New York: Doubleday, 2016), chapter 1.

10   (Re)Thinking the Black Feminist Canon

With Paris Hatcher of Black Feminist Future, 2021

Joy James I am on this journey of trying to figure out Captive Maternals. I see them spontaneously emerge. They are always appearing as teachers, rich in their ideas and in their risk-taking. Sometimes, I call the youths "baby Captive Maternals"; there are Captive Maternal youths, elders, and ancestors. I noticed that you hold Ida B. Wells as an ancestor. Wells is my favorite ancestor—if you are allowed to have a "favorite ancestor."

When I was in Harlem around 2014, I watched people—mostly women, but also men and non-binary and trans people—organize communities for their children, for their elders. This is how the Captive Maternal emerged. These people function as stabilizers, balancing life in the middle—the fulcrum on a plank, forming a seesaw, leveraging everyone into stability even to the point of the caretaker Captive Maternal's exhaustion. Captive Maternals were and are making sure that people are fed, that they get to school, they stay away from the police, from prison, from gangs. They understand their value and dignity. Particularly for children and vulnerable women who are nontypical or neurodiverse, Captive Maternals make sure that they are not preyed upon. I was humbled to watch that life-giving struggle: you wake up, even when you are tired, and you put people to bed. Even though you would like to take a nap yourself, you make sure people are fed. For me, the Captive Maternal is agender. Although most of the people whom I saw soldiering as Captive Maternals appeared to identify as women or girls, or children. Captive Maternals have stumbling blocks when moving towards political consciousness and struggles to protect and liberate their families, kin, communities.

Increasingly, academia plays curious roles in stabilizing civil rights markets and defending questionable accumulations within monied networks that annex vulnerable civilians and disparage militants confronting state violence. The most vulnerable activists mobilize in streets and within under-resourced communities. They tend to have low visibility and limited funds. In the Obama administration, surveillance data was collected on Black activists and catalogued in the FBI under a "Black extremism" index. That I would like to feed my children and not have them shot (by police) becomes seen as a declaration of war against the state. Hence, the surveillance index. The most vulnerable activists are routinely surveilled and harassed, are the most likely to be arrested, the most likely to be injured, incarcerated, or killed by police forces or white-supremacist vigilantes like the seventeen-year-old Kyle Rittenhouse, who shot three white men at a Black Lives Matter protest in Minnesota, killing two, one armed only with a skateboard. Released on a $2 million bail bond with the support of President Donald Trump, Rittenhouse, whom I've referred to as a "teenage serial killer," was able to capitalize on white supremacy and become the beneficiary of racist corporate and small-dollar donors. Before he shot BLM white protesters, he was handed bottled water by militarized police forces even though they did not check if he legally possessed the assault-rifle he carried and brandished.[1]

Reactionary and proto-fascist elites—if whiteness is existential wealth under the rule of white supremacy—benefit under these conditions of struggle as their personal identities and ideologies align with dominant proto-fascism or faux progressivism. The democratic social movements do not reflect the vigilante fascism of Rittenhouse and his supporters. But they are not accountable to the mass when violent tragedies unfold. The mass of anti-racists wants material protections. Logically, elites do not invest in popular mechanisms that could replace them.

The Black petty-bourgeois progressives are largely shaped by the desires and strategies for power. And some of it is about prestige, because people have egos. That happens. These conflicts might spur new bone growth between a class with leisure and institutional connections, and classes marked as expendable workers in hostile and underground economies, including COVID-19 essential workers and prison workers. A number of the petty bourgeoisie betray the interests of the unemployed and incarcerated. On some level of solidarity and engagement, although it is unclear which, we can forge ties: true boundaries are rarely sufficiently identified and established—I can say that from working with different impacted families, where others have lost their children to police violence, police executions. The Chicago mothers I know, Shapearl Wells and Dorothy Holmes, lost their sons to police violence. I learned much from working in support with them for over five years in the US and Colombia.

I have recently met other mothers who have lost children to police violence in Illinois, Texas, Ohio, California (as well as in other countries such as Brazil and Colombia). Activists in their twenties, as Captive Maternals, introduced me to Samaria Rice and Lisa Simpson. In the work we briefly did, lines of communication were not clear and trust was not fully established. There needs to be a separation between activists mobilizing under a set of ethics based on politics and families directly impacted by police murders of kin. Impacted families deal with their grief and trauma as primary while seeking justice for lost family members. Those of us with murdered kin who are not named in activist circles are working through our trauma with desires to help and commitments to political struggle. There are differences between primary, secondary, and tertiary traumas. Parameters and boundaries are established over time. With Holmes and Wells it took years. Sometimes organizing is like being in a pressure cooker: you are responding instantaneously to crises that heat up as they unfold. Frictions, disagreements appear among those who are trying to be in solidarity and within those families, who have their own internal and external disagreements with each other. Frictions do not completely break relationships, but it takes time to build and mend them.

Paris Hatcher Can you say more about the contradictions embedded in the Captive Maternal?

JJ The contradictions I see are the convictions of political struggle. But they are also contradictions of the unique political struggles shaped around Black captivity. There was a summit on June 12, 2021 on the Black Power Media platform.[2] The graphic we used shows 500 years of resistance, protest, civil rights, slave rebellions—scores of rebellions on a US map. Those are the conditions of siege for half a millennium. After 500 years of struggles you are going to have contradictions. What does it mean to be free? Is it a personal attribute, a position? Is this a collective endeavor? Make compromises or go hardcore revolutionary? We have no consensus.

When W.E.B. Du Bois was finally kicked out of the NAACP—he was becoming more radical and wanted to advocate for economic justice—he lamented that he had no radical cohorts. Yet, the anti-lynching leader Ida B. Wells, who originated investigative reporting through her crusade against lynching, was rejected by Du Bois who, aided by Mary Church Terrell, sidelined Wells from the founding conference for the NAACP, based on Mary White Ovington, a white philanthropist, wanting Wells out of the NAACP because Wells was "too militant."[3] Today, I read this code of denigration as "too Black." One cannot deny the specificity of our conditions to generalize the racism. It is not. It is anti-Blackness. When he had Wells as an ally, Du Bois did not want her because she was too militant. Wells would disguise herself and go to prisons to take depositions from falsely accused Black men and boys. She publicly stated that she carried a pistol in her handbag and would sell her "life dearly," warning white assailants that attempts to harm or kill her would come at a cost.[4] The historian John Bracey noted at a panel at the University of Massachusetts Amherst in the 1990s that when she moved to Chicago, people would not want her in their neighborhood, fearing that those trying to firebomb her house might go to the wrong the address. We have many contradictions. We also have political will, and we have love. In struggle, we address or resolve contradictions.

PH   Someone in the audience called Ebony says they appreciate you stating that your work is not hostile to Black feminisms, but perhaps a call to make clear Black feminism is not a monolith. Can you speak to the plurality or the multiplicity of abolitionism?

JJ   Yes, I always forget the "s": abolitionism*s*. I think we are trained to forget the "s." I don't think the academy likes plurality, it prefers order and discipline. Hegemonic discourse asserts the singular, not the plural. If the concept is singular you can better control one market. If there are multiple forms of abolitionism—or feminism—you have competitors.

I believe bourgeois feminism is dominant. The Combahee River Collective formed in Boston because Black teenage girls, Black women, were being murdered and their bodies were found in dumpsters. This meant Boston had a serial killer. Or serial killers. One of the most notorious serial killers in the twentieth century would have been Samuel Little, who killed ninety-three women between 1970 and 2004. It was not until 2014 that he was imprisoned for life for these murders (he had been arrested on several occasions but was released). Little died at age eighty in prison on December 30, 2020. The majority of the girls and women murdered were Black; the police forces did and do not consistently care about vulnerable populations, whose murders are often categorized as "NHI" or "No Humans Involved."[5]

PH   Sometimes our movement does not have teeth. Yes, violence can be generated. We try to make it palatable. We try to make it where everyone can get in around it. What do we lose? Captive Maternal is not an identity, but rather a function. Can you unpack this distinction further? You talked about it being ungendered, as well.

JJ   Captive Maternals do domestic labor. Who cooks? Cleans? Washes sheets? It is feminine or feminized labor. Nonprofits such as Kristi House focus on the trafficking of children. Most people recognize that girls and women are trafficked. But 40 percent or more of trafficked children are males. The traffickers may be disproportionately male. But there are women trafficking children as well. Boys are more reluctant to disclose that they have been sold as sex slaves. Child trafficking might not be determined by gender but by age and vulnerability.[6]

Political priorities should not be shaped by gender but by need. People need food, a clean place to sleep, need shelter and protections. One of the churches I am affiliated with has one of the few—or the only—Black teen trans shelters in New York City. That is why Captive Maternal is determined by *function*. If you think about Condoleezza Rice as a Black conservative feminist and the invasion and wars in the Middle East, she helped to start genocides with military and disinformation campaigns. She was a Black woman who grew up in Birmingham, Alabama, as a Black girl playing with the four little girls murdered in the Klan bombing of the 16th Street Baptist Church.[7] Rice is not a Captive Maternal: she is an imperial operative. You cannot work for the administration, you cannot cause and then lie about the destruction, you cannot wage imperialist warfare, you cannot shirk responsibility for the lives of hundreds of thousands of people whose countries were invaded or bombed. This is *not* a function of a Captive Maternal, but of a state-aligned and power-seeking Black feminist. Rice sits behind Brett Kavanaugh on the opening day of his testimony in Senate hearings that will appoint him as Trump's nominee to the Supreme Court, after Kavanaugh is accused by a white woman of sexual assault. Guess how many Black lives are going to be wrecked by the Supreme Court? I hope that is clear. I can name some other people as counter-radical, counter-progressive, but then people will say I am not "nice."

PH   We do *not* need to be "nice"! What are your thoughts on nonprofit employment jobs in the movement funded by large corporations? How do you see that complicated, complicating principal organizing? Specifically in the latest iteration of the movement, which has fallen deep into the nonprofit–industrial complex conference?

JJ   If you build a movement industry on top of Black death and trauma, make sure you are not building on a graveyard. There are new bones, old bones, and corpse bones. Some academic institutions instructed their students through the accumulation of Black death. If you start a freedom movement, and you are accumulating, believe me, the people who have the "real" money made an investment in you. Financial capital does not fund freedom movements.

We have to organize for sanity and for honor. Keep kids healthy and allow them to live longer and not have nervous breakdowns as a norm. Everybody should have the right to eat. But this is capitalism—to take care of our material needs we have to change the political economic order. I have worked with nonprofits before, before or during grad school, prior to becoming an academic. We are always doing "good." We try to "do good." We always confront the suffering; the sad child; the dead child's family. Then we raise money from their suffering and death—is that in good faith?

If somebody's paying for your movement, if somebody puts in $100 million—Black activists told me that foundations are donating up to $1 billion following the George Floyd protests—they are not doing it for Black freedom. I am not saying give up the job: take the resources and redirect them out. If you start lip-synching freedom songs, you are not singing anything that anybody who needs to be free wants to hear.

Whatever the Kennedys thought they knew about the 1963 March on Washington and how to control it, Black people knew more. When Barack Obama, in 2008, at Mile High Stadium in Denver, Colorado, accepted the presidential nomination from the DNC, he called out the "preacher," but would not say the name "Rev. Martin Luther King." Rev. King had delivered the famous "I Have a Dream" speech at the Washington Mall in 1963. In a late-night after-hours PBS interview with the journalist Gwen Ifill, I watched Rev. King's former assistant Jesse Jackson inform Ifill that the day that the Obama campaign scheduled for his DNC nomination was the anniversary of the 1963 civil rights March on Washington.[8] Due to Black radicals, and likely unknown to the Obama campaign, the March on Washington was set on the anniversary of fourteen-year-old Chicagoan Emmett Till's 1955 murder. Barack Obama was the junior senator from Illinois, had his residency in Chicago. If Till had been allowed to live, he would likely have been one of Obama's constituents.

PH That is right. How do you see Black academics? Can they make maroon camps around the academia?

JJ Maroon space is essential where you can create it. The question of the maroon is the question of autonomy. Are Black people allowed to be autonomous in the academy? Where is ideological adversity? How many radicals are there that you do not have to loan money to in order that they can hire lawyers and keep their jobs? Here is my read on the academy: Do what you gotta do. State universities are government entities, salaries are public knowledge. Ivy League universities are private billionaire corporations. Build a maroon camp inside a government entity, or inside a private corporation. Go for it!

PH How do you imagine Black anarchy?

JJ Lorenzo Kom'boa Ervin published his memoirs as a Black anarchist—his key work is *Anarchism and the Black Revolution*.[9] I do not know enough about anarchism to speak to it. I am not saying I am an expert on Marxism, but I value it as an intervention. Anybody who could make an intervention to create a corridor as big as an avenue or as small as a crevice in a crack helps us to slide into intellectual thinking that allows us to think and respond more rapidly and radically. Cornel West stated that Antifa saved his life, and the lives of other clergy in Charlottesville, Virginia in 2017, when white supremacists stole the life of the white anti-racist Heather Heyer.[10] If the state cannot control fascists, then it should definitely not attempt to control antifascists who are offering protections that the police refuse. Policing is duplicitous.

UN "peacekeepers" were known to rape women and girls in Haiti. The UN stood down when the Clinton administration and the diplomat Susan Rice, working within it as a Black pioneering state-power feminist, told the UN not to classify the war in Rwanda as a genocide.[11] If it had been classified as genocidal, the UN would have had to respond with material support. Anarchists are going to be part of any antifascist movement.

PH   Your last comments made me think about Black women's spaces, not only that we are going to be here but build some type of power. I think about people like CeCe McDonald, a trans woman sentenced to prison for protecting her own freedom and safety after being attacked in Minneapolis in 2011.[12] How many folks survive being punished, especially Black women or women of color and agender people prohibited from fighting back?

JJ   Vincent Woodard, the Black queer academic and the author of *The Delectable Negro*, critiques Harriet Jacobs's nineteenth-century memoir *Incidents in the Life of a Slave Girl* (1861) for taking out the violence against an enslaved Black male, who was chained naked to a bed all day to be the tortured sex object of the white male enslaver. The content is "too much" for the respectable public's sensibilities and the white abolitionists. Woodard reads a lack of respect and care for the broken captive.[13] The abolitionist movement cannot fully deal with reality. Why? Because of its phobias, fears, prohibitions. But Woodard also writes about same-sex male desire across racial and captive lines. There are limits to my theorizing about the Captive Maternal; this is not Holy Grail stuff. The function is key; politics are key. Kuwasi Balagoon, a queer Black Panther, died in prison from AIDS in 1986. Courage and love made him a revolutionary.[14] Afeni Shakur, the mother of Tupac Shakur, was jailed in the Women's House of Detention, during the Stonewall riot for gay rights which occurred a few blocks away in the Village.[15] As a Panther, Afeni Shakur began organizing inside the jail. The captive women began burning their mattresses in solidarity with the Stonewall rebellion of trans women. Solidarity exists. It always existed. It might not resonate in our analysis. But we are always learning from whoever wants to struggle. That does not diminish or dismiss the violence that happens. At the church that I belong to, teens took photographs of murdered trans women to make this huge photographic cross resting in the arms of a white alabaster angel.

I have learned to struggle and organize. I have also gotten played by people inside the movement who in late-night calls demand we "stop the summit" or "do not organize." I am played because I think the conversation is in good faith, but also because the person on the phone call is trans and thinks that I should defer to their judgment in order to prove that I am not reactionary or transphobic.

When I find out that that individual received part of the BLM settlement, or distribution pay-outs of hundreds of thousands of dollars, I am determined to support the June 2021 Accountability Summit hosted by Black Power Media and *not* to take late-night calls where strangers tell me to stand down because I'm allegedly benefiting or profiting from people I have never met and from or on behalf of whom I've received no payment, nor asked to be my "subject-object" of study. I erred because I focused on identities, not politics. The only identity that should have been known or relevant was if we were supporting revolutionary intellectuals. I will stand in defense of any persecuted group; all such groups have the right to self-defense. It doesn't mean that they are all ethical and stable and disciplined against manipulation and opportunism.

History teaches us. Joan Little stabbed the white guard who was attempting to rape her. There was a huge defense campaign. Little should have been acquitted. Little was also arrested for allegedly stealing televisions out of the homes of Black people who likely had modest or few means.[16] Black women should defend themselves from racist-sexist violence. Some work in the underground economies that harm Black communities; some work for the state that destroys Black communities. Anita Hill was verbally sexually assaulted by the future Supreme Court justice Clarence Thomas. As a Black conservative working for the Reagan administration, Hill, along with Thomas, eviscerated workers' rights by denying the claims made by LGBTQ+ people, Black people, people of color, and women concerning job discrimination and harassment cases.[17] Because she is a Black woman, I will support her, but what is she doing? What is she doing in relationship with predatory structures? I tried to organize with some others around the New Jersey Four case, centered on Black lesbians who were in the West Village in lower Manhattan, when a Black man was harassing and attacking them. Because they had been attacked before by homophobic, transphobic people, they had scissors or kitchen knives for protection. This was not seen as self-defense by police and the white judge. They were prosecuted and some did time. The judge chastised them not just for being Black, or seeing them in female body form, but for being lesbians. Part of the prosecutorial narrative was that they should not have even been in the West Village which is a white, bourgeois, gay area. The court probably did not really care about the Black man beaten or stabbed. The court criminalized Black queer/feminized personal self-defense.[18]

Ella Baker, the civil rights leader, left the NAACP because she found its leadership not aligned with the needs of Black families and communities facing racist violence.[19] Leaders had been murdered when their family home was firebombed. As noted above, Ida B. Wells was kicked out of the founding of the NAACP in Niagara Falls.

When I think of Atatiana Jefferson I realize that technology is not enough. She was standing right in front of the window, with an eight-year-old in the room. A Texas police officer shot her point blank in the chest, firing through a closed window, without announcing himself as police, after he had creeped through her backyard. She thought he was an intruder and carried her licensed weapon with her to the window; he killed her in her own home in front of the child.[20]

We have to think about security with as much importance as we think about our publications and conference talks. What does tangible security look like for ourselves? I haven't seen much public discourse on this because people have mystified violence, despite knowing that empires routinely deploy it.

Notes to Chapter 10

1   See Paige Williams, "Kyle Rittenhouse, American Vigilante," *New Yorker*, July 5, 2021, https://www.newyorker.com/magazine/2021/07/05/kyle-rittenhouse-american-vigilante; and Eric Litke, "Yes, Police Gave Kyle Rittenhouse Water and Thanked His Armed Group before Kenosha Shooting," *PolitiFact*, August 28, 2020, https://www.politifact.com/factchecks/2020/aug/28/facebook-posts/yes-police-gave-kyle-rittenhouse-water-and-thanked/.

2   See https://www.blackpowermedia.org/.

3   See James, *Transcending the Talented Tenth*.

4   See Wells, *Crusade for Justice*; and Joy James, "The Quartet in the Political Persona of Ida B. Wells," in *The Oxford Handbook of Philosophy and Race*, ed. Naomi Zack, 309–18 (Oxford: Oxford University Press, 2017); available online, https://sites.williams.edu/jjames/files/2019/05/The-Quartet-in-Ida-B.-Wells-1.pdf, accessed October 26, 2022.

5   See Sylvia Winter, "No Humans Involved: An Open Letter to My Colleagues," *Forum N.H.I.: Knowledge for the 21st Century* 1, no. 1 (fall 1994); available online, http://carmenkynard.org/wp-content/uploads/2013/07/No-Humans-Involved-An-Open-Letter-to-My-Colleagues-by-SYLVIA-WYNTER.pdf, accessed October 26, 2022.

6   See e.g. Tim Swarens, "Boys: The Silent Victims of Sex Trafficking," *USA Today*, accessed November 1, 2022, https://www.usatoday.com/story/opinion/nation-now/2018/02/08/boys-silent-victims-sex-trafficking/1073799001/.

7   Nick Manos, "Birmingham 16th Street Baptist Church Bombing (1963)," *BlackPast*, December 31, 2008, https://www.blackpast.org/african-american-history/sixteenth-street-baptist-church-bombing-1963/.

8   Attended by celebrities, and covered by global media, the 1963 March on Washington allowed no Black woman to speak from the platform, although Mahalia Jackson sang. Nor were Black queer leaders such as James Baldwin allowed to speak.

9   Lorenzo Kom'boa Ervin, *Anarchism and the Black Revolution* (London: Pluto Press, 2021).

10   See Democracy Now!, "Cornel West & Rev. Traci Blackmon: Clergy in Charlottesville Were Trapped by Torch-Wielding Nazis," August 14, 2017, YouTube video, https://www.youtube.com/watch?v=R4i61_12SGY.

11   M. Dowling, "When Susan Rice Wouldn't Label a Massacre of 8,000 People 'Genocide' for Political Reasons," *Independent Sentinel*, April 10, 2017, https://www.independentsentinel.com /susan-rice-wouldnt-label-massacre-8000-people-genocide -political-reasons/; and Colum Lynch, "Genocide under Our Watch," *Foreign Policy*, April 16, 2015, https://foreignpolicy.com/2015/04/16 /genocide-under-our-watch-rwanda-susan-rice-richard-clarke/.

12   See Chase Strangio, "CeCe is Free But So Much Work Remains," ACLU, January 13, 2014, https://www.aclu.org/news/lgbtq-rights /cece-free-so-much-work-remains.

13   Woodard, *The Delectable Negro*, 129–40.

14   Jericho Movement, "Kuwasi Balagoon 1946–1986," accessed October 26, 2022, https://www.thejerichomovement.com/profile /kuwasi-balagoon-1946-1986.

15   Hugh Ryan, "At the Women's House of Detention, the Intersecting Influences of Black and Gay Liberation Movements," August 23, 2022, http://www.hughryan.org/recent-work/2022/8/23/at-the-womens -house-of-detention-the-intersecting-influences-of-black-and-gay -liberation-movements.

16   Minnie Bruce Pratt, "A Look Back at the Joann Little Case," *Workers World*, March 9, 2006, https://www.workers.org/2006/us/joann-little-0316/.

17   Joy James, "Anita Hill: Martyr Heroism and Gender Abstractions," *The Black Scholar* 22, nos 1–2 (1992); available online, https://sites .williams.edu/jjames/files/2019/06/Anita-Hill-Martyr-Heroism -Gender-Abstractions.pdf, accessed November 1, 2022.

18   Imani Henry, "Lesbians Sentenced for Self-Defense: All-White Jury Convicts Black Women," *Workers World*, June 21, 2007, https://www .workers.org/2007/us/nj4-0628/.

19   Mary Cronk Farrell, "The Woman Who Birthed the Civil Rights Movement," personal blogpost, May 12, 2019, https://www .marycronkfarrell.net/blog/woman-who-birthed-the-civil-rights -movement.

20   Associated Press, "Trial Set for Texas Officer Who Shot Black Woman in Her Home," PBS *News Hour*, November 16, 2021, https:// www.pbs.org/newshour/nation/trial-set-for-texas-officer-who-shot -black-woman-in-her-home.

11　How the University (De)Radicalizes Social Movements

With Rebecca A. Wilcox of the Political Theology Network, 2022

Rebecca A. Wilcox How can we speak to not only those dynamics of survival, like coming to the university for healthcare, housing on campus, professors just being able to have a job? What can be said about critical Black thought in the academy? Can we rigorously talk about the things that are really critical to our work within the confines of the academy?

Joy James The academy is tricky because it is a zone that, on some level, we can retreat into in order to think with structure and support from the edifice. But it can also, you know—it's a cheesy cliché we used decades ago when I was growing up—it can eat your lunch. It's the bully. I am going back decades, I don't know how people buy food, and there's a lot of people who don't have access to food, but the whole thing about the bully within the school is that they have free license to extract from you. There's no real protection against bullies. What happens when the entire structure has or expresses aspects of bullying?

You come with ideas. You come with passion. You come with commitments. I'm not saying this is accurate, you decide—but if the academy functions as a zone of extraction then you are bringing gifts to it. Gifts that can be taken from you. Sometimes it is just exhausting; you want to give up. Like, I have this brilliant idea for a paper or dissertation and I'm emotionally invested, then people whittle the ideas/paper/dissertation down or they consume it. It's edible. They say, "I could use this in my own research," or, "Maybe we can take your idea and put it on a poster," or, "Maybe we could create a course around it."

The challenge about critical Black thought is how do we know when it's actually critical and not a commodity. Our entrance into the academy is complicated. If I did the whole historical thing about the talented tenth—the concept was popularized by W.E.B. Du Bois and his 1903 *Souls of Black Folk*, which he later repudiated—the talented tenth was engineered by white philanthropists who needed to contain the Black desire not just to learn, but to be free.

You can learn, but you may not be learning strategies to be free. However, organically in our communities, we learn and we learn how to be free or how to navigate so that we can survive.

An anti-Black or hostile world, as I've said before, is linked to historically Black colleges and universities (HBCUs). I'm glad you're from an HBCU. Take premier HBCUs such as Spelman and Morehouse. Spelman is named after Laura Spelman Rockefeller and Morehouse is named after Henry Morehouse, both white philanthropists. The point was that this talented tenth was going to be formally educated, which would lead the Black mass away from rebellion for freedom— rebellion comes in different forms, it can be how you love, write poetry, read, or give to the world. Rebellion tracks away from consumption. It tracks towards community. Once you create this "overseer" (I'm stealing from Malcolm), once you get this field–house dichotomy, the academy becomes for the state and capital the only house that can give you that stamp of approval that identifies you as an official leader.

Is it still critical Black studies when it's only engineered inside the "big house"? Is it critical Black studies if it also emanates from our communities, but not to produce commodities that the "big house" can put on the shelf or the conveyor belt? Does that make sense?

RAW In "'New Bones' Abolitionism, Communism, and Captive Maternals" and "Airbrushing Revolution for the Sake of Abolition,"[1] you make an important distinction between revolution and abolition, while outlining the ways that neoliberalism distorts revolutionary tactics with structural reforms.

Could you speak to this distinction between revolution and abolition?

J J I am always thinking about and in the community. Let me back up. My mother told me when I was twelve or thirteen that I couldn't do a nine-to-five job because I don't listen. I've been a waitress and I've done all types of work. I needed to figure out a gig where I wouldn't continuously get fired, right, because I don't listen well to authority figures. This is, in part, how I ended up in the academy. I just want to be clear, part of it is to pay my bills. I did not go to the academy to be enlightened. I love to read. I love to learn. I love to think. Sometimes, for the younger people, especially for the teachers here, that is how children survive environments that are not always child-friendly. I grew up on military bases. The last stop was Texas, which is the most interesting state in terms of predatory behavior and gun violence. Distill that down to home life and figure it out. So how do we save or preserve ourselves? Sometimes we retreat into thought. Sometimes we retreat into literature. Sometimes we retreat into ideas. We find those to be a form of respite if not salvation. I used to climb into treehouses in Texas and read for hours, and just show up at home when it was dinnertime.

Maybe this becomes the attraction of the academy: maybe we think it's our treehouse? It is a sanctuary. But that is not really how it functions. If it is a state university, it is an extension of the government. If it is private then it is a corporation, like the places I have been teaching the last decades. It is literally capital, especially at the highest form, because the institutions have multi-billion-dollar portfolios. The entities have endowments, they have stock investment portfolios that they're never going to lose in order to fight the right cause; it's about the preservation of edifices or structures that we don't control.

So back to the source of the dichotomy, or my recognition, it didn't come from text, it didn't come from the university. It came from an anti-racist gathering in Chicago.

Now, Chicago's a complicated mix bag of radical struggle and intense police repression. If you say "Fred Hampton, Mark Clark, December 4, 1969, 4 a.m.," that is when the Chicago police co-engineered with the FBI plans to assassinate our leaders.[2] We can fast-forward to today. I am not saying that the current Black lesbian mayor of Chicago functions in the same modality; but Lori Lightfoot (the Democratic mayor since 2019) enables predatory policing. Can we take an intellectual, spiritual, political stance so that our communities can survive predatory policing? If we survive it is because we engineered strategies for ourselves. The academy never said, "Oh, I have a blueprint for you." That's not what it does, but it will take our blueprints for survival and then turn them into texts, or documentaries, or syllabi.

So in November 2019 I go to Chicago with a student research assistant to the re-founding of the National Alliance against Racist and Political Repression (NAARPR) conference.[3] There, we hear Frank Chapman, an older African-American, formerly incarcerated man who was out of prison through the support of the NAARPR. That organization was formed out of Angela Davis's defense committee. It opened shop in early 1973, following her acquittal.

The NAARPR co-directors were Angela Davis, her mother Sallye Davis, and her mentor Charlene Mitchell, a Black communist leader in the CPUSA. Mitchell told me in the 1990s to research Du Bois's memoirs and why he repudiated the talented tenth. Frank Chapman is not an academic; he's someone who survived years in prison. He knew Fred Hampton's family, he is a militant and loved the people. Professor Davis gave the keynote and left the following day for another conference. I stayed for the three days. After Davis departed, Chapman says, "I am not an abolitionist, I am a revolutionary, but I will work with abolitionists." Lights are flickering in my head as I think, "There's a clear distinction between revolution and abolition."

The Chicago Police Department captain Jon Burge went to prison for obstruction of justice and perjury based on his leading a rogue ring of Chicago police who tortured Black people to make them confess to crimes. They would pick up Black people when they needed somebody to confess to a crime to make their numbers look good, they would take him to a Black op site away from the precinct and waterboard him, you know, put shocked electrodes on his testicles. Black men and Black women would be tortured to confess to crimes they did not commit.[4]

Chicago is tough not just because of gun violence on the street; it is because their cops are in another zone of predatory violence. If the Chicago Police Department can kick in the Panther leader Fred Hampton's door and kill Mark Clark and Hampton and claim they shot back at police—and it takes people years to figure out that was a lie—then the Chicago Police Department has the immunity, the impunity, the power to pull that off.[5]

So when Frank Chapman says, "No, abolitionism is *here*, and revolutionary struggle is *here*, but I will work with them," I'm like, "Wait, which one am I?" And then I say, "Okay, I don't think I'm a revolutionary." I never said I was one, I just said I know some of them. After hearing Chapman, I realized that I'm going to be an abolitionist, but *what kind* of abolitionist? The abolitionist who will listen to revolutionaries, especially as they age and die in prison or out of prison, or the young ones from Ferguson who end up shot in burning cars?

There are a lot of mothers and parents in the struggle. The story that shocked me was not from academics, or even Chapman, who startled me into recognizing that I was thinking incompletely because there are distinct entities, "revolution" and "abolition." It was when I went into a side room the next day and there was a Black mother, Melissa McKinnies, who shared her story and struggle.[6] She is a leader in Ferguson, but lives elsewhere, and she starts to talk about her young son, Danye Jones, who was not even a radical revolutionary; he was studying to pass an exam to be a real estate agent. McKinnies walks outside because the dog is barking only to find her son hanging from a tree with his pants pulled down to his ankles. How does the mother read the death and dishonor? It is because she engaged in a revolutionary struggle around Ferguson that she became a target, but rather than come for the mother they come for the child. I mean if you really want to break somebody, come for the child. She cannot even complete the task of telling the atrocity and so the father stands up and continues the narrative.

The father takes over, because the mother has to leave because she can't complete the story. And the father—though, for me, they're both intellectuals, of course—he speaks in this voice almost like someone giving a weather report. How do we keep from breaking down? We numb the full range of our emotions and our rage. He completes the story. After the panel ends, I go up and hug the mother and offer to help—but I am trained as an academic. What do you think I'm gonna do? I'm going to share their story. Maybe I'll write about it. But am I engaged on the level of strategizing and—I'll say it—confrontation? What I do know is that the predator-as-hunter has to step down even if it is only for a moment so that we get a reprieve. I know what I know because, when I can, I go into the community, and the community will tell me what is real. Do I mess it up later? Of course, I'm an academic. But I'm not so emotionally involved in academia, that I can't tell when I'm spinning and when I'm telling the truth.

RAW Right, period. I love that you ushered in a conversation about mothers participating in struggle. I want to contextualize it within the platform of political theology and that being the framework by which we start talking about God's activity in the world, and we talk about the political implications of the theological framework. For example, when we turn to the works of the theologian James H. Cone, what do these Christological things mean in light of our struggles?

In a keynote you gave entitled "Until the Next (Up)Rising" you discuss the theological implications of state violence and how distinct functions are divine through a godlike complex.[7]

And this godlike complex is articulated by Black mothers who have lost their children to the state and demand the state bring back the child who they murdered. You say in your keynote that, "If the state seeks to act like a god and take life, then it should *function* as a god and resurrect life. If it cannot then it is not a god, it is not Pharaoh, and its laws are not legitimate when they are predatory." I thought this was such an important quote because on the one hand it reflects our reality. Yes, that's what we do as organizers, we make demands of the state and for the state to deliver on.

The implication of making demands to the state is that we believe that the state will deliver our demands, right. But the way that you contextualize it is kind of subversive, that is: we actually don't believe that you have the capacity to bring back life, and therefore this godlike complex is problematic, it's predatory. On the other hand, I thought this was interesting because it reminded me of my mother when we used to not be able to pay bills and be facing evictions. My mother would pray, pray, pray, pray; and in her prayers, say, "I put a demand on God to deliver, and you know, make sure these bills are paid. I'm not asking you; this is what you *promised* me."

When I heard you make this call, I was like, "Yeah, forget the state." What does it mean to make that demand to God as a political theologian, to say, "If you're going to take life, then you should also resurrect it"? What are the implications for political theology to contend with anti-Blackness and the theological implications of anti-Blackness as a god? We don't see the ways in which God is resurrecting Black life, we only see the ways in which God is making space for, or the way that theology is allowing a vindication of, Black lives to be taken without any type of repercussions. I want to know what would you say as a demand for political theology to take up this tension—if we sit in the James H. Cone tradition—between a cross that gets redemption and a lynching tree that does not—there's no redemption on the lynching tree. What would you say to this intervention as it relates to struggle, anti-Blackness, the mothers in the movement, and this demand to "Bring back the *life* you take"?

⅃⅃   Actually, we've been making this statement for centuries, we don't always hear it, and it's not always written down in what we read.

I first started to think about the statement when I heard an impacted mother speak. I was working with mothers in Brazil and Colombia whose children, mostly sons, but also daughters, have been killed and murdered by police forces. Hearing of one mother's rebellion in Brazil when they offered money, as they do. I mean if they're not doing the godlike thing, they're doing the insurance policy thing: "We killed your kid. Sorry. Here's a package deal we can offer." It's monetary because that's all they have. It's not spiritual.

They bring the mother to a meeting after they disappear the son in Brazil and dismember him. The police/paramilitary violence in Brazil is on another level. There's serious violence in the US, but from my interaction with Brazilians, the impunity before, during, and after Bolsonaro is stunning. The US has the highest incarceration rate in the globe per capita. Brazil has the highest police killings of civilians, and they also have the largest Black population outside of the continent of Africa. So they bring the mother in to speak with officials who say, "We are not going to tell you"—because nobody ever acknowledges the crime—"who killed your son and how, but we're sorry about what happened to him." They speak as if a lightning bolt came down to take the child. No, man, it was your people.

They continue with a package deal: "Here's what we're going to offer, a basketball program, a scholarship in his name." They go to the checklist. But the mother refuses the offers and simply says, "No, bring back my son." This is an impossible political ask. This is when I start paying close attention to the narrative. The maternal/mother asks the state for what it *cannot* deliver. Right, because what do we care about more than life? There's nothing more valuable than life. Don't settle for some secondary, tertiary buy-out: a sweepstake, a car, or a new house. Those are important, but it's life itself that we desire. That loss is always the threat. Why don't we rebel? Because we want to stay alive and be able to eat.

Life is the gold standard; or platinum, whatever you want to call it. Nothing matters more than life. If they kill your kid, you say, "Okay, you could pull that one off; now return the child." If you cannot, then why am I talking to you? Anything else you offer—name a school after the child—doesn't matter. I'll say it again, my go-to twentieth-century Captive Maternal is always Mamie Till-Mobley. Once you're dealing with murder and torture (and I would see the attack on Emmett Till also as a sexual assault, which nobody talks about because he was embodied male in the frame of a fourteen-year-old boy), there's nothing holy except for your love and rage. That's why you can have an open-casket funeral for a mutilated teen and totally disturb the mortician when he tries to clean up or reassemble Emmett's face. Mamie Till-Mobley said "No" to conventional politics and violated every rule of decorum under theology or politics—what is a ceremonial burial? An open-casket funeral for the teen you murdered. Since you cannot bring them back alive, you will imprint with your love and rage their memory on the nation, on the globe, which is what she did when the photographs circulated. Back to the Brazilian mother. She cannot pull that one off, but her refusal to be coopted becomes the honor of not just herself or her family but also of the child who was supposed to preside over her burial decades later. I see this in the Jamaican sociologist Orlando Patterson's *Slavery and Social Death* (1982)—his concept of "natal alienation."[8] White supremacy, capitalism, imperialism, and misogynoir rupture the timeline for us. We're supposed to grow old, our children are supposed to attend our passing and have some good things to say about us—but even if they don't, at least we tried.

When you violate not just individual families, but whole families within the carceral-captivity framework, we suffer on different levels because our families are imprinted with the sign of "Blackness." Then time doesn't work for us the way it works for other people. Honor doesn't work for us. The state can take life but it cannot return or restore it, so the state doesn't work for us. Police said Kalief Browder stole a backpack and then they said he didn't, but they kept him in Rikers for several years as a teenager. Two years after his release he committed suicide. They hold him because he doesn't have $50 or $500 for bail.[9] Look at the state's policing now. Who's the mayor of New York City? Eric Adams, a former Black cop. The new police commissioner is a Black woman, Keechant Sewell. We respond to signs and symbols that tell us there is progress.

RAW What are the stakes for political theology, what happens when not only does the state not meet our demands, but God isn't meeting our demands either?

JJ Let me ask you, what does a resurrection look like? I don't know. We die. We come back. Where's Malcolm? Maybe he's here.

I won't even ask the deity to throw down on this one. I am asking us to throw down first. Then, we can ask the deity, "What's your plan?" But if we don't have a plan? I'm not a theologian. I was in seminary. James H. Cone and Cornel West were my advisors. I walked into seminary after returning from Africa to New York City. On the continent, it felt different. I thought different. I realized that I need more spirituality in my life. So, I go into seminary to meet the gifts of God. I leave early because the store isn't open. What the heck, why did it become a store? Because it's shaped like the academy?

To the extent that we embody the deity, we bring back life. I don't know, the way you teach your five-year-old, your fifteen-year-old, how you teach your students in the classroom. Whatever they tried to kill that is worthy and relevant to our freedom, that is what we bring back alive. Is that blasphemy, you know, like strike me down now, I don't—I didn't really swear, I just made a gesture towards it. At some point, because we've been struggling for decades, some of us for thirty or forty years, it is *your* game now. You cannot keep asking us questions. Okay? Because if we were able to pull a freedom movement off, we would have pulled it off because we love you so much.

There are people inside who've been incarcerated for decades. Sundiata Acoli, Mutulu Shakur, Leonard Peltier, Mumia Abu-Jamal. They let Russell Maroon Shoatz out when he has stage-four cancer, just before he dies. They have been killing us while we've been breathing in prison. We did not get political prisoners out with the volume and rapidity needed. Is freeing political prisoners an impossible feat, that only a god can do? What about feeding the babies? I just don't know to what extent we ever decided to risk everything for agape.

RAW This is ultimately the thing that leads you to the Captive Maternal. This love and care that is compounded upon by the state. As you put it, every time we stabilize the state builds upon that stability for its own coherence. Then you pose a question back to us: "So, what's next for the Captive Maternal?" It's like you set up an impossible paradigm: we're going to stabilize; we're going to free them all; we're going to bust them out of prison. You walk us into this impossible task and you then note that this resistance, this level of revolt, not only is Blackness capacious for it, we have the capacity, because of the amount of endurance and suffering that we have to go through, but then the state has the capacity, too, as long as we're stabilizing: the prisoners can produce the prison labor, right. As long as you all are okay and take care of each other, then we'll be okay and you'll take care of the state. When you talk about agape, I ask, if love becomes the stabilizing force for the state to build upon, then what is to be said of love?

JJ I go to Renaissance Church in Harlem. Pastors Jordan and Jessica are a husband and wife team. In a 2022 sermon, Rev. Jordan spoke about different kinds of love: erotic, familial, fraternal, sisterly, etc., but elevated agape as the highest form, because it requires political will. According to Rev. Jordan, we have to love people we don't like. I had to sit with that, because I prefer to love people whom I like, it's easier. If I don't like you, why do I have to be bothered with you?

Community has the same contradictions. The commitment to community transcends disagreements and conflicts. All forms of love, the love you have for your parents, your partner or your partners, your multiples, for your kids or your kid, your comrades, that's because they give you something back. There's some reciprocity on a good day. What does it mean to love people who want to be capitalists, or work for ICE and be prison guards? It is totally jacked up to deal with them. I'm thinking, "Oh my God, what am I supposed to do with you?" Agape is a form of love but it's not the love of the marketplace. It's not on the level of, "Here's a masterclass on love." It's not on the level of, "We have a TED Talk." It's not a narcotic. It is a journey. I'm still figuring out the sacrifices embedded in it.

What happens if we know we're going to lose, even if we win? Jonathan Jackson, the seventeen-year-old high school student, had a particular love for his imprisoned brother George Jackson, the Black Panther Party field marshal, who prison guards threatened to kill (he died August 1971). The high school teen was shot and killed by prison guards at the Marin County Courthouse on August 7, 1970, when he attempted to take hostages, using guns registered to Angela Davis, for a barter exchange for the life of his brother and other Black prisoners. Jon's love and risk-taking politics shortened his life (although any police officer could, with impunity, have killed him at any time).[10] Yet, his love for his brother, and for those tortured in prison, has radiated over half a century. That love had a huge impact on me and my kin, a Panther who said because Jonathan did it as a teenager, he didn't have to do it when he was a teenager, risk his life to attempt to free his older brother, a Panther who went underground into the Black Liberation Army, who was caught by police and tortured inside The Tombs prison—the Manhattan Detention Centre—in New York. It's the sacrificial love. One of us does it, and now we know it's possible. Will all of us sacrifice in this manner? I totally doubt it. We're being conditioned to shop and also to shop in our own movements. You can make money off of Black suffering. We know that now. Over the last couple of years, we had rebellions and people marched, millions did. Then some people got a ton of money. How did this happen?

It's extraction, accumulation, and then sell the movement back to the people. Still, we sacrifice our time, resources, health, and livelihoods, if not our lives, because we don't want to buy simulacra. This isn't a linear response to your query but I will tell you what I know, and what I will know until I transition. I have seen people love so much that they would die or be caged for decades. Do I love like that? No, I don't think I could pull that off. But I know it's real. So, if they can do it, some deity or deities—could be Ogun, Oshun, or Yemoja—it exists throughout time and space. It is transcendent. That is why the academy cannot eat your soul, because there is something greater than it, just as there is something greater than the state that can take life but not restore it.

RAW I'm just sitting with that for a second. What you're setting up is a relationship between a very central claim in political theology, which is "God is love," and then Revolutionary Love. I think of the entanglements. What love requires, what it produces, its capacity to transcend, these are always predicated upon Black suffering. So, taking your examples, the capacity for one to be caged because they love so much or for one to stabilize the state because they love so much is the very vehicle by which Blackness becomes capacious, right? Blackness has the capacity to endure and this puts into question the project of endurance by way of love. If love is going to be this vehicle by which we have the capacity to transcend—I wouldn't say "transcend," but to endure and maneuver—the antagonisms that come with Black suffering because of the people we love, then love also becomes the vehicle by which the suffering is durable. Suffering does not overdetermine the conditions.

JJ   I am trying to figure this out in real time. I'm talking to you about my interpretation of people who've spoken to me or at me. What hooked me with the Harlem church assertion—the pastors collectively meet before they write their sermons, one person delivers it but they meet collectively, so there's community—it's not specifically a hierarchy. It is political will. I am like "Okay." Tina Turner asks, "What's love got to do with it?" So, what does political will have to do with it?

Maybe that is the endurance: when you want to leave and you cannot. You could; clearly a lot of people have already left us, they just talk for us and about us but they're gone. They're like, "I'm out, and I'm going to cash in, it's an investment portfolio." And I get it, I mean, why would anybody want to suffer? It's like, where's the exit door to this? People find it and hop the train or plane and they're gone. They'll explain our suffering to bourgeois whites; they're not really explaining it to poor whites, they're definitely not explaining it to the white supremacists who have come up from the underground to above ground and are proto-fascists, if not full-blown fascists, waiting for an opportunity to use all their weapons.

I'm not saying you should get a weapon. I grew up on military bases. I lived with an officer who was likely destabilizing liberation movements around the globe. I watched troops do their thing. The level of violence that we're not prepared for is absolutely real. We are not prepared. We're used to random cops killing civilians, shooting or choking someone out. It is horrific, but state entities and employees do not randomly inflict violence unless they are sloppy. There are strategic plans to get violence to produce desired outcomes. Police forces don't deploy violence haphazardly, unless they are lazy and unstructured. If they are efficient, they figure out the greatest return they can get on a specific amount of violence or a targeted group.

What about the performative violence, using people as scapegoats or as martyrs? The state's capacity to intimidate you is based on its capacity to kill what you love: freedom, family, honor, dignity, intellectualism. They're like, "We can wipe it all out, and then have you watch Netflix all day." You would have to undo that capacity for violence. Those other loves that I mentioned are insufficient without the political will.

I have never—from raising kids to seeing parents transition—loved anybody without suffering. There is no way you love without suffering. Oh, you want no damage? Then don't love that much. We know people who just gave their whole hearts, that opened and burst. Somehow all that molecular matter ended up absorbed by us. My kids refuse to watch the documentary *Who Killed Malcolm X?* (2020) with me because they find it too scary and they want to go listen to some rapper. Before they leave, I say, "You know Malcolm loved us, right?" They respond: "Yeah, I know." That's all they need to know. Ten to twenty years from now, when they need reassurance that we loved each other, hopefully, that knowledge will be useful.

RAW Your work has been positioned as not only a critical and necessary intervention to Black feminist thought, but also a pseudo-alliance with Black male authors in what is a now burgeoning Black male studies discourse. Recently there was a social media debate between Black male studies and Black feminists around the Black Panther Party. Some forms of Black male studies were trying to insinuate that the critique of the Black Panther Party as being sexist is rooted in white feminism and white supremacy. I want to return to the Captive Maternal because it makes a critical intervention to discourses such as Black feminism and gender studies when thinking about the nature of anti-Blackness and predation.

You define the Captive Maternal as "an ungendered phenomenon whose generative powers"—which would be what we just discussed, love and care—"have been stolen by the state." You expound on the nature of anti-Black violence and the issue of gender as it relates to Black feminist critiques of cis-hetero patriarchy within our sociopolitical movements. Then you make this turn in your research to political prisoners and radical actors such as Erica Garner, Amílcar Cabral, and George Jackson to discuss the function of Captive Maternals as ungendered phenomena throughout history. Can you discuss why it's important to think of the Captive Maternal and the capacity for love, care, and stabilizing as ungendered or genderqueer rather than gendered?

JJ   The Captive Maternal emerged in my mind from my being attentive and watching how people of all genders— nonbinary, male, female, trans—provide services for the most vulnerable, which would be the child or the elder who is transitioning or frail. Fragility freaks us out most, at least me. I understand how much we suffer. I didn't quite understand how much we *feel* that suffering. Sometimes knowing what that feels like makes you very protective of the children, of the elders. I am in the middle. It's the fulcrum on the seesaw. I'm going to try and balance the plank and have folks bring that garbage (dishonor, disrespect, violations) to me because I want to deflect it from the other sectors, those who are younger or older, frail and vulnerable in different ways. The commitment to protect them is a foundation. It is a guiding light until you start allowing children and elders to be indoctrinated by the state and capitalism in order to offer them "security."

For example, last year when activists and communities asked the Chicago mayor Lori Lightfoot to control the spending on hiring more cops—I already told you how violent the Chicago police are—her pushback was to rhetorically ask, how would Black and Latinx people get into the middle class? Having jobs in policing and subjugating people become the vehicle for having money and economic stability. That's stage one of the Captive Maternal. I don't even know if I would even let them in the door on to the stage, but since I don't control the concept, people do whatever they want with it and others might include them.

We are full of contradictions. You keep moving on to those latter stages towards revolutionary struggle and it can be pacifist, and some people are militarist. I think sometimes feminists have problems with me because I don't completely condemn the militarist aspects. I will tell you again, I grew up in the military within the context of an imperial army that was always at war or planning wars and they were always invading some former colonial nation.

The Captive Maternal is nongendered; it is a function, not an identity, so it encompasses all genders or has no gender-identity marker. I only figured that out because people ask me questions. When I was finishing the draft of "The Womb of Western Theory," a trans academic, intellectual editor—who had asked me to contribute the chapter to a volume of the *Carceral Notebooks*[11]—raised the query about the gender of the Captive Maternal. You could read the entire draft without the gender of Captive Maternal being identified. Then I realized that the Captive Maternal was and is a function, not an identity.

There are women like Condoleezza Rice who are also on the masterclass roster, co-teaching with Madeleine Albright something like diplomacy after they devastated the Middle East using false claims of weapons of mass destruction, orchestrating an embargo that kills 500,000 children in Iraq. They would never be Captive Maternals. They don't function that way. They function for empire. Someone can be a Captive Maternal if they play with empire out of dire necessity: they need this low-level job to feed kids or get housing. However, if you are one of the architects willingly engineering the stability of empire and imperial warfare there is no way you are captive. You're an *operative*. Obama was the first Black *imperial* US president, not because he was captive, but because he wanted the job.

We can go from Obama to Kamala Harris, all the way down the ladder. Sometimes you have to take the job because you have to feed yourself and your kin. Those jobs are *not* called "president" or "vice president of the United States." If you can get that gig, you don't have to take it, you can get another job. You could teach high school.

The desire to be famous and powerful and wealthy closes the door on the *function* of the Captive Maternal and opens the door to predatory behavior because the state and capital back or invest in your endeavors. Jeff Bezos gives the abolitionist Van Jones access to $100 million and the Koch brothers pay Jones too, as an abolitionist. Bezos and Amazon eviscerate workers' rights. The Koch brothers are chewing through what's left of climate. We need *clean* water—we need *clean* air. There's no way to justify, "Oh, they gave money for abolitionism, so I can roll with them." No, I'm sorry, if you *do* you're not a Captive Maternal; you don't *function* as a Captive Maternal. There is actually a logic in this; I'm just trying to be consistent. There's a pimp, and then there's a trafficked child. This is my dichotomy in life right now: You're either a pimp or you're a trafficked kid; or an ally of that child who stops the pimp. I play along that spectrum and if you're making money, then for me, you are clearly not captive to anything. Unless you're Dan Freeman—the protagonist of Sam Greenlee's 1969 novel *The Spook Who Sat by the Door*. The plot of the book—and of the 1973 film of the same title, directed by Ivan Dixon—centers on Freeman, who pretends to be an "Uncle Tom" in order to be accepted by the CIA as their first Black recruit—he infiltrates the agency as a revolutionary seeking to learn the skills of the world's premier counter-revolutionary organization, he takes resources and training from the CIA to share with the besieged Black community in rebellion.[12] Unless we channel our education, training, resources, and influential networks into vulnerable communities, we remain alienated from material struggle and political ethics. We can funnel funds into underground schooling, housing, feeding people, freeing imprisoned folks, securing health care, rescuing Haitians and Africans deported via ICE and returned to destabilized countries where they are likely to be killed.

The older I get, the clearer I become about empire: You cannot rehab predatory structure. You would not try to rehabilitate organized crime, you would simply say, "You all have to go find another line of work." That is the situation we're in. This corrupted state functions as organized crime. Everybody knows it, but do they and we want to have a strategy to deal with it?

RAW You just dropped the mic. You have quite a few questions here in the chat. Let's start with: "I've heard Dr. James mention in previous talks/discussions about the betrayal stage of the Captive Maternal. I am curious to hear if she could elaborate on what that is, especially in relation to what has been spoken about today regarding love."

I love this question. We have talked about the betrayal stage because I thought you needed another stage of the Captive Maternal.

JJ   It's true, a year ago you asked me, "What about the stage of betrayal?" Somebody else said, "We need to 'off' the Captive Maternal." My response to that was: "Oh, me? Stop! I have to change my address now?" It's not funny, but it's kind of funny. The truth of the matter is—I've said it before—the younger generation was betrayed by the older generations. We lied by omission to the youth. I was in Canada, giving a talk a couple years ago. And it was mostly sisters and they were diverse, some were in the academy, others were dominatrices. I grew up in an era where progressives asserted—as per Audre Lorde—that you cannot use the master's tools to undo the master's house, right?[13] When I quoted that, as the oldest person in the room, the sisters roll back and they say that we can use the master's tools. I replied, "Wait. Audre Lorde said you *cannot*." The Black youths responded: "We don't care." I started thinking: "Okay, people are improvising here . . . they plan to survive."

This relates to our relationship with violence. To link it to "'off' the Captive Maternal" is not my preference because I'm implicated in betrayals given my contradictions. I also want to be candid. You cannot just roll up on people and think that they don't have a plan. Some people you should just leave alone because they're not all grounded in spirituality. But, if we could agree as a community and hold a line of ethics, you do not betray us. However you want to make your money or build your brand, you don't pimp us, right? Us being the collective movement who agree to be disciplined by agape, and agree to sacrifice and suffer not, hopefully, 100 percent, not every single day, but to some degree.

Because the idea of who we *could* be as free is greater than the reality of the minutia of twenty-four hours a day, seven days a week, twelve months a year. If we could agree, however, respectfully, lovingly, that we will confront betrayal, then you have the right to criticize me when I betray our struggles for liberation, justice, peace.

You guys are inheriting what we left you. Our lies of omission meant we couldn't tell you what we actually saw and knew to be the world. How violent it is. How predatory and unloving it is. Still, there's beauty. There's this tenacity to love more and give more and risk more. I don't think we were ever clear about that with you. Definitely the academy is not clear—it has to make money and build its brand.

We lied to you by omission. People can say, "Oh, no, you're lying now." Whatever. I'll just tell you my part in it. There were things I would not probably say in a classroom or in a conference based on how violent I see the world to be. But I keep trying to gesture towards you, that if I tell you that I grew up on a military base, I'm not stupid about this.

I'm only talking about my father in the last year or so. I was in Nicaragua during the Contra war and met with Salvadoran victims of US-backed terrorism who had been macheted during the Reagan era. There's so much horror that the US has exported around the globe. For us to recover, we would have to do something absolutely brilliant and breathtaking; and we will likely do it, but it won't be my generation, it will be yours. You have the right to say, "You've betrayed us," and it's not cancel culture, it's an analysis and it's astute because you have receipts (or maybe you do not). You understand how capitalism and imperialism work, if you can take Black suffering and cash in on it, that is betrayal.

You have a right not to be turned into prey by anybody. And you have a right not to be battered or dishonored or humiliated by anybody. At the same time, you have to contextualize the personal abuse or the group abuse with the larger terror, which is that we're moving towards (proto-)fascism and we came out of enslavement.

Whatever we do to each other will never rival those zones of terror. We do need to stop throwing broken glass and garbage at each other and at women, trans, LGBTQ+, children, neurodiverse people—all of those rights have to be respected. Let's be clear: everybody died for us, including cisgender men who were probably a pain in the neck and patriarchal. Everybody contributes who is disciplined to agape. Agape is not the personal property of any gender or any sexual identity, agape is the wild card. Not everybody will throw it down even if you're the right intersectional identity that's supposed to be the leadership.

The only people who lead are the people who commit, and the only people who commit are the ones who are willing to suffer and love simultaneously. That has no gender. How do I organize? I only want to organize with women because it's easier, but that doesn't mean all the women that I know are nice people or honest. There's no virtue in your identity construct. The virtue is in the capacity to love and to keep loving when people become a pain in the neck.

Everything we do for the last 400 years has been turned into a commodity. The gender wars is a commodity now. People are trading in it like it's a brand. We're smart enough to know when we're being played, aren't we? But if we get too emotionally involved in this stuff then it's like a crusade—for what? Feed the kids, stop the devastation of the environment, and deal with the empire, as well as our relationships around

gender, sexuality, the murder of trans women, the dishonored, etc. But you can't isolate those and think that the empire
is not playing you. The state/corporation is cashing in on our
conflicts. I'm not saying hide the conflicts, I'll go full-blown
open. I'll write about anybody, from Barack on down. But.
You know, if we can't find the capacity, the political will—now,
I understand better what the pastor was saying. We don't have
to *like* each other. Agape as political will means that we have
to *love* each other. We have to be disciplined. We don't have
very much discipline right now. Everybody's doing their free-
range-chicken stuff. I would discipline myself to a strategy if
someone threw one out that I thought had integrity, and then
I would want to tinker with it. If the collective or community
told me to shut up, I would stop doing these pod things. I
don't have a problem with that. However, if people are building brands out of conflict, I don't have time for it.

RAW On the one hand there is the brand of it all, and then,
on the other hand, it's a real antagonism that people suffer
through. Anti-Black gendered violence is something that
people *actually* die from. I think—referring back to the point
that you made earlier around Orlando Patterson's notion of
social death[14]—there is a misalignment. When we talk about
the function of Patterson's natal alienation, the critique is not
only of the family, of kinship, of this idea of love, what I think
the critique is situating us in is that these formations, this
discipline that you're calling for, become the impossibility
because of the antagonisms.

JJ   I think I understand and I'm sorry that I wasn't clear.
You have the right to self-defense. That is not violence. Self-
defense is not a synonym for violence. I've talked about this
with people I was in seminary with, who went on to become
directors of Harlem programs about intimate violence, family violence. A number of us are survivors. We are survivors of
rape or survivors of beatdowns. We agree, "You have the right
to self-defense."

Rebecca, I could have led with that, and then we could

have shortened the conversation. But that narrative is prohibited in public. Do what it takes. Do what you need to do to be safe and unviolated. But do it with your crew. This verbal back and forth? I don't consider that self-defense. You might see it as some kind of armor, and you'll go ahead and write and speak more. But know that the nitty-gritty is material reality. It is a confrontation with violence. If we won't confront a violent state, are we then going to physically confront domestic battery? We're going to go to the house of the rapists down the block and confront them? This is about strategy.

I left seminary early maybe not just because it was a business, maybe because I may not be a complete pacifist. There is a strong possibility that I am not. I wasn't trained for pacifism. I was in Reserve Officers' Training Corps for years: I am not trained to be a pacifist. But, I *want* to be a pacifist. This is like when *Millennials Are Killing Capitalism* asked me how could I refer to the "hyper-masculinist" George Jackson as a "Captive Maternal" (see below, p. 255). How? Because he *loved* people.

But then he threw down, and most could not deal with that. He threw down. You have the right to survive without being battered, humiliated, sex-trafficked, raped. Disproportionately, it's women and children, trans and cis women, who are subjected to these abuses, but so too are males. In the absence of having a public strategy and making it clear that there will be a community response for harming us, *we go to words*? I mean, come on. If you want to throw down, I'm totally behind you; but then you throw down on every metric. You do not stop at level three or therapy. What is the material plan without having to rely on the cops or therapy only? You would have to have a plan, and it will likely look a bit militaristic, security-focused. So, if you don't want to do that—I can only say, after decades of writing about feminism and the need to stop rape, joining a lesbian dojo to offer protections to people—I don't have anything else to say.

RAW Let's go to the next question. Can you speak to the role of celebrity in contemporary Black movements? I'm thinking about both the celebrity of academics, who formally were a part of radical movements, and members of the entertainment class. What does it mean, for example, for Angela Davis and Cardi B to write a foreword together?

JJ   My assumption is that people want to be remembered. The best way to be remembered is to be a celebrity. Being a celebrity is not the same thing as agape.

It's a different function; it's not a Captive Maternal function. I am not talking about any specific individuals or collectives, who you're talking about is sometimes the same folks I'm talking about, sometimes not. Put the people up on your fridge with a magnet and deal with it.

This society is driven by entertainment because it's a deflection from material struggle. What we really want to do is address our sorrow that we have to fight this hard. It's freaking me out—when does it stop? It doesn't stop. So, we distract ourselves with entertainment: "Oh look at that, we are so cute, we get to be president, we get to be rich, they're going to do a biopic." Success like that might make us feel like we have power. That's not power over economies, militarism, proto-fascism, voter disenfranchisement, neo-slavery. It's distraction.

The real brilliant people I know, you don't know their names. I'm sure you know brilliant people and I don't know their names. Because they're behind the scenes. But here's the flip side, the most predatory people—I know we're not supposed to use the word "evil"—but the most violent people empowered to structure military invasions and drone strikes, we don't know their names either. The people you need to know, you don't know who they are, because they are behind the curtain. If you want to be entertained, maybe just choose sixty minutes a day and say, "I'm just going to do fluff." Listen to the celebrities that tell us how to organize a revolutionary struggle while they look out from the mountaintop in their mansions. They're embedded in white (imperial) power. I realize that the places I teach are white power bastions. Where do you think I'd be teaching?

If academia needs a Black unicorn, they'll get one. I don't want to talk about celebrities too much, other than to see if there's a line where I can study them to track where they/we came from in terms of struggles. And where we're going in terms of the mutation of the struggle into commodification. I only want to watch them in order to figure out the trajectories.

Everybody works for white power given who the funders are. Certain people get out of jail or don't go to prison. These are moments of study to figure out where we are on the graph. We were in rebellion half a century ago, and then people got shot up, murdered, and put in prison—think COINTELPRO. Other people survived. They have the right language, but then somehow become embedded in the Democratic Party, and are jet-setting around the globe. Now, I'm gonna say something really controversial because that wasn't. *We cannot do it alone.* All the revolutionaries knew that. There are the Indigenous people doing resistance around Standing Rock. What are the white rebels doing after Kyle Rittenhouse shot them up and then walked for two murders?

There's no way we pull this off solo as Black people. It will be revolutionary-minded lovers joining forces with revolutionary-minded lovers, it will not be an all-Black formation. That's why I led with the current male mayor of New York City (Eric Adams) and the current female police commissioner (Keechant Sewell), both are Black. It makes the struggle even more painful because I just want to throw down with my people, but Black people have already told me that I am a pain in the neck.

Any sincere gesture to move forward—so that we leave youths something that is not just ripping their hair out or asking, "What the heck is this, it makes no sense!"—means that we must work with other rebels who love.

RAW I think that's important. The hard part is finding the rebels that are not anti-Black.

JJ But I didn't say they were anti-Black. A rebel is a rebel is a rebel. If you can figure out who's an authentic rebel, work with them. I did not say to have dinner with them every Friday or invite them over to your house. I'm just saying that they have strategy and analysis.

RAW Right, and they are a means to an end.

JJ   I don't know if they're a means to the end. In rebellion, they need you and you need them. You talked about the Captive Maternal. There was a Latina. Her name was Margarita. Notice I speak in the past tense. She was a doctoral student in one of the University of California campuses. She contacted me to write a dissertation on the Captive Maternal. I told her it was really a "Black thing," but I sent her links to articles; she said she was going to write the dissertation anyway. But with the lack of support in the academy, her lack of support at home, being undocumented and with limited resources, her exploitation on the university campus as a teaching assistant mentoring stressed out and under-resourced youths, she committed suicide. Rebels depart faster than anybody else. Our job is to keep rebels on the planet as long as possible, because we need them and because we/others love them.

RAW This is going to be our final question. It really speaks to what you just said: "Is there a way for institutional Black studies to embrace the thought of suicide? I ask this from a place of theorizing the university as a site of a plantation, where I think one can argue that Black studies has developed a neurotic attachment to the university that prevents it from embracing the abolition of the university."

JJ   I brought up Jonathan Jackson before. I don't know why, but Jonathan haunts me. Not in a bad way. He is not a spirit that I fear. But he is a spirit. At Jonathan Jackson's funeral, after white prison guards killed him in the Marin County Courthouse parking lot, Huey P. Newton called it "revolutionary suicide." There is a complicated narrative, maybe some people were supposed to show up and offer backup but they didn't for varied reasons.

California prison guards had/have a mandate to stop all potential escapes, even if they kill everybody, which they nearly did that day. They killed seventeen-year-old Jonathan Jackson and the incarcerated James McClain and William Christmas, as well as a white judge, Harold Haley.[15] At Attica Prison in New York in September 1971, the month after George Jackson was murdered by prison guards, white National Guardsmen shot through white prison guard hostages in order to kill imprisoned Black rebels.[16] Apparently the worst thing in the world for a white-supremacist empire is a Black rebel.

I went to seminary in a faith in which political suicide is written into the scripture. I don't care what they call it . . . if you agree to go up on a cross, there's some transactional politics. Sorry. Forgive me if I went there. But literally, I'm going to give up a life to the beloved so that you guys are going to live. We do that every single day. Parents who don't have enough food in the house, give their food to the kids or to the elders. Or, they take that second, third job to feed their families. Adults work in dangerous underground economies because they are willing to sacrifice life and dignity in various ways so y'all get to live and grow up.

That is our inheritance. For some people who are not us and who don't live under the conditions of terror that we live under, it looks like we—a population mutated through enslavement and genocide and a deep entanglement with death and dishonor—are committing or facing suicide in small dosages or spectacular ways every single day. "Revolutionary suicide" as described by Black Panthers; "political suicide" as defined by the comprador classes. Don't fear it. Comprehend it. The "suicide" to having a happy family, or a successful career. I can't explain to you how I got tenured or got to these elite spaces, because I just followed the best I could the love of the mass in rebellion. For whatever reason, the academy said: "Yeah, we can use something like that, but we're going to put it in a petri dish, stick it in the freezer, hide it in a cubicle."

I rarely wavered. That doesn't make me better than anybody else. It just means that I try to resist the reality of suicidal practices. I'm talking not about pills or walking onto the train tracks or overdosing on drugs. The practices of sacrificing at this level are organic to who we are as a people; we've done it for centuries, perhaps we don't have a narrative that we want to hear.

Jonathan still follows me. He is a comfort. I'll repeat what my Panther vet kin said: "Because Jonathan did it, I don't have to do it." We only need to know that one of us is capable of sacrificial love. We don't know the limits in terms of possibilities, because there's no limit to loving in a slave camp.

The love mutates. The more they bring the terror until they break us into the grave, the more we emerge from the grave. We come back into memory and political will, as did fourteen-year-old Emmett. Rosa Parks, I believe, was thinking about Emmett when she wouldn't give up her seat to a white person on a segregated bus.

We die, but we don't die. We suicide, but we manifest. The point is to embrace each other enough that longevity becomes more of a practical possibility—not the longevity because we sold ourselves within slavery, the point is to reclaim ourselves under enslavement.

RAW I love this as a closing remark. Particularly in thinking theologically. I love the juxtaposition between the Christological story and Jonathan Jackson. I think this is important because, on the one hand, there's a Captive Maternal—we think about Jonathan saying, "This is my brother, George: I'm going to go for it in order to save him." On the other hand, you have Jesus saying "Take this cup from me." His Father is saying "I'm going to raise you up in three days." So, the sacrifice is not equal because Jesus gets raised up in three days but Jonathan is like, "I'm through with this."

JJ I just said Jonathan was with me. Jonathan got raised. He's here. Y'all are still younger, you might not focus on time but I am moving towards my death. That's just how it works. That's the architecture. It doesn't change. Death, as scary as it is, it's a death of the body. I'm not even doing the religious thing right now. Departure came with the agreement. You can show up, but then you're going to go out and you won't determine the time or place.

Have you ever watched an elder die? A mother? You came out of her body and then you're just trying to give her a shred of dignity in these half-assed nursing homes because your brother is in charge of everything now. And people are saving money with the refrain, "They're going to die anyway, why spend *real* money?" To me that is maddening. But when they transition you calm down in your grief because you realize that they didn't leave you. Nobody who loves you, even if they hated you while they loved you, leaves you.

That's why you transcend. That's why you know you love. That's why you know you are better than whatever garbage people try to shove down your throat. That is why they will keep trying to kill us but will never succeed. The soul—I don't even know what it is—but Jonathan keeps popping up. So, it's real. And that's good enough for me.

Notes to Chapter 11

1   Joy James, "'New Bones' Abolitionism, Communism, and Captive Maternals," *Verso Books Blog*, June 4, 2021, https://www.versobooks.com/blogs/5095-new-bones-abolitionism-communism-and-captive-maternals; and Joy James, "Airbrushing Revolution for the Sake of Abolition," *Black Perspectives* blog, AAIHS, July 20, 2020, https://www.aaihs.org/airbrushing-revolution-for-the-sake-of-abolition/.

2   See *History.com* editors, "This Day in History: December 04 1969."

3   See https://naarpr.org/.

4   *Chicago Tribune* staff, "Jon Burge and Chicago's Legacy of Police Torture," *Chicago Tribune*, September 12, 2018, https://www.chicagotribune.com/news/ct-jon-burge-chicago-police-torture-timeline-20180919-htmlstory.html.

5   See Taylor and Haas, "New Documents Suggest that J. Edgar Hoover Was Involved in Fred Hampton's Murder"; and Conway, "The Government Murdered Fred Hampton."

6   See McDonell-Parry, "Ferguson Activist Claims Son Was 'Lynched.'"

7   Joy James, "Until the Next (Up)Rising," keynote address at "Imagining

Abolition: Beyond Prisons, Wars, and Borders" virtual gathering, April 14, 2021; available online, https://www.youtube.com/watch?v=giq5oABfI7s, accessed October 11, 2022.

8   See Orlando Patterson, *Slavery and Social Death: A Comparative Study* (Harvard, MA: Harvard University Press, 1982); and "mumbletheory," "Collapse of the Paradigm," *Mumble Theory*, January 14, 2021, https://mumbletheory.com/2021/01/14/collapse-of-the-paradigm/.

9   Jennifer Gonnerman, "Kalief Browder, 1993–2015," *New Yorker*, June 7, 2015, https://www.newyorker.com/news/news-desk/kalief-browder-1993-2015.

10   Freedom Archives, "The 50th Anniversary of the August 7th Marin County Courthouse Rebellion," accessed October 26, 2022, https://freedomarchives.org/projects/the-50th-anniversary-of-the-august-7th-marin-county-courthouse-rebellion/.

11   Perry Zurn and Andrew Dilts, eds, "*Challenging the Punitive Society*": *Carceral Notebooks* 12 (2016); available online, https://www.thecarceral.org/journal-vol12.html, accessed October 26, 2022.

12   Sam Greenlee, *The Spook Who Sat By the Door* (London: Allison & Busby, 1969).

13   See Audre Lorde, "The Master's Tools Will Never Dismantle the Master's House," in *This Bridge Called My Back: Writings by Radical Women of Color*, ed. Cherríe Moraga and Gloria Anzaldúa (New York: Kitchen Table, 1981); available online, https://monoskop.org/images/2/2b/Lorde_Audre_1983_The_Masters_Tools_Will_Never_Dismantle_the_Masters_House.pdf, accessed October 26, 2022.

14   Patterson, *Slavery and Social Death*.

15   See Tracey Onyenacho, "Black August: Marin County Courthouse Rebellion," *ColorLines*, August 14, 2020, https://www.colorlines.com/articles/black-august-marin-county-courthouse-rebellion; and *SFgate*, "1970 Marin County Courthouse Murders," slideshow, April 18, 2017, https://www.sfgate.com/news/slideshow/1970-Marin-County-courthouse-shooting-144014.php.

16   Burton, *Tip of the Spear*.

12   Angela Davis Was a Black Panther (AKA "Pragmatism vs Revolutionary Love")

With Too Black and Ryan of *The Black Myths Podcast,* 2021

Black Myths Podcast The myth was, "Angela Davis was a Black Panther."[1] I do want to underline that this series is not meant as a shot at Angela Davis. Anything we say is within a larger context of trying to understand our history, our struggling on liberation. And anyone can get critiqued within that framework. Angela Davis is not a god or a perfect person.

In the first part, we wanted to walk through the timeline to lay out who Angela Davis was, what she was involved with.[2] The fact is, she was not a member of the Black Panther Party, but she did work with the Black Panther Party primarily as a member of the Communist Party USA. She worked with the Black Panther Party to help organize political education within that party. She also had strong critique, she thought they were sexist. She didn't particularly care for the nationalism. She was not a member of the party. Her critique of the BPP is collapsed and gets lost in history, when you just add it in because she had a 'fro, you think she was angry. A lot of times the aesthetics of Black radicalism—or as I called it in the first episode, "Black Militant vibes"—just get collapsed into this single category, this amorphous idea of militancy that doesn't explain really any politics of what people stood for, it's just guns and Black fists and afros. It's just a vibe. There's really no articulation of what needs to be done. These things are ahistorical and revisionist. They don't really explain anything. How do we understand this idea of Black radicalism, how it gets watered down, how it gets sold back to us?

In your interview with *Millennials Are Killing Capitalism* you emphasize "I'm not a revolutionary" (see below, p. 257). You kept saying it. Is that in reference to what you're saying about now, as far as academics?

Joy James Yeah. I say the "go to" is I'm a librarian, like you and the *Millennials Are Killing Capitalism* hosts. You all read Davis's autobiography so closely. It's pretty magnificent the way *Black Myths* parsed it. I was thinking, "Oh, I forgot to teach that. I don't even remember that part."[3]

BMP You can be this revolutionary, at least aesthetically, you can also have some privilege. I don't know if people don't throw around the word "revolutionary"; very often nowadays they throw around "radical" at least. You can have these politics, but there's no real suffering that has to come with it other than maybe the troll on the Internet. Hope I'm not stepping out of line.

Alicia Garza got on Twitter and was talking about how she had FBI threats, and the Justice Department came to her door and told her about death threats. She was warned, as one of the founders of Black Lives Matter. I just found that to be interesting. I don't want anything to happen to her. I'm going to clarify that. I'm just saying that's not normal either. If you're really fighting it is not normal at all for the FBI to be protective, given its lethal, criminal history of COINTELPRO to destroy Black radicalism. Given the structure, that's just an odd relationship.

JJ   It's about integration and assimilation as alternatives to radical resistance. Back to the integration matrix. The wave of private elite school integration was likely fueled by the middle classes. Davis's family did integrate into these Northern elite schools, and they express their racism as "Can I touch your hair?" It is offensive, but it doesn't look like a lynching. That tells you that the world, the democracy, is probably accommodating to Blacks. I mean, it can be dangerous because you know people who died, but nobody's trying to kill *you* in the private white school or wealthy neighborhood, and nobody's even spitting on you in school. The teachers are kind or trying to be kind, and you get invited to white people's homes for dinner, whatever. So that tells you what the possibilities are; there's a class division here. If you're the scholarship kid who lives in the Bronx and you end up at Yale, then you have a story you can run with for the rest of your life. What percentage of Black people end up like that? What percentage hopefully won't end up in Rikers? What are our choices for the mass? People are starving and we throw food away; we waste water. What is a revolutionary struggle without war?

I am not only talking about material war. It could be psychological warfare, which the state wages all the time; the universities and colleges function as ideological factories. I only trust people who will tell you that they don't have the answers. I think a lot of people say they have the answers. But how could you have answers if you tell me this is not a war zone, and so we do not have to prepare ourselves for war or create a security apparatus, not just a physical but also an emotional, psychological one. Elites tell us that if we work harder, vote more (I voted for Obama) that it's going to be okay—for me. I'm petty bourgeois. The way I suffer is not how impoverished others suffer, or the incarcerated suffer at Rikers or in maximum security.

BMP George Floyd, his neck gets stomped on, and that somehow has something to do with somebody getting hired at Chase Bank. I've been screaming this on every episode.

JJ   That's brilliantly stated. Our deaths fuel capitalism and accumulations—industries of care and leadership get born whether the catalyst is our physical death, work death, shattering of honor from being spat on or raped. Sexual assault isn't/wasn't just women or girls; it's also men and boys. The accumulation from our lives in our death is just like clockwork. The difference now, maybe most noticeably so, is that Black people can also accumulate more. It used to be the state and whites killed you, ran you from your land. We went from Blacks owning 20 percent of farm land at the turn of the twentieth century to 1 percent today. Only way we lose that much land is when they (state, law, police, white supremacists) terrorize us off the land. State, capital, whiteness accumulates through terror. But now they can accumulate through social movements. It's so painful and traumatic. I don't think individually we can claim anything. I think the only legitimate claims have to be collective, and we have to be disciplined to that. Does that mean you let the whole neighborhood move into your house now? It does mean that you're going to have to cede ground. I'm directing this to the Black leadership that is publicly the Black leadership. There has to be an accountability metric with the mass. Elites need to stand down, because if you can't get our leadership to stand down, they will continue to accumulate, and by the nature of accumulation, they will become increasingly alienated from working-class and poor Black communities.

BMP Can you clarify what you mean by "stand down"? I'm just curious how you're defining that.

JJ I wrote "Airbrushing Revolution for the Sake of Abolition"[4] after talking with graduate students who were being intimidated by faculty to look like "reasonable radicals"—i.e., more like the older academics—and to maintain distance from impoverished and working-class communities, such as the one where George Floyd was born. Contemporary elite academics write about those communities. In "Airbrushing," I was trying to gesture (not bash) and address the (un)ethical by calling out the simulacra and profiteering around struggles that disproportionately terrorize the laboring and working classes. Obviously, I was pissed when I was writing it to some degree. I had been waiting for people to stand down or stand up and call out the performance politics. If elites know more wealthy conservatives and progressives than members of the Black working class or militant collectives, then "stand down." If you can accumulate hundreds of thousands or millions of dollars—that nobody even knows about until years later—on behalf of "the movement," that is problematic. How many houses do you need funded by movement trauma in order to elevate your profile as someone who cares about or speaks for Black people or shares their pain or plans to lead them against capitalism and imperialism? Stand down. Individual faculty can earn $500,000 to $900,000 per annum, salaries based on their public profiles of explaining racism or Blackness. I am sure white faculty earn more. This is capitalism, but how do the wealthy get to discipline the radicals as being too abrasive and unreasonable? And bash radicals who take more risks? If you're doing that to those who take more risks or live with more precarity, I just feel you're taking out a political competitor or gentrifying the neighborhood.

I'm not an Afropessimist. I know some of them who were actively radical, but they don't organize anymore. I respect the contributions they did make. If you're bashing because you have to be the authentic Black left leadership but won't follow the leadership of non-elite laborers and workers or even unionize your nonprofits, then stand down as gatekeepers. Unless you have something that grounds you in the mass, something more than rhetoric or aspiration, you're likely to retreat or conform. In the music video for their 2012 song "The Guillotine," Boots Riley and The Coup replay *The Wizard of Oz*.[5] The Scarecrow, Lion, Tin Man, and Dorothy are Black. The wizard is a capitalist. The sister, Silk E, who plays Dorothy struts in in red slippers singing, "We were in a war before we fought one." COINTELPRO was lethal but that was just the tip of the state's violence.

In the stages of the Captive Maternal, the maroon camps (maroonage is the stage of rebellion for sovereign life) have all kinds of multiracial allies in solidarity: their defining characteristic is their function as rebels for autonomous zones. Grapple with the tragedies that we've inherited from enslavement, rape, rebellion, and militarized forces to destroy resistance. Inside those tragedies and traumas, there's a coda, there's a script. There are analyses to push things forward so that our children are less terrorized, and the same for our elders. As you get older, you're going to care for your parents and try to help them find dignity while they transition. We should not have multiple layers of trauma impeding our abilities to be free. In order to live and thrive to some degree, we would have to agree that celebrity leadership is done. Maybe I'll go to your movie when it comes out, but once you start marketing our freedom struggle as an extension of yourself that's a dead-end road. Or it's circular, so that you just come right back and end up at the Pentagon or Deutsche Bank, Wall Street. It then remains about capital and control.

To come to terms with grief and our loss means to come to terms with reality: we have to agree that all our heroes in material struggles were not crazy, even if we do not agree with their strategies and choices. All of our celebrity heroes, were not inherently heroic for the mass. Sometimes you are just caught between a rock and a hard place and you do stuff to survive; and people tell the story. The South African ANC communist leader Chris Hani is assassinated, but pro-capitalist and liberal Nelson Mandela is your mentor. I cannot really ride with you other than down the block, because we're not going anywhere.

Also, to your point about not looking around the corner, you're already in the midst of the violence and warfare. Maybe it's just time that we acknowledge how vulnerable we are? Physically, emotionally, psychologically. Stop pretending we are not. Politics that are performative pretend that, "We've got this, that if you do A, B, and C, we're going to get 1, 2, and 3, and maybe not in your lifetime but one day we'll be free." We would have more clarity if we were clear that we are raw. This is Black August. George and Jonathan were raw. I wouldn't necessarily want to live in the same communal home with them, because police forces and reactionaries would always be coming for them. But I have to tell you, because they existed, another dimension of me can exist, even if it's only on the level of "What if? What if they had survived? What if they had made it to Cuba? What if an international movement had been able to contain imperialism? What if . . . ?"

Instead of binge-watching Netflix or some distraction from the pain, face it. What if we flipped the pain? What if our children live to old age? What if no mother or father ever has to look at their child in a coffin as a mutilated being without features? I don't want abstract freedom dreams because we know too much. I think it's dishonest based on who we are and what we've gone through in captivity and its afterlife. I think we can handle it. I don't know what we will mutate into, but we're not going to mutate into crazy people. We're not going to only retreat into pathology. I've been talking about Revolutionary Love. Some of us are going to mutate into a highly disciplined cadre that follows Revolutionary Love wherever it takes us. It doesn't have to be militarist, but don't allow people to sell you simulacra.

BMP I was going to ask you about Attica in relation to pragmatism. One of the craziest things we've been discussing is capitulating to capital, which people tell us is basically more "pragmatic." It's more practical. At the same time, we're sitting here talking about how—not even just for the Black poor—how crazy this makes even the Black bourgeoisie look, because the discipline and the structure of it forces you to lose yourself in many ways. What about capitulating is really pragmatic? My original question was, how does the Attica rebellion, partly inspired by George Jackson, complicate our idea of what's pragmatic in the face of war? The incarcerated did write petitions and things of that nature. They didn't just take over the prison on day one.

JJ   I question how pragmatic are the things we've really been trying that our leaders tell us we should do? I don't know. I know we can say it keeps us alive. I don't think we should go prematurely or violently, or starving, or without necessary medicine or medical treatment during pandemics. I don't think we should suicide or OD either; or be snuffed out in prison or turned into sex slaves. Basic stuff here. There's nothing pragmatic about any of these things that I just ticked off like a laundry list. Violence is deeply embedded in this culture. This is not a pragmatic culture. What you're talking about is a hustle. You can call it a pragmatic one. You're still hustling in a predatory zone. That means people do tricks. All kinds of tricks, you know, card tricks. The kind of trick in order to stay alive or get more money and security. What's "pragmatic" about that? What is pragmatic about burying your murdered child? There's nothing practical under racial capitalism, misogynoir, misopedia, imperialism. You cannot tax us. Okay, I'm serious. I mean, the state does. If you don't pay, it'll take your house and your car. When we pay taxes, I'm literally paying for police forces to kill people. Then I'm paying for the compensation packet after they murder you. One-point-eight million dollars for Fred Hampton, Mark Clark (murdered by the FBI and Chicago police during a predawn raid on December 4, 1969), twelve million for Breonna Taylor's family. Six million for Tamir Rice's family. Just let me pay for pre-kindergarten. I don't mind giving my money to the collective, but this is not practical or pragmatic. This is predatory.

Don't confuse the predatory with the pragmatic, because if it's a hustle around the predatory, so you can live long and have multiple homes and a lot of cars or just put food on the table, I totally understand stage one of the Captive Maternal. It's contradictory that the work that we do diminishes us. But I'm going to do it because my kid needs to stay in the school or I need to keep this job. Then we move to protests about exploitation and torture in prisons like Attica, where the imprisoned waged a struggle to be recognized as "human" (however, you want to define that). The movement, the takeover of the prison and the building of the maroon camp inside the prison, was the next stage; then the declaration of war from the state, because any attempt to be free from whites as a Black captive is seen as war. This is pathology. We can find other key words besides "pragmatic." Accumulation keeps skewing towards the top. There used to be a lot of millionaires, and now you have billionaires becoming the norm for the ruling class. Biden is better than Trump. But tell that to a woman who was in one of those ICE camps, a Haitian sister who met the womb-collector who gave her a forced hysterectomy. She will never have children. Her man leaves her because he wants to. There's nothing pragmatic about consistently breaking and humiliating people. A Rochester, NY Black pastor said after George Floyd was murdered: "If you kill us, we'll kill your economy." That was in 2020. I was listening to WBAI (NYC radio), and that statement keeps radiating. It doesn't even have to be "killed." How about "neutralize"? How can we make people—police forces—understand that there will be a cost to killing us? I'm not saying that we have to do it the way George Jackson did it. Jonathan was doing something different: a really high-risk liberation strategy. The rational thought would be that the state would want its white judge, assistant district attorney, and stenographer to stay alive. There were two women jurors in the van. The assumption that the state would not kill middle-class whites is erroneous. In war the irrational and terror dominate. For example, Marine Corps drill officers reportedly asked unseasoned troops during the US war against Vietnam if they knew what their jobs would be. Correcting their ignorance, a drill sergeant told them: "Your job is to make your enemy die to protect his country."

The violence at Marin County administered by the state went beyond practicality, just a utilitarian function for its predatory behavior. The point is not to be pragmatic. The point is, how best to contain a predator on all levels? You wouldn't let the predator roam through kindergarten with your kids in it. But you let the predator roam through your community? The point is not to be pragmatic. The point is how to deal with the predator. Is there a pragmatic way to deal with the predator? You know, we're going to be practical. This is my understanding of us as a people. If we were pragmatic, we would never have had rebellions. Nearly 200,000 Blacks fought in the Civil War. The only reason the

US sketchily looks somewhat like a democracy is because Black captives were never pragmatic. We made demands when they said they would kill us; and not just kill us but kill our entire families. And sometimes they did. Lynching is a collective phenomenon. If we were pragmatic, we wouldn't have any civil rights because they came out of risky movements stalked by white-supremacist terrorists. I'm saying just keep it real. You think the practical is what got us this far? No, it's the imaginative. It's a risk-taking in the culture. Let's go back to Birmingham, Alabama, Davis's birthplace. The 1963 16th Street Baptist Church bombing and the murders of four tween/teen girl activists.[6] Few talk about the fact that a sector of the Black community wasn't "pragmatic" after the Klan murdered four girls in church. The working-class, laboring, lumpen section of the city decided to burn down part of Birmingham. We are focused on the trauma and the laws. Don't forget our agency (even if you disagree with our choices). I am not saying we could have done a prayer circle rather than put gasoline on downtown businesses and start fires. Of course, more Black people died from that uprising because white people came out to shoot you and sheriffs were out there to shoot you. But the expression of their rebellion left an impression. You don't think the white city managers got a clue of the future of business if white Klan/police kept murdering Black children and kin? Some likely feared that Blacks would burn down the entire city. They're stunned because Klan/police thought we as Blacks were broken and there would be no resistance, only grief; there was both. Did Klan/police come back even more lethal? Probably. But we still keep resisting.

If you're going to use the term "pragmatic" to discipline radicals, my preference is that you say nothing. You can feel "pragmatic" all day, all night. If you want to discipline rebels then pony up something tangible: raise bail funds, pay for their attorneys, feed their kids while they are inside, or try to get them out.

You cannot lecture risk-taking people about being politically "infantile" out of your fear or out of your accumulations. It was their protests in the streets that led to donors giving millions if not billions to quell protests or ease consciences. There's nobody we admire who is pragmatic. I've said this before: Malcolm could have taken and kept the money. Martin could have just gotten a little quiet church somewhere. Everybody could have been "pragmatic." But if they were, we would not have any ancestors. What does it mean to be a people without ancestors? You don't exist. Nobody loved you enough to do something impractical so that you wouldn't have to work through a killing field? I would rather take the love than the pragmatism.

Notes to Chapter 12

1   Angela Davis's *Autobiography* (New York: Random House, 1974) conflates the Black Panther Political Party (BPPP)—a study group organized by academics and former SNCC members—with the Black Panther Party (BPP) by deleting a letter "P" from the former organization, and throughout the rest of the memoir only references the BPP as a single party, as opposed to two diverse and oppositional parties: see Joy James, "The Architects of Abolitionism: George Jackson, Angela Davis, and the Deradicalization of Prison Struggles," paper given at Brown University, April 8, 2019; available online, https://youtu.be/z9rvRsWKDx0, accessed October 6, 2022. Davis's political autobiographer, Keeanga-Yamahtta Taylor, writes in their September 2022 *NYRB* article, a review of Davis's reissued autobiography, only that Davis was a member of the Black Panther Party Political Party, a study group. In *The Black Power Mixtape 1967–1975*, Elaine Brown asserts that Davis was a friend of the BPP: Göran Henrik Olssen, dir., *The Black Power Mixtape 1967–1975* (2011); available online, https://www.youtube.com/watch?v=O_dCL2F571Q, accessed October 11, 2022: Elaine Brown at 49'55".

2   *The Black Myths Podcast*, "Myth: Angela Davis Was a Black Panther," August 20, 2021, https://blackmyths.libsyn.com/myth-angela-davis-was-a-black-panther.

3   See Joy James, *Contextualizing Angela Davis* (forthcoming).

4   James, "Airbrushing Revolution."

5   Beau Patrick Coulon, dir., "The Coup: The Guillotine," 2012, music video, https://www.youtube.com/watch?v=acT_PSAZ7BQ.

6   Manos, "Birmingham 16th Street Baptist Church Bombing."

Part III
Communities in Conflict and Care

Troubling Black Feminisms

With Momodou Taal of *The Malcolm Effect* and Khadijah Anabah Diskin, 2021

What actions are most excellent? To gladden the heart of a human being, to feed the hungry, to help the afflicted, to lighten the sorrow of the sorrowful, and to remove the wrongs of the injured.
—The Prophet Muhammad

We recognize the devastations of lack of clean water, adequate food and shelter but the cause of those deficits cannot be remedied through policy. If so, then there is no need for confrontation, only accommodation with colonialists and petitions for greater benefit packages.
—Amílcar Cabral, *Return to the Source*

I'm sick and tired of being sick and tired.
—Fannie Lou Hamer[1]

Momodou Taal Joy James began one of her lectures by quoting three individuals. She quoted the Prophet Muhammad, the pan-Africanist and anticolonial leader Amílcar Cabral (who engineered the liberation of Guinea-Bissau and Cape Verde), and the Mississippi civil rights leader Fannie Lou Hamer (who co-led the Mississippi Freedom Democratic Party and SNCC) for reflection and mediation. Likewise, in similar fashion, I want to quote the Prophet Muhammad today: "Whoever does not thank the people has not thanked God."

I started today with those words, because I just want to thank my guests: it's very rare you find people who challenge all the assumptions you once held. I also have with me

Khadijah Diskin, who's been on the show before. Welcome to you both. I'm going to go straight into this question: "Is there a place for academics in revolutionary struggle?"

Joy James You have already stated the mandate: Whoever feeds the people . . . and, revolutionary struggle is spirit-filled and godly. There are different manifestations of deity, but a day job is a day job. There is a place for people who garden and farm, for people who mend the roads, for the people who soothe the elderly and the sick and dying. Then there's a place for us as academics and intellectuals, as long as our university day jobs don't become a form of deification.

Khadijah Anabah Diskin I love that sentiment because I think a lot of the time when I've talked to people about radical politics, when I talk to my students, they often get this deep sense of dread, you know, "Well, what's my place in this? What can I do?" I would say there's space for everyone; it's about finding where you fit and it's about finding how you can resist. Dr. Joy's statement is just so potent in reminding us, exactly, that there is space.

MT Dr. Joy, you have said you no longer call yourself a "Black feminist." I've shared this amongst a lot of Black feminists with whom I'm in community. They were a bit taken back. I'd love to unpack that further with you.

JJ No insult to anyone who's found their path, comfort, and intellectual capacity through Black feminism. Having walked those roads for decades, I've found the limitations. Where the road leads is nowhere I currently want to go, or rather it looks like the road is leading me in a circle. I say that because the United States presents as an imperial formation. It accumulated for its version of democracy through chattel slavery and genocide.

Its feminism increasingly takes on the tenor of state feminism because that's where power accrues in the US under capitalism and (neo)imperialism. Embedded in empire, we are paid to conform to state edicts and preferences, or we are punished when we do not. I do not see how Black feminism escapes that kind of disciplinary regime unless it is embedded in under-resourced communities.

And that is not what the academy does. It does not embed within working-class or struggling or militant communities. It embeds in structure. If it's a large university or research institute, it's about elites. There are people who teach 4:4 or 4:5 classes a semester or term, but not in the sectors where I've been privileged and conflicted in teaching. On the elite academic levels, elites drive the definitional norms of Black struggle because they have the money, stature, position, book contracts, book prizes, Zoom talks, etc., to do so.

That doesn't mean that in our regular lives—or in our lives outside of the academy—language and culture are not created. It just means that when it's disseminated through industries, book contracts, lecture halls, academic conferences, it is bourgeois or petty-bourgeois Black feminism that dominates. I'll give you an example. The anniversary of the Combahee River Collective is talked about a lot, and rightly so, because of its contributions.[2] The origin story is based on material conditions under which this collective and this manifesto about identity politics embedded in progressive politics emerges: it was predatory violence and the murder of Black girls and women that was a catalyst for the creation of the Combahee River Collective. In the current reiterations of it, that origin in violence and the resulting confrontations against the violence arrayed against girls, women, and sex workers in underground economies, that origin story becomes diminished, if not disappeared. Our lives in the United States and the Americas by necessity focus to survive captivity and predatory violence, not coming just from work or labor or domestic sectors, but from the state itself. I shifted to the Captive Maternal decades after co-editing *The Black Feminist Reader* and editing *The Angela Y. Davis Reader*.[3] I am seeking something that I cannot find in conventional Black feminism or (petty-)bourgeois Black *feminisms*—in their plurality.

KAD To ground ourselves in the context of what Black feminism means in the United Kingdom requires or has a specific genealogy, but a lot of our inspiration comes from the Black feminisms of the US. How do we have this conversation? I've been, since reading Dr. Joy James's work, more intentional about distinguishing myself from other types of Black feminisms. I got my Black feminism from the works of the journalist and activist Claudia Jones and Angela Davis. I'm now seeing this sort of mobilization of Black feminism in commodified and transactional ways. It's unsettling.

In the UK, we don't have the potency of Black feminism within the academy the way it exists in the US. What we are seeing is a crude interaction of Black feminism, which has become what I call "white liberal feminism in Black faces." It is a very transactional thing. We're seeing the Black feminist case being made not for radical politics, not for abolition, not for ending carcerality, not for decoloniality and all these other critical ways around which we've historically seen forms of feminism mobilize. We're seeing it become about representation. We're seeing it become about a particular type of reformism that not only wants to see itself represented within the state, but also wants to see itself *paid*. Paid, given money and opportunities—I mean, "Cash up a Black woman for her labor!" And I'm like, "What the hell does that mean?" How is that radical?

JJ I go back to capital and it is related to what I was trying to write in my post on the Verso blog, "'New Bones' Abolitionism, Communism, and Captive Maternals."[4] US presidential elections occur in four-year cycles, sucking up all political organizing to elect one of the parties' leaders as president; it's a duopoly system. Neither candidate is progressive. Voting is fear-based. We do not want the (proto-)fascist so we settle for the liberals or neoliberals, who still expand AFRICOM and drone strikes; abandon starving babies; pollute water in Flint, Michigan; and put Haitians, Cameroonians, and Africans in ICE camps, before deporting them at disproportionate rates as Black people. In the US, some think that the detained children who are worth saving are brown and *not* Black. Betrayal of human rights is not based on chaos; it is based on engineering and the fact that people want to get paid under an imperial state. I voted for Obama; he turned out to be the first Black *imperial* US president. I do not vote for imperial presidents anymore unless it's a buy-in for a temporary insurance policy against a proto-fascist candidate. If the choices of Black women are (neo) liberal or conservative policies, by default we defect to state politics. The US elected Kamala Harris, Barack Obama. So, what do Black people get from electing a Black female vice president and a Black male president in the US? Black enablers for an imperial state built on white supremacy, interventions around the globe to destabilize every liberation movement. Why would Black feminism be spared state violence if it were actually a liberation movement? It is spared and leveraged because it is reduced to personal liberation or accumulations by Black elites. This new Black feminist politics works as an agent of the state.

KAD It reminds me of when the British state mentioned that they would be criminalizing fathers who did not pay child support by taking away their passports. And so I reacted! And initially I saw many Black feminists saying how this was a great achievement and how we need to "lock up the deadbeats." And I was like, anytime the state gets to mobilize in this way, anytime the state gets to make the case that it can remove people's passports—when we have had the case of Windrush[5]—we know who it's specifically targeting. That was a crucial moment, where I was like, what is this thing called Black feminism? Because this is actual violence now, this isn't just commodity; this is now actively working as a border force agent on behalf of the state.

MT Dr. Joy, something that rings in my head is that you said that you don't believe that the state will fund its own demise. When we have our movements, a lot of the time leaders would be the Black feminists or "pan-Africanists" who are culturally pan-African but aligned to the state.

Pivoting away, to give context: right now, the UK's largest union elections are taking place, with approximately 1.2 million members. Our home secretary Priti Patel has enacted probably some of the most racist immigration policies we've seen. She is a woman of South-Asian descent, the daughter of Ugandan-Indian immigrants. Patel has spoken down on Black Lives Matter movements and has directly instituted legislation that penalizes BLM protests.[6] How do we develop a language with which we can critique the pushback as right-wing folks weaponize identity politics? Running for election to become general secretary of this union, a middle-aged white man said that we should deport Patel. The Black people in my circles would say things like, "Oh, he can't say that, he's a white man." He had to apologize. He said, "All I'm saying is that I hope she gets subjected to the same nasty policies she puts on some people of color." Black people were saying, "No, no, no, no, no. We agree with you, but you can't say that." And it kind of made me think of the kind of conversation you get around Chicago's mayor Lori Lightfoot, as well, when people criticize her. "Oh, she's a Black lesbian woman. You can't really criticize her." How do we develop a language?

JJ   We just keep it plain. I worked with these wonderful Black mothers in Chicago, Shapearl Wells and Dorothy Holmes, who lost their sons to Chicago police violence. I've worked with them in the US, but also in Colombia, in different formations, including bringing them to the college campus to speak. They are clear about the betrayals of Lori Lightfoot. For them, your opposition is your opposition, it doesn't matter—their skin color, gender, what shade or what kind of pumps they wear. Opposition is opposition. "Identity-based" protective language, like therapeutic language, is not always effective in the midst of dishonor, abuse, and annihilation taking form in deportations, incarceration, disposability. Race/gender/sexuality does not make you an inherent ally or opponent.

The 600,000 COVID-19 deaths in the United States (1.05 million by October 2022),[7] showed that the US did not adequately leverage money or competency to save lives. Money and competency were never for poor people. I'll use the phrase "people of color," but it wasn't *every* person called "a person of color" who was most vulnerable not to only COVID-19, but the violence of white supremacy—basically being shot by cops and white-supremacist terrorists. As you know, the US has the most guns per capita on the planet. I pay taxes for policing. Police have not actively and consistently sought out white-supremacist terrorists but they will define Black activists as "identity extremists" and create bogus FBI files labeling them as an "internal threat." Your ally is whoever shows up for material struggle. It is not necessarily someone who looks like you. The state has longevity because it knows how to mobilize proxy soldiers. They tell you that you can't critique a Black lesbian, Lori Lightfoot, who is pro-police? As a former prosecutor, she gets a pass? If we allow that to happen, then our politics are not strategically dealing with material conditions. That is ideology fabricating false coalitions that don't hold water. If you pour water on these coalitions which are fragile as thin paper, they dissolve. The CIA does commercials now recruiting Black lesbians. Black women, historically enslaved, raped, and battered, can now buttress and support the imperial state. There are always opportunists. Clarence Thomas is on the Supreme Court and he's Black. If you think there's Black solidarity writ large, then you're not operational in the material world. If you think there's female solidarity writ large, then you're not operational in the material world. Remember how Amílcar Cabral and Patrice Lumumba were assassinated by the US, NATO, and Portugal. Not everybody is your friend in a liberation struggle. If you plan to actually participate in struggle, accumulate networks, then you can *pretend* as if everybody's your friend while doing the real work off camera with close collectives.

MT   Absolutely. You often quote Amílcar Cabral and his book *Return to the Source*.[8] Could you unpack that a bit?

JJ   I always listened to activists. I don't say they're my prophets, but when they tell me to go read something, I do. I did what my Panther friend told me to do, and Cabral became a comfort and a catalyst.

What is the source? I can't speak from it, but I know I've seen it in material reality. I know from decades ago when I went to the international women's gathering, the World Conference on Women, in Nairobi, Kenya, for the UN's Decade for Women. I stayed in the compound of the Women's International Democratic Federation that formed in 1945 as an international antifascist/anti-capitalist organization. In 1985, so forty years later, I'm in this compound with women freedom fighters from all over the world. This is still the former Cold War against the Soviets, who were not all noble or nice but they did fund certain kinds of movements. At that site I saw a different kind of source. I saw international women, including women who'd been guerrilla fighters who morphed into diplomats once their nations assumed some stability.

And so what is the source? The source is anything that struggles against fascism, the source is anything that feeds babies, the source is anything that comforts the ill and ailing, the source is not structured by academia, corporations, nonprofits, think tanks, the CIA, the democratic governments—all which still accumulate through expropriation and intimidation.

Through Cabral, I could see a kind of activism that I would never have participated in when I'm not from Guinea-Bissau or Cape Verde. But I thought I could hear when I read him speak about a culture that is based on Revolutionary Love, on the need to survive, and the need to have honor and dignity in that survival.

I said I was a seeker. I didn't say I had the answers. I just said I was continuing to look. A seeker would try to recognize the source if it appears and when it appears in its inevitably, and deal with the demands that people in struggle make. I understand my contributions, but also my contradictions.

We don't have any ground rules for integrity for the encounter. I don't know what disciplines anymore. There have been so many betrayals for so many decades and centuries. I don't even know how we would trust each other, but I still think we continue to do it. I know we continue to do it. So, there must be some kind of catalyst, spark, energy, or maybe we're just all seekers. If that's the case, that's good enough for me.

KAD Is there any hope for Black feminism?

JJ   To the extent that state feminism has gentrified Black feminism or entered and started to redesign Black feminism, it cannot be held. I moved to theorize the Captive Maternal because I saw agender, nongendered, diverse-gendered people love people to the point of sacrifice and to the point of faltering while still building capacity to save what we value. There are stages. The celebratory, conflicted caretaker, who makes their kid go to the private white school; your kid's going to be traumatized, but you compare it with the kid going to the under-resourced school with the metal detectors and the cops. Both are forms of trauma.

It's been seventy years since the publication of *We Charge Genocide*,[9] which was written in 1951 by the Black communist Civil Rights Congress, including William L. Patterson, and signed by W.E.B Du Bois and Paul Robeson. The document was delivered to the UN and the international community and focuses on anti-Black terror and US violations of civil and human rights. It's been fifty years since the Attica Prison rebellion and its violent suppression. When the incarcerated created a maroon camp inside the prison walls, they created sites for educational programs, medical, food distribution, and culture; they sang to themselves and each other to calm their nerves. Not everyone self-identified as "male" although they were classified as such by the state. Diverse genders typify Captive Maternals. Their maroon camps contained imprisoned intellectuals.[10] The National Guard shot through white guard hostages in order to kill Black rebels; after the retaking of Attica, prison guards would torture, sexually violate, and reportedly murder those who had resisted barbaric captivity.

What's the stage after that warfare and repression? What is the stage of a veteran survivor, or the stage of a betrayer? What is the stage of the ancestor who comes after that to heal or haunt you? The Captive Maternal, for me, is an attempt to shake off shackles and imperialism filtering into our movements as we watch how we move towards freedom through time and space.

Notes to Chapter 13

1   Fannie Lou Hamer, "I'm Sick and Tired of Being Sick and Tired," speech delivered at rally at the Williams Institutional CME Church, Harlem, New York, in support of the Mississippi Freedom Democratic Party's congressional challenge, December 20, 1964; available online, https://awpc.cattcenter.iastate.edu/2019/08/09/im-sick-and-tired-of -being-sick-and-tired-dec-20-1964/, accessed November 3, 2022.

2   See Kristen A. Kolenz, Krista L. Benson, Judy Tzu-Chun Wu, Leslie Bow, Avtar Brah, Mishuana Goeman, Diane Harriford, Shari M. Huhndorf, Analouise Keating, Yi-Chun Tricia Lin, Laura Pérez, Zenaida Peterson, Becky Thompson, and Tiffany Willoughby-Herard, "Combahee River Collective Statement: A Fortieth Anniversary Retrospective," *Frontiers: A Journal of Women Studies* 38, no. 3 (2017).

3   Joy James and T. Denean Sharpley-Whiting, eds, *The Black Feminist Reader* (Hoboken, NJ: Wiley, 2000); Joy James, ed., *The Angela Y. Davis Reader* (Hoboken, NJ: Wiley, 1998).

4   James, "'New Bones' Abolitionism."

5   Windrush: the British political scandal which began in 2017 after it was revealed that hundreds of Commonwealth citizens who had emigrated to the UK from the Caribbean had been wrongly detained, deported, and denied legal rights.

6   See PA Media, "Priti Patel in Fresh Bid to Push Through Strict Anti-Protest Measures," *Guardian*, May 21, 2022, https://www.theguardian .com/politics/2022/may/21/priti-patel-in-fresh-bid-to-push-through -strict-anti-protest-measures.

7   World Health Organisation, "United States of America Situation," updated October 10, 2022, https://covid19.who.int/region/amro /country/us.

8   Amílcar Cabral, *Return to the Source: Selected Speeches by Amílcar Cabral,* ed. Africa Information Service (New York and London: Monthly

Review Press and Africa Information Service, 1973).

9   Civil Rights Congress, *We Charge Genocide.*
10   See James, ed., *Imprisoned Intellectuals*; and Joy James, "American 'Prison Notebooks,'" *Race & Class* 45, no. 3 (January 2004).

14   The Plurality of Abolitionism

With Felicia Denaud and Devyn Springer of *Groundings*, 2021

Felicia Denaud Abolition is growing as a means through which people are seeking and conceiving liberation, which also means on the flip side, that it's just more vulnerable to "neo-radical handling": infiltration, containment, funding, contestation over method and strategy. Talk to us about abolitionism. How do you define it? How has it informed your own political analysis and your commitments? What are some fundamental questions you're still working through or starting to formulate as we enter this new period of struggle?

Joy James I'm puzzled by abolitionism and how it's come to be the buzzword, the term for political mobilization when it was not the term used decades prior. Abolitionism does not exist in singular form: "abolitionism" comes with an "s." Historically, Frederick Douglass had a different form of abolitionism than the white liberal abolitionists, some of whom were struggling with their own sense of racial superiority in regards to Black captives. Douglass was among others more radical in the community of Black activists, and his abolitionism would be distinct from the abolitionism of Harriet Tubman or the abolitionism of John Brown. When we make "abolitionism" a singular concept, it's easier for elite sectors to define its meaning. The mainstream take is a unitary concept that says: "This is what abolitionism is"; such a definition most likely would meet the needs of the elite, not the captive. So, the notion of this unitary Black, the idea that you can talk about Black people without differentiating or highlighting class differences or ideological differences—that simplistic approach to us in general has bled over into abolitionism. We become a stereotype or a caricature of one unified formation.

Abolitionism, I would argue, has become a stereotype of *ideals* about struggle. When it's conflated, the whole notion is in a nice package of whoever's written the last book that becomes a bestseller, or gives the most-viewed talk on TED, or whose book got the *New York Times* review, or who got this prize in literary achievement, etc. Archie Mafeje in his 1998 article "White Liberals and Black Nationalists: Strange Bedfellows"— meaning white liberals and Black radicals within the African contexts—describes setting up a hegemonic norm to define the terms, the language.[1] If you're using hegemonic terms and language, then strategy, logically, would also be derived from those terms and language. We need to look at the diversity of abolitionisms and then decide which forms are worthy of our attention.

Critical thinkers and radical activists might not be the most popular ones. So I stick adjectives in front—"academic abolitionism", "celebrity abolitionism"—to differentiate. I work in the sector of the academy. It's not an industry that I believe is going to lead people towards freedom. That's not its mission or its goal. It's a state or corporate apparatus that reproduces itself. It reproduces elites, hopefully with some skills. If I say I'm an academic doing abolitionism that doesn't mean I'm always doing academic abolitionism. For example, when I went to Brown University and invited former political prisoners to campus, I wasn't doing "academic abolitionism."

I brought rebels to campus who weren't apologetic or seeking redemption and inclusion. Their position was that this democracy is predatory; it has no civic virtue; there's nothing of quality to integrate into except for a liberation movement against the state apparatus and the liberal hegemony that supports and intellectualizes the state's right to exist, only with minor reforms. There seems to be one hegemonic abolitionism in the minds of the people funding "abolitionism," who think abolitionism should be compatible with the academy and not embrace rebels or calls to radically confront the state apparatus.

FD   I wonder, should we concede that ground? I like this idea of a plurality, especially as you root it in an analysis of slavery. There were different lines, different streams of abolitionism, but should we cede the ground? Should we not say that's not abolitionism? Or do we add the adjective? Do we give them that ground, that this is "academic," and this is "revolutionary"? Or do we hold the line and say, "That's not abolition"?

JJ   A really great question. I think it depends on you as a strategist. I'm not going to argue with you about words. Except if you claim to be Indigenous or Black when you're not. If you make false racial-identity claims, I'll just cross the street. We shouldn't be on the same sidewalk 'cause we'll bump into each other or something. I guess you could say slapping an adjective on it is the coward's way out. But confrontation is inevitable because if your goals are radical, elites or management will tell you that you're *not* the real abolitionists.

I don't think you have to make the first move once you become visible as a political thinker and strategist. In my experience, people ignore you as long as they can. And then they just do the *bochinche*—gossip—as their form of "cancel": "Don't meet that person . . . Don't invite them to . . . Don't talk to them." If people see you as competitor or opposition they pay attention to see if they can counter or coopt. When they cannot contain the message, then there's agitation: "Oh, my God, the horses got out of the barn!" They don't ask why the horses got out. The horses got out of the barn because the barn was burning and so the horses kicked down the stalls. They needed to survive. That's why they ran for it. If your barn was a safe place to be in, they would've stayed. Because there's some hay; it's kind of warm. It's a little crowded, can't move around a lot, but I'm alive within the structure.

People move to other intellectual political concepts because they *need* to do so, it's not like we have a ton of leeway. I do have leisure time as an academic. I'm not hustling three jobs to put a roof over their head and feed folks. I'm trying to acknowledge my own privilege. But I'm not trying to create concepts just to sell a brand.

I'm trying to theorize a world on fire. People tell me to stay in the barn, and then the language they give will only take me to the edge of my stall, left or right. But it doesn't allow me to kick down a locked door to get out. That is, not kick down a door to say, "Oh, I want to manage the barn." I don't want to manage the barn, I want out. And I think the worst thing about the abolitionism that I look at, and I'll just call it academic abolitionism, is that it has this abstract goal and it's tethered to freedom dreams. And so it's pretty open-ended, meaning that you could put anything in there, but I'm like, what's the plan? Like what's this strategy? I mean, is this dreaming? How long was the dreaming going to last? For the rest of our lives? This is aspirational, but what's the strategy or the plan to confront the predator? I don't trust dreams that don't allow for the possibility of nightmares. That's not even how the brain works. You're not consistently going to have these wonderful dreams, pastel colors. There's always the flip side of that; you wake up in a cold sweat; you have the scissors under your pillow.

You can't say this freedom dream will mobilize me into a higher level of abolitionism: we've been organizing for centuries, we've always been mobilized. I understand that this mobilization is a logical, rational, biological, emotional response to threat. Asking me to dream more aspirational dreams does not neutralize the threat. Nor does it confront the nightmares that are not just in my emotional, intellectual landscape but exist in the material world of violence and deprivation.

Black people don't live in a dreamscape unless they have enough money to live in an alternative world with rich white people. In the absence of having a gated community that doesn't even need to put up a physical gate because "other people" are never going to roll up, you have to provide a strategy. Talk to me then about the aspirational landscape and how dreaming strengthens my defense rather than becoming a form of narcotic that turns me away from analyzing how democracy was built on incredibly deep violence.

Devyn Springer One thing that comes to mind is the historian and activist Walter Rodney's concept of the "guerrilla intellectual."[2] I've written about this concept in the past.[3] Seeing academia at its most transparent, academics, academic work, the university are commodities. They are cash cows. They're arms of the state. Thinking about that term, what Rodney was saying was that, if they're aspiring to be this intellectual guerrilla, the role of the academic should be to redistribute whatever they can get their hands on from the university, to redistribute the tools of knowledge production, to redistribute resources, money, whatever it may be. That's their role, because they ultimately want to subvert it and build something better. I'm curious if you think there's a place for such a concept in the year 2020, the year of hell on earth.

JJ   Those academics do exist, the guerilla academics, but they tend not to be the elites. There are folks that you loan money to because they need to hire an attorney when the university is trying to fire them because of their radical politics. Or the ones that move around because the university makes it so hostile for them that they're thinking, "Let me get out of here and go to another gig." But the new gig is just like the old gig, with the same hostility. The guerrilla intellectual is a beautiful concept; it is principled and understands that sacrifice is necessary in order to use our intellect in a way that is ethical.

There's no way to be ethical intellectuals without sacrifice under these systems and regimes. Yet, you have the possibility to accumulate wealth, seriously, real money, if you play by the rules of the state and structure. I make money. For some reason, younger people know what everybody in the academy makes. Sometimes they tell you what people make as elite academics. Salary, book sales, talks—some people can charge $40,000 for a keynote. The standard is $500. If you can get $40,000 this becomes a moneymaking site, and folks are not going to say radical things that mess up the flow of dollars from the left to the right.

Today, the academy is definitely an extension of the marketplace, in part because academics have become pundits. This coexists with the rise of technology and the way in which "news" is coupled with punditry; "specialists" appear on news programs that promote the latest books we are told to read. The books win awards, sometimes because of quality of content, sometimes because of promotion, or perhaps both. The news promotes the award-winning book. The award-winning book becomes a documentary or film. The award-winning author is hired as a consultant on the Hollywood movie. The film is marketed and distributed through corporations. Entertainment, commerce, trade become part of the swirl of the academy. The academic appears in the world through press releases that increases their value to the institutions that can market them to raise more money.

Do you see the loop? It's moneymaking every day. You will get your cut as an academic, but the university will get theirs in terms of prestige and standing and the rankings in *US News & World Report.*

What do you do when Black suffering has become monetized? It was monetized in the antebellum era when we as Blacks were literally chattel slaves. One key question then was, "How much are you worth on the auction block?" It's monetized after the enslavement era through the Thirteenth Amendment to the US Constitution, which legalized slavery in prison. Blacks, when arrested, became sold as prisoners and so became the joint property of the state and corporation invested in mining, lumber, manufacturing, etc. So Blacks are worked to death on "plantations" that are in fact work farms belonging to the state and Northern capital while it industrializes the South. Those most likely to be incarcerated would be poor laborers and workers. Our death rates went up significantly after the Civil War due to this convict leasing system. Decades later in the civil rights movement era, it would be the petty bourgeoisie that commands leadership because government and capital leverage or help pick them for Black leadership.

When Martin Luther King is chosen to be the public face of leadership for the Montgomery Bus Boycott in 1955, it is partly because he is middle class, has a PhD in theology from Boston University, and is the pastor of a respectable church. When he becomes a guerrilla intellectual, after marching, organizing, and suffering with Blacks of all classes, he is radicalized and understands that the war in Vietnam is immoral and illegal and that means US citizens must oppose imperialism and capitalism. That is when King's funders largely disappear. There was nothing to capitalize off of in terms of Black suffering.

For King there was only solidarity. If you're going to fight, you're not just the victim. Now you have agency and then your agency is tied to rebellion against capitalism and imperialism. Two to three million Vietnamese died in the Vietnam War. The US lost 55,000 personnel. For the Vietnamese, it was a genocide. The US state losing that many people was seen an investment in "foreign interests" and empire.

Blacks were some of the soldiers "fragging" white officers in the Vietnam War. Black troops appeared to be sent to their deaths at a higher rate by white officers. As Blacks, we were and are monetized because we were and are reduced to monetary objects and that's tracked us through and into rebellions. Yet, our rebellions also became monetized. We start off with street protests and then there is an incredible flood of money coming from large liberal—but not really humane or justice-minded—corporations. The multi-millionaires or billionaires made donations to some form of Black Lives Matter offshoot as corporate leaders exploiting workers, devastating the environment, and supporting police unions. When do we know the abolitionism is real? When do we know that the academic is really a guerrilla academic? Those are brilliant questions to put on the table because they mean you're interrogating and not buying the whole package.

If I got a button or social media profile with a Black Power fist on it, some might think, "Oh, that must be radical. That must be abolition. That must be something that can deliver." Actually, it is just symbolism. People have become "experts" on and "profiteers" off of Black suffering and, weirdly, Black rebellion. My position is, "How would you know anything about a rebellion unless you actually fought in one?" I'm not an Afropessimist. Maybe they adopted me somewhere down the line. I think the antipathy towards Afropessimism, the way it's construed, is because Afropessimists are often guerrilla intellectuals engaged in an intellectual rebellion defining an anti-Black world. Afropessimists are not asking you to do anything tactical, but they are saying that you can't reform the US democracy as a racial-imperial project. I've written in "Airbrushing Revolution for the Sake of Abolition" that "revolutionary reforms" are an oxymoron.[4] I'm really tired of people making up political language. I understand if it's culture and it's coming from the streets, or from artists such as Noname. But for academics to think that we're creating Black radical/revolutionary culture from the academy, that's just a straight-up hustle. Academics don't create culture. We create artifacts that are compatible with the industry.

It's the people as a mass who decide political paths. I'm not romanticizing the masses. People tell me that I don't know what I'm talking about on a regular basis. My response is: "Okay, let me see." I am still going to do what I think is right. The shift of power should be towards the mass. If the mass is being disciplined to follow the state/corporation, then power shifts towards the elites who speak on behalf of the mass and interpret their suffering. People were counting the numbers of folks who came out after George Floyd's slow murder by the police officer Derek Chauvin. Showing up is important, but that doesn't mean that everyone who marched and protested changes their commitment to capitalism or racism.

"BLM" does not mean "Black Liberation Movement," it means "Black Lives Matter." If you have to explain that we matter to an imperial nation, with grown-ass people, I mean, come on. They didn't know? They know—they don't care. And some are poised to tell you that Black lives do not matter because they can accumulate from your suffering. Obama, Trump, and Biden all rejected the term "defund the police." If they could not truly support "Black lives matter," by reining in police violence, then what do you think their position is on a "Black liberation movement"? They would criminalize a Black liberation movement; they did that decades ago with COINTELPRO. It's not hard to figure out the government's positions. It's emotionally hard to accept what we figure out.

FD   There's a passage in Frantz Fanon's *The Wretched of the Earth* where he writes that decolonization equals the flight of capital.[5] This is lodged in my head just as a metric. Where is money pooling? Where is it drying up? It's just a baseline that flight of capital is a sign that you're onto something.

JJ   There's so much violence right now. You are put on a surveillance list if you resist. It's horrific that the white supremacists have their own capture or kill list, I don't know how they describe it, but obviously the state does too. It doesn't matter whether it's a Democratic administration or a Republican administration—any rebel is a cause for concern because they encourage the flight of capital, which makes sense because rebels are trying to undo a predatory economic system: capitalism ("predatory capitalism," if you need adjectives, or "monopoly capitalism"). Capital is protected by violence. Try a strike, try a demonstration. Logically, you know who's going to show up to suppress the strike and suppress the demonstration.

One question would be, "What's the role of the academics in this?" Are we the buffer zone between the cops and the mass? Decades ago, I would have said, "Yes, we are, or could be." But there's something about the academic industry: its aloofness or engagement exists within the modality of the classroom. Now, prisons become our classrooms and also our laboratories, it's where you go to study people or study their writings. There are admirable things that we've done as abolitionists, but we could not call ourselves *revolutionary* abolitionists unless we actually opened the gates of the prisons. It's kind of biblical. I mean, the Jericho Movement—now doing a 2021 tribunal on the 1951 *We Charge Genocide* document (see above, p. 50)—works to free political prisoners. Their name evokes the biblical seismic change when the walls come tumbling down.

Sundiata Acoli, Mumia Abu-Jamal, Leonard Peltier. There are others that I'm forgetting. Forgive me. It's an important endeavor to free the political prisoners. The academic abolitionist's method is going to be aligned with liberals that fund "radicals" (radicals that get their money from liberal funders). We're not going into churches, mosques, or synagogues passing the plate for our endeavors. Instead, we ask if folks can write a grant proposal, or have their university sponsor a conference. That is where the tens of thousands—if not hundreds of thousands of dollars—reside. Look at the money. Obama had his senior advisor Valerie Jarrett meet with Koch personnel to discuss prison reform and "abolitionism."[6]

The language doesn't even work if you can't distinguish a "radical" from a "liberal." Rebellion is prohibited as "bad manners." Reinventing the world is beautifully frightening because it's a full-blown, 360-degrees wrap of struggle. You cannot do 90 degrees, or 180 degrees. Everything is unstable, including the very meaning of what it means to be "free." That sounds overwhelming, but on a good day, it can be thrilling.

DS   One last point on this because I'm not in academia, I'm "academia adjacent." It's really me getting to glean in on the insights of you two. Capital is guarded and maintained by violence, but it's also created and generated by violence. This is something Dr. Jared Ball recently helped me to really understand. I'm thinking about capital being generated and created from the violence of colonialism and slavery till today. And if we think of these economies of representation, the representation industry being linked with the academic industry—those two are almost one in the same at this point—then capital that's being generated by these academic abolitionists, and academics in general, must also be generated through some form of violence or exploitation, hyper-exploitation.

JJ   If somebody signs up for your class and they don't drop out by a certain point, they have to keep on with the class in order to get the grade to accumulate grades that they're passing in order to get the degree, to be able to launch themselves as not laboring poor or working class. Look, I got the paper, so they hired me as a white-collar worker. When the next round of COVID-19 comes, I get to stay home and I'm not going to likely die prematurely as an expendable essential worker. If the captives are the raw material of our factory work, then yeah, we should pay them. But more important than paying them, we should free them.

We're part of this machine that is consuming the lives of the captives. But we tell ourselves that we're contributing to their wellbeing by putting their stories on page or on film. Unless they have a percentage of the royalties, their lives became the property of others. Who gets to own other people's stories? To own their story means that to some degree you own their politics, and dictate to them what political responsibility is. That is the parental voice. This is when we were talking about the Captive Maternal or *in loco parentis* (the state or social worker in place of the parent); or *parens patriae* (the state itself as the parental authority).[7]

The only way to shift the violence away from the subjects that we say we care about is to better understand the violence of the state and neutralize that violence, deflect that violence, or allow that violence to go somewhere else, but not into our communities and the communities we care about. I agree with the abolitionists and the aspiration that prison should not exist. I also know that predators of all types exist. I don't care what you call it; they're going to have to go somewhere until we work this out.

Police are a predatory formation for the democracy. What I think is key is not defunding the police per se—that is a budget thing and people keep moving money around.

The state donates to public programs after rebellions, a few years later they slice the money back from the basketball program or the arts. Money follows rebellion; once a rebellion settles, the state/corporation takes the money back because the mass/rebels did not control the bank. We have to control the violence. Violence is going to exist. The question is, "Who will control it?" If you can control the violence, people are better equipped to demonstrate for their needs, protest for their needs, without that violence being successfully turned against them.

If we can come up with these therapeutic modalities to deal with violence inside our communities, that is terrific. I will definitely support that, have always supported that. But a therapeutic modality will not deal with the police, with ICE, the CIA, the FBI, the National Guard. Those sectors of organized violence do not deal in therapeutic modalities with you. They deal with control, capture, elimination. Academic abolitionists, if we want to take a risk, would focus on violence and money. We would be transparent. We would tell people how much we make for our gigs, how much we got in book royalties. This would be public knowledge. We don't want to be predatory capitalists. We want to be transparent about our revenue streams. And then if you want to tithe, whatever your percentage is/would be, put something in a common fund.

You can't dance with the devil and come back with two feet. We need to explain candidly what freedom dreams are about when working with the Democrats, because those dreams don't seem to be streaming on the same line as people held captive by police/prison due to policies developed by the Democratic Party. To the best of my ability, I've tried not to dance with the devil, but I have done a do-si-do here or there.

The last thing I would say echoes the Black Panther leader and veteran Kathleen Cleaver. I paraphrase here from a PBS interview she did with the Harvard professor Henry Louis Gates in the 1990s (see above, pp. 72–4). I think her analysis was brilliantly stated, but I don't hear academics talking about it much. Cleaver said that the liberation movement—Black Panther, third party, Black Power movements—presented a false united front that the Black (petty) bourgeoisie and Black radicals were aligned together. They were not. But Black radicals felt that in public or before the "white gaze" they had to appear unified, as if only one form of abolitionism existed. This was a false front. There was no unified Blackness. The Black middle classes were anti-revolutionary, pro-capitalist, and did not support anti-imperialist wars. Black radicals had more in common with movements in the "Global South" than with Black people writ large. What happened to those anti-colonial movements? Short answer: the CIA. But there were betrayals inside Black communities. To echo Cleaver, Black intellectuals lied, thinking that an all-Black performance or projection of a united mass would somehow deliver. It did not. It betrayed us.

We have to disaggregate ideologies among Blacks. We don't all share the same politics. Some people's "freedom" is the ability to purchase. I'm not just talking about Prada bags. I mean, purchase access to powerful people. You become "essential" as a Black person when you can bring this many Black people to a rally, voting booth, access to the apparatus. Then I'll have your ear.

FD   There was a lot of this discussion about the money we receive at Brown University being tainted; any demand we make, we're already swimming in it.

JJ   Look at the Catholic Church. They've been paying out a lot of money for their abuses against children and women. Some people still go to church. Some people were totally turned off, viewing the church as a pedophile ring or something, but the edifice still exists. The question for the people I know who stay in church is, "How do you transform its authoritarian ethos—its indifference to children and women and LGBTQ+ people—its racism—how many stained-glass pictures of white Jesus need to exist?"

There's a difference between the churches that become mega-churches—accumulating money over money—and the smaller churches I know in Harlem that are really trying to work their way through Scripture. They will not call themselves "guerrilla intellectuals." But if you tell them there's a war between good and evil and God is on their side and they can humble themselves to a higher power, they would likely risk their lives to do good. Churchgoers have done this for centuries. There was the sanctuary movement in the 1980s harboring victims of US-funded Contras and death squads in Latin America during the Reagan administration. There's the Black church leadership during the civil rights movement. We can navigate the duplicity of our environments.

Frederick Douglass stated that people don't give you power. You take it. As an academic who can pay their bills, I understand exactly what I'm saying in terms of the implications. I have met people who risked their lives and some transitioned in order to pursue freedom and liberation, not just for themselves, but for the entire collective. I understand that to be a worthy life. And I'm not saying that longevity and comfort are equivalent.

FD   You dedicated your book *Seeking the Beloved Community*[8] as follows: "To the cyborg maternals and ghost warriors . . . all who made and make the impossible demand to the omnipotent state, its allies, and apologists: 'Resurrect the child you killed.'" Can you talk about the political condition of Black children and mothers and how that has informed your work.

JJ   When you have proximity to Black children, and you have responsibilities to them, then you really understand what terror is, because you realize you cannot protect them. On one level that is so humiliating. You've been around for so long that you think, "I've got chops, I got game; I know what to do and I've got money." But the principal is racist. If they go to a school that has fewer resources and metal detectors, the cops are just roaming around the kids. Their outcome is going to be more limitations, and their precarity or vulnerability to incarceration or violence is going to increase. So, you're going to put them in this fancy school just to keep them from harm. But you know, too, here's the conundrum, that the principals are racist. So, when they go to that school, the principal and their staff are going to harm them. Those are your choices. "How do you nap?—With one eye open." We need freedom schools and we need autonomy. But the vast majority of time, we make choices that are going to be harmful. We just try to mitigate the degree of harm to our children. Kids are going to be harmed. That happens. How much harm should they be exposed to? Obviously, such queries mean that we are not a free people. The child's position would be: "I don't want to be harmed. I don't agree to 15 percent vs 25 percent, or 40 percent vs 60 percent. No harm, period."

As adults, we forget how much we've suppressed about the violence against the most vulnerable, who rely on adults for protection. The adults never clearly told you that they could not offer stable protection. Perhaps they were mortified by that fact; or maybe they did tell you, and gave instructions to grow up faster. What's the point of having a childhood? What was it? Two minutes long? It would be painful to redirect ourselves to the needs of the child, but it would be amazing. Some would sing ballads about us, about what we do for the kids. They will remember us forever with ballads because of the movements we built for liberation.

When we align with the children, then all struggle is for the children. All power is for the children. And it doesn't mean we don't have structure. We're not always nurturing and raising, but at least radicals are not creating cogs in a factory. We're not creating cops and prison guards. We're not creating wonks who talk about trauma rather than addressing their own trauma and acknowledging that the trauma of others is not a commodity. You can never meet the needs of children. We will always feel before children just like we feel before the divine, because we're flawed. I think that brings sanity to our lives in humility and aspiration. And it gives us meaning, that's the way I see it. The bottom line is, "Don't let the state pimp your kid. Don't let the social worker pimp your kid. And you, don't pimp your kid."

DS   I can't help but think of my time in Cuba and how one of the very first things I noted spending real time there with organizers is that they're not coordinating childcare for their organizing meetings and their educational circles so that a couple of adults go watch the children in another room. The children are sitting in the circle, listening half the time, contributing, even in off-the-record conversations or the hot spicy conversations. In reality, you should be brought up and nurtured and situated in a circle and in a community of organizers and activists. I've had eight-year-olds in Cuba school me on the Cuban Constitution. Here I am an adult, I can barely quote two sentences of it.

JJ   All revolutions are imperfect. The Cubans have a revolution which they must defend and we don't have a revolution to defend. The examples to study are those in which children are valued, and where we acknowledge that adults don't know everything.

Notes to Chapter 14

1   Mafeje, "White Liberals and Black Nationalists."
2   See Walter Rodney, *The Groundings with My Brothers* (London: Verso, 2019; originally pub. 1969).
3   See e.g. Jesse Benjamin and Devyn Springer, "*Groundings*: A Revolutionary Pan-African Pedagogy for Guerrilla Intellectuals," in *Critical Understanding in Education, Volume 1: Keywords in Radical Philosophy and Education—Common Concepts for Contemporary Movements*, ed. Derek R. Ford (Leiden: Brill, 2019).
4   James, "Airbrushing Revolution."
5   "The spectacular flight of capital is one of the most constant phenomena of decolonization": Frantz Fanon, *The Wretched of the Earth*, trans. Constance Farrington (New York: Grove Weidenfeld, 1991; originally pub. 1963), 103.
6   Fabian, "White House Meets with Koch Officials."
7   See Rajan Bal, "The Perils of 'Parens Patriae,'" *Georgetown Journal on Poverty Law & Policy blog*, November 21, 2017, https://www.law.georgetown.edu/poverty-journal/blog/the-perils-of-parens-patriae/.
8   James, *Seeking the Beloved Community.*

15   On the Rise of the Black Bourgeoisie

With Jason Myles and Pascal Robert
of *This Is Revolution*, 2022

Jason Myles In the 1980s, the creation of the Black welfare queen was used as a scare tactic, a tool to gut public goods programs that benefited the poor and working class. Bill Clinton, who was sold to the American people as a savior from twelve years of neoliberal rule in the form of Ronald Reagan and George Bush, doubled down on the right's assault against public goods governance with the omnibus crime bill in 1994 and the poverty-increasing welfare reform in 1996—what we call the fifty-plus-year counter-revolution against the New Deal and the Great Society programs.

How have we gone from the racist images of single mothers of color living fat off the system to "Black girl magic" and a growing Black bourgeoisie? Has the Nixonian ideal of Black capitalism finally replaced underclass ideology as a tool of containment for the ruling class? Today, in the face of the current Supreme Court nomination of Judge Ketanji Brown Jackson, who was appointed by an administration with the first Black US vice president, Kamala Harris, we will discuss race, gender, and class in the current American context.

Joy James Maybe there's a metaphor here for what we're talking about in terms of the rise of Black women through empire. You have the 1980s with Reagan. Reagan's two terms come after two terms of Richard Nixon, who has incredible racial animus against Black people as well. Nixon is elected president in 1968 and re-elected in 1972, he should have served until 1976, but there was the impeachment. You have four years of a Democratic president, Jimmy Carter, who comes from the South; same with another Southern Democratic president, Bill Clinton, who positions himself as a centrist. The white Southerners Carter and Clinton perform as anti-racist: "I'm used to being around Black people, so I know how to talk to them and deal with them."

You still have no sustained gains where wealth becomes shared among the working class and the poor, but opportunities increase for Black/brown/working-class people to enter into government. Nixon would've been one of the first to promote integration to quell radicalism given his position on affirmative action. The larger context is that you have these movements for justice or equity: the civil rights movement, Black/Red Power movement, feminist movement, anti-war movements. This is galvanizing people, not just in the US, but also across the globe, to critique the US as a racist-imperial project.

These presidencies that follow these movements tamp down that desire for struggle. I would argue they have the capacity to tamp down the skills for struggle. That once you start hiring Black people, once Black people enter into white corporations or firms, the government itself, or the academy (which is where I've worked for the last two to three decades), or the state starts to absorb Blacks into its structures; we become part of the infrastructure of the state itself.

That project, obviously, wasn't just a personal pet project of Nixon or of Reagan, again, with a little four-year gap with the Democrat Jimmy Carter between Republican presidents. Other presidents followed, including the disastrous George W. Bush, who got us into a bogus war in the Middle East. But integration into capitalism as a form of "liberation" is also the product or the project of Barack Obama, the US's first Black *imperial* president. The legacy of the executive office or presidency is to maintain the state and to allow it to expand and to accrue.

For centuries, accumulations have come out of our labor and out of our loss. I think the question that we're going to tangle with today has been split into a focus on gender formations; some would argue that we no longer have the solidarity of the 1960s militants in terms of identifying the state as opponent and being willing to move against it.

JM   I want to ask about what you mentioned about the Black introduction into government roles. This is shown in pop culture of the time. The 1974 movie with Diahann Carroll and James Earl Jones, *Claudine*, where it actually gets into the weeds of "You can't have a man in your home." There were people that worked to get the men out of the homes. That's part of that story, where in one of the scenes they are hiding James Earl Jones's underwear or something like that.

Pascal Robert   Very Daniel Patrick Moynihan (see above, p. 37).

JM   Very, very, very Moynihan-esque. But let's remember that these programs were born out of not wanting even women to work in the public sector when they were rolled out in the 1930s. That's what a lot of that was for. I can't remember the original name of welfare, but it was designed for non-working females.

JJ   Welfare was designed for white women. Particularly white women who were widows.

The whole notion of the family is a white project in a white-supremacist nation. If the nation was born out of genocide and enslavement, then part of what it disposes or tries to kill is the very notion of family cohesion and community cohesion in Indigenous and Black communities or nations. This is where it becomes really complicated for me when I try to see what the fulcrum is on this seesaw; how do you balance this? The nation when it works for women is designed to really work for white women (with means); but to some extent it had to include Black women within the category of "human." To some extent. Well, if you were performing the duties of the state, you can entertain whites and serve them. But there are penalties for human rights protests, as the Black artist and actor Eartha Kitt found out in 1968, once she came out against the racist war in Vietnam and confronted the First Lady, Lady Bird, President Lyndon Baines Johnson's wife.[1] President Johnson supported civil rights and voting rights (he gave to Rev. Martin Luther King the signing pen of the

Civil Rights Act of 1964); he also expanded the US imperialist war in Vietnam and used the CIA in an attempt to destroy Eartha Kitt's career. On a visit to the White House, Kitt "made" the FLOTUS cry while scolding the administration for drafting and killing poor/working-class Black youths to fight in Southeast Asia. You're told—as a Black woman or feminized Black—that if you can entertain and sing or dance, or make a movie that non-Blacks like, after you have historically nursed their kids on your breasts for centuries, if you can reproduce the family integrity of others, you are tolerable. If you seek agency, autonomy for civil rights and human rights, you're a pain in the neck and maybe you should disappear in whatever way: lose your job, housing, freedom, go to prison . . . or, like Malcolm and Martin, lose your life.

JM   As those original aid packages were being rolled out, as the New Deal was getting rolled out, I think in 1935, divorced women could not get it. Non-widowed women with children couldn't get it. So, there were definitely caveats on who could get aid and who could not get aid. But what I wanted to add to your very, very astute point about adding Black people into the government apparatus is that when these people were part of the system, so to speak, there was a unified voting bloc with the people that were a part of the system receiving the aid, and now some people have moved up into a new middle class. In the early 1970s those who are part of the same system are voting in unison to keep these programs.

You definitely see this in the more major metropolitan Northern cities. When you look at a place like Atlanta, it has its first Black mayor in 1973, Maynard Jackson, who increases the business sector. You turn the city of Atlanta, the soft drink megacorporation Coca-Cola, the massive airport—it all becomes a hub. Private capital is now hoisting the same Black people into the middle class. They're not so aligned with their poor and working-class Black neighbors. I believe towards the end of the Jackson administration we actually see the destruction of a lot of the government or public housing in Atlanta as well. So, there's an interesting juxtaposition when we talk about including Black people into the government apparatus. Trying to protect the system, if you will. When you have private capital the demarcating line is almost about class.

JJ   This has a practical or pragmatic aspect. Once you're included into an apparatus or structure, then the logic would be that you would protect it. Once you have Black people protecting state accumulations, corporate accumulations, those who are left behind are just seen as even more deficient. This is part of the reason I avoid the language that we've inherited today about, not just "Black girl magic," but also "Black excellence." As if everybody else is mediocre or substandard; this is so aligned with the language of white supremacy and predatory capitalism. How do you know you're excellent? Is it because you got the corporate job or you got the degree, JD, PhD, or whatever gains you achieved under this system?

The larger picture is this is a capitalist society that was built on slavery, rape, and genocide, and that the accumulations always accrue to the top. If you are ethical, you would want to tinker with that machinery and not just be seduced by all the glitter. The glitter could be a Tesla. Back in the day it might have been a Cadillac. We have to think about our collective position on something that looks like a mixed economy or a socialist economy. How do we stop these buy-outs that make those who remain in certain zip codes disposable, and vulnerable to poisoned water? Think of Flint, Michigan. Poisoned air, disproportionate exposure to police violence and civilian violence—all negative and deadly impacts on our communities.

PR   Like any other people, Black people have class conflicts, internal stratifications. Unfortunately, because of the way in which society portrays Black life as a unified underclass phenomenon, these stratifications of class—which have been a reality of Black life going back to the days of "free people of color" societies—is completely obscured to the majority. This is true not only with white Americans, but also with many

Black folk as well, who are not necessarily connected to those within these communities because they are more proximate to capitalist power or are the gatekeepers or the racial ventriloquists, if you will.

So, the narrative that you are very eloquently exposing is very much in line with what we try to do by complicating the notion of collective community. In other words—and you may disagree with this, and I respect you if you do—it's very important for us to complicate the notion that Black people work as a unified community. Black politics is contained and used as a pawn of the ruling class because the ruling class will choose—undemocratically—the racial ventriloquist who speaks for the masses, while the masses have no say in the agenda and they're moved like a piece on a chessboard. So Black politics becomes a politics of containment in the rendering of collective community. It's something that we on our show try to challenge effectively. I like to make the argument that there are multiple Black communities, not just one Black community, if you will.

JJ   That's great. It's making me think there are multiple Black feminisms in the plural, not just one form of Black feminism. That should also be stated for abolitionisms in the plural; there is not just one form of abolitionism. I totally agree with your analysis. When you're speaking, I'm starting to think about how we were warned about this. When Malcolm was talking about the dichotomy between the "big house" Black workers/laborers and the field Black workers/laborers. The "big house" today could be Deutsche Bank, Bank of America; or those working for the State Department and its foreign projects who are working for the Department of Justice.

Kathleen Cleaver was the first woman to sit on the Central Committee of the Black Panther Party. This is Oakland before things went one way and the Cleavers left the country and the BPP fractionated, partly because of the violence of COINTELPRO, partly because of internal contradictions and violence (largely originating in the Oakland leadership).

In 1997, Kathleen Cleaver states in her PBS interview with Henry Louis Gates (who's obviously in the "big house" called Harvard) that the Panthers thought they had to pretend that Black people were a unified front against racism. They had to project a false unity, so they thought, as a political strategy. Yet, they clearly knew that the Black middle class, the petty bourgeoisie, bourgeois Blacks with means, money, and ambition, were going to be hostile to the Black Panther Party as a revolutionary or proto-revolutionary formation.[2] Also, bourgeois Blacks would be hostile towards the Panthers supporting liberation movements in the "Third World" or Global South fighting US imperialism. There have always been sectors of the Black communities, in plural, that have been trained or prone to seek an opportunistic portfolio, i.e., to work for the state and corporation. Impacted people working in these zones would be an extension of anti-Black violence, but this time with Black faces.

PR   I appreciate that assessment. One of the things that we definitely see is that the more there is this incorporation into the apparatus of the ruling class by what we call the "Black political class" over time, the more and more the importance of symbolic representation becomes the focus of what is deemed Black political aspiration, and the less redistributive policy trying to change the material conditions of poor and working-class Black people becomes the focus. To the point where—I'm reading a book on Black political history—cynically, the Democratic Party recognizes in the 1980s that they literally can offer Black people the symbolic representation of appointments and political candidates instead of actual policy that changes the material conditions of poor and working-class Black people. What we find is the further and further we get away from the civil rights movement, the easier we find that Black communities, plural, are intoxicated with that politics of symbolism and less willing to demand any kind of truly redistributive materialist agenda for working-class and poor Black folk, who are the majority of Black folk.

JM   Would you add to that that there's something to be said about the civil rights movement really pivoting away from the communists and socialists, getting them out of the movement, and instead having the movement be about inclusion?

PR   Preston H. Smith II's book about racial democracy in Chicago talks about how part of the problem of the civil rights movement is that the limitations of the Cold War deny the capacity of the leaders of the civil rights movement to really put forth a materialist pro-working-class agenda. As a consequence, they focus on what Smith terms "racial democracy" or "racial inclusion." His argument is that whenever there are Black politics or policies premised on racial democracy, it basically becomes a wealth transfer to the Black petty bourgeoisie or the Black professional-managerial class or Black elites. There's no redistributive agenda in racial democracy.[3] Racial democracy can mean that we literally have a ruling class that is 14 percent Black, 60 percent white, and 18 percent Latinx, and now that's democracy and everyone else can basically be either a slave or a serf or a tenant farmer.

Those politics don't make a difference as long as they're *proportionally* represented in every level. What Smith's arguing is that what was needed was social democracy, which was a redistributive materialist agenda that would have changed the actual material conditions of poor and working-class Black people's lives instead of just simply asking for racial inclusion. Even Dr. King and Bayard Rustin and A. Philip Randolph, in 1965, realized that the traditional civil rights movement is not going to do what is necessary to change the conditions of working-class Black people's lives. That's why they asked for the Freedom Budget for All Americans in 1965.[4] The Vietnam War denies the ability to really fund it.

JJ   I thought what you just said was pretty real. What's more real than that?

PR   One of the persistent themes that we have on our show is the way class stratification amongst Blacks facilitates a Black political class that works as racial ventriloquists for the majority of working-class and poor Blacks in exchange for economic patronage and enrichment from the ruling class, largely to the detriment of the Black masses. Where do you see the contemporary Black academic and Black academics in general in this particular hierarchy? Particularly with the rise of the Obama and the post-Obama Black political class, are Black academics more likely to challenge this class hierarchy or reify it?

JJ   Howard University professors I believe are on strike right now. That is about the conditions under which they labor, which means teach. But the students had gone on strike months before. That was about the conditions under which they lived: mold, lack of security, substandard housing. The faculty are paid by Howard. The students, through tuition or grant money, are contributing funds to Howard University. Howard also is an expression of both state and corporation.

If we look at where we are today, I would say we're in a slog. We're in a marsh. I mean, I can keep throwing things out like "mud" or something like that. In my opinion, there's no solid stable ground in the academy to speak with the integrity, honesty, and brilliance of intellectuals in open communities seeking justice. The academy is an imposition upon intellectualism tied to freedom. Its function is not to march or articulate a clear agenda or strategy for curtailing a racist-imperial project, also known as US democracy. There's been so much money flooded into the academy in terms of how the administrative strata—how many provosts do you need?, etc.—have turned into state or private corporations. Those of us tenured decades ago, I will include myself, were able to secure certain types of monetary packages with health benefits.

But the academy is mostly without unions or they're union-busting.[5] Academia's work is often about extraction from the students—their ideas, energy, tuition, and of course extraction from faculty (even the conservatives, who are not really committed to social justice). Don't look to academics for answers. I wouldn't even read some of our books unless

you have leisure time and can afford them. Hopefully librar-
ies have some. But as academics we're not trained for militant
political struggles. Before and during the 1960s there were
"race people"; that was more legible in terms of struggle and
service; now, we're not well trained to serve Black communities. We're trained to treat knowledge as a commodity and
then put it on the shelf and hopefully get enough buyers so
that it looks like our brand has some content behind it. Even
some of the writing about these movements is not imaginative; it doesn't take risks; it doesn't speak with the voice of the
people who created the movements. I think at times about
Erica Garner, for instance, transitioning at twenty-seven, leaving a seven-year-old and a four-month-old behind. I wasn't
even aware of her health insecurity.[6] I was living in Harlem
during the 2014–17 uprisings against police murders of civilians (starting in 2014 with the deaths of Eric Garner—Erica's
father—in Staten Island and Michael Brown in Ferguson). I
would make a donation or go to a march or something like
that. But I didn't understand Erica Garner's vulnerability of
not having sufficient personal support, better doctors, healthcare, more alliances. I and other academics could have been
much more helpful in advocating for impoverished/work-
ing-class rebels. I'm not saying we could have stopped the
death, but we could have been much more helpful in these
movements. We tend to write about movements and tragedies, package content in between two book covers, go on book
tours. I'm not saying that's all bad; it is a form of knowledge.

JM   That is the reality and it's a very stark one when you
think about it. Because I think one of the better books, let's
just take the Eric Garner case, was not even by an academic. I
think the journalist Matt Taibbi wrote one of the better books
on the Eric Garner situation, really bringing broken-windows
policing to light for a lot of people.[7] But all that being said,
sadly, we live in a world where a lot of this stuff is just easily
digestible. How many people are actually even reading the
books?

JJ   Then, what's our function now? I mean, as academics, how do you see academics? You can ask me, I work there, but you are the core consumers. I'm supposed to be a producer, but I don't own the company. So, I'm really a worker.

JM   Did you ever read Barbara and John Ehrenreich's work from the late 1970s about the professional-managerial class (PMC)?[8] I think the academy is definitely a part of the PMC and produces more people that go into that class.

JJ   I wonder to what extent? I understand we're a factory, we are churning out people with degrees who then become managers. I'm wondering to what extent we would own up to the fact that there's something much more nefarious about that.

PR   Universities are not created to be counter-hegemonic institutions. I mean, the purpose of the university is to reify a ruling class that maintains the status quo of a functioning capitalist empire, which is the United States, or Western imperialists, or the West overall. Universities are not designed to build revolutionaries. They're designed to create people to solve problems so that you don't have a revolution.

JJ   But when you get to this moment after the movements, where people want Black studies, women's studies, LGBTQ+ studies, Chicano studies, ethnic studies, it all looks like that this is—at least the right wing says it is—an "assault on the academy." Like corruption of its core purity, which is its white supremacy. But why do we believe, or do we believe, that because now we're writing about movements or writing about feminism or writing about—fill in the blank—all the good fights—why do we believe that this knowledge from academic sites is trustworthy?

PR   There was a time in which radical politics within Black spaces demanded things like Black studies or Africana studies or African-American history departments. Can we evaluate the efficacy of that demand if the quality of material life of Black people is degrading as the existence of these institutions proliferate? Is it not fair to say that perhaps the utility of these institutions is counter-indicative to the quality of life of

Black people over time, and they're serving a purpose other than actually helping solve the problems of Black people?

JJ   So, they're like a Trojan horse.

PR   I think that there's logic to that argument.

JM   I mean, commodifying education to me is extremely frustrating. The fact that I just can't learn something to learn it, it's kind of a waste of time. I have to spend my money learning something to be some sort of cog in the machine of capitalism. That's the reality for a lot of people. Now we live in a world where we are the commodity and we're very well aware of this. When they go Google something on their phone, people know that they're going to get hit with a whole bunch of ads. Either they ignore them or they succumb to them. But no one seems to mind that they themselves are the commodity. You can turn that commodity, now yourself, you can make some money off of it. I mean, we have the rise of hustle culture in which you guys talking about the ineffectual nature of the academy is kind of one and the same.

JJ   Can we pose an alternative to it? Can we build an alternative to it? Like, after COVID-19 they were having those pods? Wealthy people were creating pods that were thousands of dollars to buy in, like a poker game stake, for their children who could not go to school. Other people, in Brooklyn, got their nieces and nephews and cousins and kids together for a communal hook-up when the schools closed. People began to better understand that education cannot or should not belong to the state; and, it cannot belong to the corporation.

As I said before, there are two types of universities in the upper tiers. There are the state universities like the University of Texas at Austin, or the University of California, Berkeley, and then there are the privates. The Ivies: Harvard, Yale, Princeton, and Stanford. Then the private elite colleges where I teach. How could we create an alternative zone of intellectualism and critical thinking, knowing that the academy, as you both rightly pointed out, was never designed for that? It was designed for elites.

Remember what we know about the talented tenth: these schools were designed to create a managerial elite. The tenth, it's one tenth of y'all. Du Bois signed on to it in 1903 when he popularized the concept in *The Souls of Black Folk*. Yet, Du Bois notes in his memoirs that when the US government was persecuting him during the McCarthy era he could not trust Black elites who feared losing their status or influential jobs. Only trade unionists and radicals publicly supported Du Bois against the communist witch hunt.[9] Kathleen Cleaver said in the 1990s, Malcolm said in the 1960s, this Black elite sector is engineered for betrayal, but it still has credibility because it has shiny diplomas and degrees. So, how do we change the very meaning of education and wrestle it back from state and corporation?

JM   First and foremost, we have to start thinking collectively and not so individually.

PR   I want to go to a basic question which is that we have to come to the reality that most people in America, Black or otherwise, really don't do counter-hegemonic thinking. In other words, most people don't organically see the system as a problem. They see the fact that they can't participate in the system as the problem, but they don't see the system as the problem.

JM   Pascal, I want to get you and Dr. James's take on this. Would you say that we live in a country that is literally based off of hero narratives? That one good person can get into this system, which isn't so much corrupt as it just has bad actors? We see the judicial system that way all the time. That it's not a flawed system as much as that there's just bad people inside. There are bad judges, bad prosecutors, but the system itself was built on honor. I think breaking through that line of thinking is the really, really hard part, because it's baked into the idea of American exceptionalism.

PR   Absolutely. Particularly when it comes to the law. I studied law, I practiced law, that's what my academic training is in; and, one of the most effective ways the charade of

American exceptionalism is perpetuated is in the reverence of the American legal system. When you challenge the efficacy of the American legal system, what you will get from people trained in it is that there's no better system in the world. Where else in the world do you have the protection of the rights that you have in the United States?

My response to that is that America creates the illusion of those rights. America has the luxury of extraction to create the comfort that denies the capacity of other people in the world to have that justice. The US siphons off much of the global resources to create this level of diluted comfort amongst its citizens. It's no actual argument to say just because you are eating spam instead of dog food that you have the best meal in town. So the comparative mediocrity of justice in the Western world doesn't make America great. It just means America is the best at masking its mediocrity because everyone else is so bad.

JJ The mediocrity of American justice is driven by predatory behavior. It's like: "How many people could you kill?" Nobody can keep count on the international and the national scales. Here, you get this weird patriotism that's tied to consumerism—if you get to shop it must be a working democracy? The US is exploiting and extracting from other countries, regions, continents. The Ukraine war is horrific, but that's not the first war we've ever seen.

When I think of NATO, I think about Amílcar Cabral.[10] Who assassinated the anti-colonial African freedom leader?[11] Portugal, the CIA, and NATO were aligned. Portugal was the first European country to get into African enslavement in the 1400s and the last one to get out in the 1970s. I wonder if we would remember our losses, if that would stop this fetish for this democracy, which is really incredibly violent. But as long as that violence doesn't personally touch us, we seem as if we can accommodate or be compatible with it.

JM You see that with the right-wing push against critical race theory. The idea that this law theory is being taught in public schools and it's being reduced to, "Well, slavery is not going to get taught anymore." We're not really going to say bad things about white people and, damn it, we're not even going to talk about the Civil War or the betrayals of Reconstruction anymore. That's all "critical race theory."

PR I've come to a position, largely as a product of not only doing the show, but really just reading a lot of American political history, that the notion that America is a center-left country is a canard, is a charade. America is a reactionary right-wing country and it always has been. I see this as a significant problem of all factions of America: left, right, so on, so forth. People take the *anomaly* of the period between 1944 and 1971, i.e., the Bretton Woods period, post-World War II, the massive expansion of American largesse, the quality of middle life for white men, because it was really white men who had the jobs. To *The Adventures of Ozzie and Harriet* (1952–66) sitcom narrative of the American family, the standards of what normative patriarchy is, the standards of what a normal family is.

All of these things were an exception to the normal way American capitalism functioned since its beginning. Largely to save capitalism from radicals who wanted something more revolutionary, which brought forth the New Deal. But because that period of time, from 1944 to 1971, is perpetuated through media as the example of America being great, "Let's make America great again!" No one's talking about the Lower East Side in 1913 when they're saying, "Let's make America great again." When they're saying, "Let's make America great again," they're talking about 1954 or 1952, *Ozzie and Harriet*.

JJ The actress Donna Reed comes to mind, too. But we as Blacks were always seen as the problem and so largely absent on screen or in integrated public settings. "America's great . . . but something's going on with Black people." We're talking about the 1950s. Pascal, when you were speaking it made me think about Mamie Till-Mobley with a child corpse on display to the world. An open-casket funeral for a child murdered by white supremacists, for me, is a declaration of war against the state. Then the photos go out everywhere around the globe. I think in some ways in relation to us, I just feel like we catch the hell, the brunt. It's not just from the cops. This is an anti-Black nation and zone, but it seems to me that they're always looking for Black people to prop up to prove that this is not as lethal, as violent.

In September 1963 the Klan put a bomb in the women's bathroom of the 16th Street Baptist Church to blow up civil rights activists, who are children.[12] After Martin King delivered his "I Have a Dream" speech at the Washington Mall for the August 1963 March on Washington, the next month the Klan asserts that about the dream for reconciliation: "It's going to be a nightmare." I still believe in us as Black people, as being the wild card. I think that's how the state sees us as well, which is why it seeks a Black (vice) president, Black Supreme Court justice, a Black woman cop to head the NYPD, a Black NYC mayor: "One of y'all" to police radical movements and show that the US is not white supremacist to the core.

PR I really want to respond to that. Jason and I have an ongoing debate, and I'm going to be very honest with you, we have a problem with the trope that exists on the left that Black people are the vanguard of the revolution. I'll tell you why. Because it denies the fact that, number one, what makes Black people revolutionary is not the melanin in this skin, it's the material conditions under which Black people are forced to live in a capitalist society in America and in the world that renders them surplus everywhere, stemming from chattel. Number two, when you position Black people as the vanguard of revolution, it denies the fact that large segments of institutional mechanism in Black societies, plural, are premised on reactionary politics, ideology, and world views that are sexist, misogynistic, anti-poor, pro-capitalist, abusive. Whether they be schools, universities, churches, membership societies, you name them. Can Black people be revolutionary? Absolutely. Do Black people have revolutionary capacity? Absolutely. But it's not because of the melanin in their skin. It's because they are ground down disproportionally because capitalism requires an N-word, and capitalism requires an N-word so that, unfortunately, white poor people don't believe that there can be revolution.

JJ   I don't disagree with that, but I want to trouble it, or stir it in the pot. You're right; there's nothing inherently revolutionary about our color, per se, except for how people respond to it. Meaning police forces, vigilantes, white supremacists, etc. I don't believe that all Black people would mobilize in a freedom movement because that's not how it works. It never quite worked that way. It's not working that way now and it won't work that way in the future. I appreciate your saying, "Don't project some romanticism that 'we as Black people' have a unique role and that we were anointed." But I do believe that there's something about what we've accumulated in our consciousness, in our memory. We remember whatever stories our grandparents told us about lynching or racist violence in Mississippi. We understand lineage and inheritance. We also understand that the future could just shift and go either way. Not for people like General Colin Powell. Those people as "Black leaders" can work for President Ronald Reagan in the 1980s of reactionary and lethal interventionist politics—including Contra terrorists in Latin America—and still be happy about being a military general, secretary of state, or UN ambassador—an imperial career trajectory after coming out of the Bronx and working class.

There are still political prisoners today. Young people organizing, walking away from academic degrees, the academy, and the corporation. The material conditions, also the psychological and the emotional conditions under which we live—eight minutes to choke somebody, George Floyd, while he's crying for his mother—that has an impact. That forms a consciousness.

JM   It does, but let's be honest about that. That ain't affecting everybody the same way. This is where I take a little bit, I don't want to say offense, but it hits me a little in a personal place because I grew up in—are you familiar with the Bay Area?

JJ   I lived in Oakland for a short period.

JM   I was born in Oakland and I grew up in Richmond, California. So, you're probably familiar, mildly even, with those areas. I've lived a bit of an economically precarious life. I don't have felonies, but I've spent a long time driving without a license because I couldn't afford car insurance and my license got suspended. I remember there was a time when I couldn't pay a ticket and I was driving without a license. All told, I think I drove seven years without a license.

If I get pulled over by the cops, I'm going to get effed with. I might even get my butt kicked. Because I don't live in a good area, I'm driving a crappy car, and I'm driving it without a license. They might want to tune me up just because they can. The prisons are filled with people that committed serious felonies, didn't get tuned up on the way in. Cops know who to mess with and who not to mess with. I think what happens is, and this is where I get a little upset, there becomes this "They're getting all of us" thing. It's like, not everybody is going to face police violence the same way.

PR   This is a statistical fact, Dr. James. At the exact time the rate of mass incarceration increases post-civil rights—which starts in the 1960s by the way, before the end of the movement—the mass incarceration increases for Black males, and eventually females, without a high school diploma, it starts to increase *precipitously*. But the amount of carcerality or imprisonment of Black males, and eventually females, with *any level* of college education drops like a rock.

What happens is that mass incarceration is not exclusively an issue of Blackness, it's an issue of Black race and class. As James Forman Jr. eloquently demonstrated in his 2017 book *Locking Up Our Own*, the likelihood of a college-educated Black male having an adverse interface with a police officer compared to a Black male with no high school diploma, it's like ten to one.[18] Even in terms of the wealth of the zip code you live in. Over $100,000 of per capita income compared to those under $30,000, the chances of even having a police interaction are skewed. So, one of the things that I don't like is even talking about "we" when we talk about Black people. I don't want to say "we." I want to say there are poor Black people and working-class people who have been ground to dust, and their class enemies.

JJ   This is really helpful because now I understand better, and will try to articulate better.

JM   I'm not trying to be antagonistic, if I'm coming off that way.

JJ   No, no, no, please. I have a thirteen-year-old, I know what antagonism looks like. This is really helpful because you're both right, and I've got to figure out how my language can be clear. Look, when you're talking, I'm thinking about how after Henry Louis Gates was arrested in 2009 at his Harvard home when neighbors thought there might be a burglary, he goes to a "beer summit" on the White House lawn with President Obama and Vice President Joe Biden, and the white cop who arrested Gates. Gates was arrested essentially for talking back and being indignant; the Harvard prof was yelling that as a Black man he should not have to show his ID if he is standing in his own home. Sometime around the "beer summit," the Harvard professor traces the cop's genealogy and informs the public that they both share Irish ancestry.[14] This type of arrest and resolution—that absolves police from abuse of power—does not happen to most, and definitely not to non-elite, Blacks.

It reminds me of what the legal theorist Derrick Bell says when he describes being stopped by police when he's driving at night in the Deep South. Bell has the name and phone number of a prominent white judge. Bell is the architect of *radical* critical race theory. He writes about calling out the name of the white judge during his interrogation by police officers so that the white cop knows that Bell "belongs to" an influential white person.[15] There are segments of the Black communities (in the plural) who don't care about the working class, who don't care about the poor, who don't care about environmental devastation. That's not us, but then I'm trying to figure out what is the language, or should there not be "us" as a Black mass called the "Black community"? Should it just be radical Blacks, and then what is "radical"?

JM   We had a show the other day, Dr. James, on our *This Is Revolution* channel that sadly YouTube pulled down, where we spoke with a man who was on the cutting edge of house music. If you're familiar with house music, that really comes out during the mid-1980s and 1990s. In our discussion, we're going back in the roots of house music, which is of course disco, and he had made an interesting point about how culturally disco was supposed to be the antithesis of funk in a way.

If funk is their music, it's ghetto. It's not refined. When you think of a band like Chic and Nile Rodgers, they are the proggy funk. They are the refined funk people. This is for an elevated class of individual here. You can see it in the way the shows looked, how different they were. So, I think it is just baked in. We keep talking about how, and that's why I'm bringing up these kinds of contradictions, because we have to understand how, baked into even popular culture, there is always an otherizing. There's good Black people and then there's always the bad. There's this disassociation. In that documentary on Deutsche Welle about the burgeoning Black bourgeoisie, it starts off with, I believe he's the richest Black man in America, right?

PR   Not *the*, but one of.

JM   I'm sorry, *one of* the richest Black men in America, that real estate magnate, and he's got Aston Martins and multi-million-dollar condos. And he says, "I don't live like those rappers."

JJ   It would've been a version of, I guess among white Europeans, their version of old money, aristocracy in comparison to crass new money, which is boorish and rough and has no "culture." Their money becomes their culture. Their students go to private elite schools. They don't socialize with the riffraff, which probably includes people on this call [*Jason* *laughs*]. What is their radical project in the face of that? I'm asking in terms of the betrayal.

When I talk to Black doctoral students, some of them don't come out of means, they come out of the Bronx. They grew up with Cardi B, their families were in the underground economies. They say when I talk about Captive Maternals instead of about Black feminism—because I'm trying to think of caretaking as a nongendered function—they want to know if I'm willing to engage in the zones of betrayal. Then one of them actually says we should "off" the Captive Maternals who betray us. I'm like, "*No*," because that could include me. I have contradictions, too.

So, how do you see the politics now that you've differentiated between the posh and the polish, and those who can be invited to the White House to get a medal? Our luminaries include Toni Morrison, who received a 2012 Presidential Freedom Medal from President Barack Obama, and a 2000 National Humanities Medal from President Bill Clinton. How do you see us, or do you not see us, forming political alliances that will not be subverted by the rich and powerful?

PR I think that you have to have something that we have never had in this country, which is a working-class Black politics.

JM Have you been following what the young man Chris Smalls has been doing with Amazon?[16]

JJ I've been following the labor union on Staten Island.

JM I interviewed him a few years ago when the story broke about him. What I found fascinating about Chris was that we had similar stories as far as how we came up and even where we were working. One thing that people don't really take into consideration, and we talked about this a little bit on our show, is a lot of people on the left got very dejected and confused about Bessemer, Alabama not voting to unionize.[17]

One fact that I felt people on the left didn't take into consideration is that that job was more money than most of them people had *ever* made before. I spent time working in the South on oil rigs. It's a non-union place. The South historically is not a very unionized area. To think that you're going to get cats that, a lot of them, this is unskilled labor. This is the surplus labor we talk about so much when we love throwing around theory. Surplus labor is getting $19 an hour in a place where $19 an hour can probably buy you, not a house, but at least a nice double-wide. I don't say that with any sort of disrespect. I say it as far as people need shelter, and that's affordable shelter.

JJ   That's food on the table.

JM   That's food on the table. Why would you want to upset that apple cart? I'm not saying it's justified to not vote for worker protections and some sort of labor power. I just think that a lot of us are a little disconnected ideologically here from the idea that some of these people in these areas are making more money than they've ever made before. It's very risky to try to organize around that. The one thing that got Chris radicalized was COVID-19 and people literally dying on the shop floor.

PR   If the majority of Black people are working class and working poor or poor, what sense is there to have politics that's not rooted in the actual material condition of most Black people?

JJ   It makes no sense, but let me try to parse this out. I'm wearing multiple hats here. I got the academic hat on, which feels like I should take it off, but then that would be dishonest because I get paid with the academic hat. Then there's this other thing, like when was I last a waitress? I did those "menial" jobs at some point, too, but those years are way in the past, decades in the past. From my setting now, my lifestyle, my employment sector, I can read about the disposition or dispossession and disposability, but I'm not on that shop floor.

During the first wave of COVID-19 in New York City, I'm in my middle-class apartment, but on one side it's multi-million-dollar and the other side is New York City Housing Authority (NYCHA), public housing. In New York

City, they went from losing twenty people a day dying in their apartments to some 200 a day dying in their apartments. Then they stopped reporting the numbers to the public, likely until they could bring them down. The body bags were only coming out on the right side of my apartment building, the side where NYCHA was.

That radicalized me, but I wasn't going to be in a body bag. Because I was like, wow, this is the middle class. We're the fulcrum on the seesaw. We got one foot on either side and we're just going to balance. We're not multi-millionaires. So, we're not going to jet out somewhere. But, we're also not in public housing and we're not forced to show up as a nanny or a babysitter, whatever, just to keep food on the table. What is the role of the people who are balancing between the two zones? They're never going to be millionaires, but they're never going to be poor and unhoused.

PR   Well, you are a scholar of Amílcar Cabral. I think Cabral had the great, great, great formulation: class suicide.[18]

JM   But you know what's the neutralizing factor in the idea of class suicide? Hustle culture. "You're not working hard enough."

PR   In other words, if you are middle class and you're not a millionaire, how come you're not selling Bitcoin? How come you're not driving Uber at night to get those extra hours? Why aren't you doing overtime? You mean you don't have your own business? You don't have four limited liability companies?

JM   Even beyond the idea of "Everyone can be a millionaire," just the fact you are busy, constantly busy, is a function of—not so much success—but every week at work you have to be working over forty hours. If you're working forty hours, you're not working hard enough. We're going to hit you up all the time and the moment that you stop and say, "I need to take my kid somewhere, I need"—Nope! There'll be someone else to replace you that will work twice as hard. That is very, very prevalent in the PMC culture. When I say hustle culture, I think people just automatically think, oh, you mean like Bitcoin and those guys.

No, I mean, the idea that you have to constantly be working and the moment you're not working, you should feel shame.

J J　　The *New York Times* picked this up with the Supreme Court nominee, Ketanji Brown Jackson. A woman writer said the nominee had to balance being a mother and how she's raising her daughter and feeling guilty.[19] How do you even make it to this level of a job offer unless you are putting in more than eight hours a day over decades? But then that is expected if you're to be worthy. Worthy of what? I've called this a predatory democracy. How do you disentangle your value from the state's metric?

P R　　Class suicide, class traitorism. I think it's a matter of reorienting. I mean, for me, I grew up in a middle-class family in Queens, New York. My parents didn't have elite jobs, but my parents also were Haitian immigrants and they came from an upper-middle-class kind of Haitian elite in Haiti. They had middle-class jobs. My mother was a nurse, my father was a car mechanic, he owned a couple repair shops. But because of the time I grew up in New York city, we had a nice middle-, upper-middle-class lifestyle.

But at the same time, the reality of the precarity of life does not obscure me from the fact that people can be ground to powder. Everyone can be ground to powder. That all of my education does not stop me from—possibly—literally being on the margins for health reasons, personal reasons, economic reasons. At the same time for me, part of the process of realizing this is spending a lot of time with poor and working-class communities of Black people who have been ground to dust.

I went to college and law school. I was in a Black fraternity, so I was amongst Black potential PMC career types throughout my teens and twenties and early thirties. Then I joined a community. Basically, I converted to Islam. I became a Muslim. And I was dealing the same way I was dealing with those professional-managerial-class-aspiring Black men. At thirty years old, my social sphere was Black men who had been ground to dust in prison for years who accepted Islam as adults. What I found is that those men had more integrity in character than the career-professional-managerial-type guys that I had known my whole life. I started to realize that the politics of that first coterie of men has a large role in determining the quality of life of that second coterie of men. That was a radicalizing experience for me. I'm not saying that we should demand that of everyone. But I think that there's got to be a process, to indulge in that class suicide or that class traitorism, to have people realize, like, "Listen, this ain't working for most people."

JM   I don't think most people understand the statistics. There's a common statistic. You hear people like Richard D. Wolff, the economist, talk about it all the time. People are producing more now than we've ever produced before, working more hours, and making less money. I think that's hard for a lot of people to wrap their heads around, especially people who are in the salaried world. Because they took that job knowing, like, "I'm going to be probably working a lot more, but I'm making six figures. I'm working my way up to elite status." There's a ladder that they can see that includes those 100-hour weeks. How do you get those people to see that those 100-hour weeks is a sham?

JJ   I think in part they already know it. I think people are miserable, and they can shop and want to be entertained. How many Netflix series can you watch? To go back to what Pascal was saying, if the people who are captive find a spirituality and acceptance of themselves that is not dependent upon running around a hamster wheel, and working for a predatory structure, then that opportunity is open to everybody—if you're willing to let go of the propaganda or the internalization of values built on a capitalist economy.

To be willing to let go of those, what would be the incentive? One, would be your misery. Two, would be your compassion, because you see how the world is being devastated. But three, I think, would actually be your courage. It would take a certain kind of courage. It's not like people just say, "Oh, here's the door. Have a nice day." Your opponents or critics tend to track and punish. I mean, the point is there's not supposed to be an "out." When you start creating these avenues or crevices to get out of a kind of machinery, it's not as if statist/corporate/managerial people celebrate that. I mean, the people who are receiving you do. However, the people who are looking at your back as you're departing, from my experience in academia, they're going to want to destabilize and delegitimize you. Once you turn your back on the edifice, it's like saying that the emperor has no clothes; and that's not a narrative you're supposed to be publicizing.

Maybe there aren't any contradictions and I'm just letting my head get in the way. But let's go back to Black women. The way we are trained as Black women and girls is to compensate. Even the "leadership" is a compensation packet in some ways, which includes a Trojan horse. The way I always looked at it, whenever we got a promotion and stuff, it was another form of "domestic labor," not in terms of physical, manual, and low-paid labor but the historical relegation of Black women during and after chattel slavery to the position of house servants and wet nurses, distinct from the field slaves and sex/rape camps. You were there to clean up somebody's mess. They put you on a grant, you're there to clean up. They want you to build Africana studies, it's because the institution thinks, "We're looking a little racist here. Come tape something together."

You're never actually in control even though you're given these positions that look like you have institutional power. The fact is, you do not. It is as you say: more labor, more grind.

JM We had so many questions and this conversation has been so wonderful.

JJ I'm pacing around the office muttering "What do I think, what's going on?!"

PR I have a question based on the judge. Judge Ketanji Brown Jackson is currently being nominated to the Supreme

Court. Though Judge Jackson has surpassed the rather low bar of having some progressive elements to her judicial record, there is a certain danger to the way neoliberal identity politics was used to advance her nomination. When asked by her Senate questioners as to what value there was to having diversity on the bench, she stated that diversity lends and bolsters public confidence in our system. Can you problematize how that assertion further illustrates the classed nature of the Black political project in terms of what the system means for most Black people who are on the margin?

JJ I would say Obama already problematized that assertion when he said he wasn't a president for Black people, he's the president for "everybody." For me, it's the dictate of absorption, that you have to absorb and be absorbed by the state and capital, then you have to perform functions of maintenance for state and capital. This happened to Michelle Obama. She wrote that thesis at Princeton that was critical, a bit, of racism in America. Then she spent the next eight years apologizing for it by being "the mom of the nation."

The US should be balkanized. That's my position. I would say, let the white supremacists have Idaho since the state won't adequately surveil and derail them—but the land belongs to the Indigenous, so you can't do that. You still have to fight white supremacists. There's a way in which our desire to belong—as if we thought that belonging was an insurance policy—trains us to articulate constantly that we're "safe" Black people. That we have no autonomy and that we don't even want it, no matter how much the white-supremacist underground starts to play around above ground. I think that conformity becomes the moment when we cut our own Achilles heels.

The logic is you can't expect anything much from Black officials because they work for the state. The state has already indicated that it is about accumulation through force, and it is not about distribution of equity or goods or material sustenance for the people, for the mass. I've tried to stop being disillusioned every time a Black woman assumes some level of power at a corporation or within the state. Condoleezza Rice should have cured everybody decades ago of that desire for Black feminism as fetish, or even in academia or in one of these movements.

I've made little queries—maybe snarky—about "movement millionaires." But, how do you monetize Black suffering and end up a millionaire? I mean, how does that even work as a movement? Of course, the state and corporations and whites have been doing this for centuries. There's a template. The way you don't want to romanticize Black unity or Black community, I will not romanticize Black women just because they belong to the Democratic Party or they go to church or they're kind or whatever.

The only subjects that have a true autonomous persona and independent thinking would be those people who understand the state must be not only critiqued but also opposed. Once you take a job within it, then you become the opposition to freedom movements that emanate from the base. Whether the movements are environmental, labor, right to be trans, right to abortion, there are different issues that we have to deal with. I really appreciate you both because if I had a tendency to romanticize Black people, you definitely killed it [*Jason and Pascal laugh*].

I just have to figure out where I go from here. But that whole thing about Black women are going to lead you somewhere? No. You've negated the false concept that "Black people" as Black people are going to lead you somewhere. People who theorize, who will engage in material conditions and material struggles and be accountable to the people they say they represent, that becomes a collective leadership to which we can contribute.

Notes to Chapter 15

1   Zinn Education Project, "This Day in History—Jan. 18, 1968: Eartha Kitt Spoke Truth at the White House," accessed October 12, 2022, https://www.zinnedproject.org/news/tdih/eartha-kitt-spoke-at-white-house/.

2   PBS *Frontline*, "Interview: Kathleen Cleaver."

3   Preston H. Smith II, *Racial Democracy and the Black Metropolis: Housing Policy in Postwar Chicago* (Minneapolis, MN: University of Minnesota Press, 2012).

4   See A. Philip Randolph and Bayard Rustin, "How the Civil-Rights Movement Aimed to End Poverty," *The Atlantic*, accessed October 12, 2022, https://www.theatlantic.com/magazine/archive/2018/02/a-freedom-budget-for-all-americans-annotated/557024/.

5   See Mary Ellen Flannery, "'We Stepped Up and Fought Back': Behind the Explosive Growth of New Faculty Unions," *neaToday*, November 29, 2020, https://www.nea.org/advocating-for-change/new-from-nea/we-stepped-and-fought-back-behind-explosive-growth-new-faculty.

6   Martin Pengelly, "Erica Garner, Black Lives Matter Activist, Dies Aged 27," *Guardian*, December 30, 2017, https://www.theguardian.com/us-news/2017/dec/30/erica-garner-dies-black-lives-matter-eric-garner-daughter.

7   Matt Taibbi, *I Can't Breathe: A Killing on Bay Street* (New York: Spiegel & Grau, 2017).

8   See e.g. Barbara and John Ehrenreich, "The Professional-Managerial Class," in *Between Labor and Capital*, ed. Pat Walker (Boston, MA: South End Press, 1979).

9   See James, *Transcending the Talented Tenth*.

10 Cabral, *Return to the Source*.

11 Sa'eed Husaini, "The Socialist Agronomist Who Helped End Portuguese Colonialism: An Interview with Peter Karibe Mendy," *Jacobin*, October 17, 2019, https://jacobin.com/2019/10/amilcar-cabral-portuguese-colonialism-biography.

12 Manos, "Birmingham 16th Street Baptist Church Bombing."

13 James Forman Jr., *Locking Up Our Own: Crime and Punishment in Black America* (New York: Farrar, Straus and Giroux, 2017).

14 Ta-Nehisi Coates, "The Arrest of Henry Louis Gates," *The Atlantic*, August 12, 2010, https://www.theatlantic.com/national/archive/2010/08/the-arrest-of-henry-louis-gates/61365/; *Oprah.com* editors, "The Importance of Ancestry," *Oprah.com*, March 9, 2010, https://www.oprah.com/oprahshow/dr-henry-louis-gates-jr-start-your-ancestry-search/all.

15 For key texts by Derrick Bell, see *Faces at the Bottom of the Well: The Permanence of Racism* (New York: Basic Books, 1993) and *And We Are Not Saved: The Elusive Quest for Racial Justice* (New York: Basic Books, 1987).

16 See e.g., Gloria Oladipo, "'The Revolution Is Here': Chris Smalls' Union Win Sparks a Movement at Other Amazon Warehouses," *Guardian*, April 6, 2022, https://www.theguardian.com/technology/2022/apr/06/chris-smalls-amazon-union-warehouses.

17 See Michael Sainato, "Amazon Workers in Alabama Vote

Against Forming Company's First Union," *Guardian*, April 9, 2021, https://www.theguardian.com/technology/2021/apr/09/amazon-union-vote-result-latest-news-bessemer-alabama-plant.

18   "To retain the power which national liberation puts in its hands, the petty bourgeoisie has only one path: to give free rein to its natural tendencies to become more bourgeois, to permit the development of a bureaucratic and intermediary bourgeoisie in the commercial cycle, in order to transform itself into a national pseudo-bourgeoisie, that is to say in order to negate the revolution and necessarily ally. In order not to betray these objectives the petty bourgeoisie has only one choice: to strengthen its revolutionary consciousness, to reject the temptations of becoming more bourgeois and the natural concerns of its class mentality, to identify itself with the working classes and not to oppose the normal development of the process of revolution. This means that in order to truly fulfill the role in the national liberation struggle, the revolutionary petty bourgeoisie must be capable of committing suicide as a class in order to be reborn as revolutionary workers, completely identified with the deepest aspirations of the people to which they belong": Amílcar Cabral, "The Weapon of Theory," address delivered to the first Tricontinental Conference of the Peoples of Asia, Africa and Latin America, Havana, January 1966; available online, https://www.marxists.org/subject/africa/cabral/1966/weapon-theory.htm, accessed October 26, 2022.

19   Molly Jong-Fast, "What Working Mothers Heard in Judge Jackson's Words," *The Atlantic*, March 23, 2022, https://www.theatlantic.com/family/archive/2022/03/ketanji-brown-jackson-hearing-working-mom-guilt/627595/; Jackson was confirmed to the court in June 2022.

16 We Remember the Attempts to Be Free: Part I

With Joshua Briond and Jared Ware of
Millennials Are Killing Capitalism, 2021

Jared Ware Today, August 7, 2021, is the fifty-first anniversary of Jonathan Jackson's raid at the Marin County Courthouse, in which Jonathan would be killed by police prison guards, in a plot to liberate his brother George Jackson and the other Soledad Brothers, including William Christmas and James McClain. We want to start with the Captive Maternal to frame this conversation. You talk about this concept in a lot of your work. One of the things you state—in "The Womb of Western Theory"—is that "leverage, rather than 'feminism' or 'intersectionality' or 'progressivism,' might be a useful term for recognizing power and predation."[1] Can you discuss your concept of the Captive Maternal, and that quote about leverage?

Joy James Let's start on the anniversary of the state killing of the seventeen-year-old Jonathan Jackson (see above, pp. 154–5). Because "my concept" is not my personal concept of the Captive Maternal but my formulation of the Captive Maternal as a descriptor of function in terms of what I saw when I was in Harlem watching parents trying to get protections and services for Black children. This is, you know, an incredible feat, like Sisyphus rolling the boulder up and it falls back down on you. It's a predatory state. It's imperial. It's white-supremacist. It accumulates through terror. Blacks are primary targets; the Indigenous are also targets; the working class, poor, LGBTQ+ people, trans women, and so forth.

With this seventeen-year-old, the leverage would have been that if they could take "hostages"—literally by

definition they were hostages but the raid was actually a barter exchange—it would not be to accumulate. It wasn't to rob,
as was and is the case with Deutsche Bank, which is a criminal enterprise anyway (or any bank that comes to mind). It
was an attempt to save the brother's life. Seventeen is technically still a child. Legally, right? The Captive Maternal as a
function can be embodied in a child or "minor" (Jonathan's
mother Georgia Bea Jackson says her son was a "man"), in
a teenager, in a male, a trans or nonbinary person, and in
a woman or girl. It is not personal liberation or the liberation defined within the framework of bourgeois feminism
which has become hegemonic. Now, conventional feminism is multiracial and rainbow. The liberation sought by
Jonathan Jackson is tied to the freedom of a people, that can
only be materially manifested if you defeat the predator.
It's not like the state or predatory capitalism/imperialism
says: "Here's some land, a plot, and we won't bother you as
you seek autonomy from us." That's not how accumulations
through terror work. They're predatory because they hunt.
The Captive Maternal on these various stages resists the
hunt. The seventeen-year-old goes into Marin County, having weapons registered in the name of Angela Davis—that is
how Davis becomes involved, Davis is not actually functioning in this capacity of rebellion or resistance to save the life
of George Jackson, the brilliant theorist who will die a year
later in August 1971. Jonathan died on August 7, 1970, in the
Marin County Courthouse raid. The September 1971 Attica
Prison rebellion would follow George's death.

The Captive Maternal gets to the level of rebellion, after
they've tried cooperation, stabilizing the state, trying to be
the "good" Black person, through all of these different stages
of compromise and protest. When I talk about Attica I will try
to break it down, hopefully, more clearly. All of these stages
exist but when you get to the point of sacrifice—which for
me is inherent in all of the stages of the Captive Maternal,
because it's organic in struggle, you might find that you will

risk your life in order to save a life. By saving that life, you leave a legacy, even if it's a "technical failure"—and it's not low-tech, right, because people die.

Even if it's read as a failure, it becomes in some ways a victory. Because we're talking about the raid on the Marin County Courthouse some fifty years later. *We remember the attempts to be free.* We remember the attempts to turn the hunt against the hunter. The leverage that this seventeen-year-old wielded—by walking in with the weapons and saying to the state, which is always weaponized, "Now I'm in charge"—is vocalizing, for me, the materialization of a form of the Captive Maternal who has reached the zone of rebellion that will start to look like the sacrificial lamb within an hour or so.

The mandate from the state was that there would be no escapes, even if they had to kill Judge Harold Haley, which they did. Even if they made the assistant district attorney a paraplegic, which they did. Even though they would kill the Black teenager, *which they happily did,* along with the two other Black incarcerated men, McClain and Christmas, and wound Ruchell Magee, who is still incarcerated as the longest-held political prisoner in the United States.[2] This would be the statement of the state: "Captive Maternals who seek those latter stages of rebellion and resistance will be eradicated." Still, Captive Maternals keep manifesting.

Back to "The Womb of Western Theory." I open that analysis with an Iraqi feminist who I watched on YouTube saying how great it is to be in the US. As she speaks, I'm thinking, "Wait!" I'm old enough to remember what went down here in Iraq decades ago. Claims of nonexistent weapons of mass destruction held by Saddam Hussein, the disinformation campaign from the Bush administration which included Condoleezza Rice. Even though she's a Black feminist, Rice is not a Captive Maternal. She works for the state, which is the predatory formation and which is the hunter. That Iraqi feminist TED Talk[3] is interesting, fascinating, and implicates the US, but has no critique of the US because it was celebratory:

"Oh, I'm here in the land of the free, the home of the brave." I juxtapose that talk with the Black Liberation Army (BLA) narrative of the wounded, tortured feminist, a Black one, Assata Shakur. The Iraqi woman has fled a war zone to seek freedom in a democracy which is a war zone for all rebels against predatory accumulations. (The blowback against the "Captive Maternal" is to challenge whether I am a feminist anymore because the Captive Maternal is nonbinary.) When you juxtapose the two women, you see that feminism is not a stable concept. It is always contextualized. But antifascism is stable.

An Iraqi woman seeks refuge in a war zone. A Black/African-American woman flees the same zone that the refugee/immigrant seeks as sanctuary. "The Womb of Western Theory" explores the TED Talk narrative. That Iraqi woman stated that they wear red lipstick so when the sniper shoots to kill them they will know that they "killed a beautiful woman." That's very poignant. It has its place in our struggles. But so does 500 years of being tortured and raped. Under regimes of enslavement and dishonor in which they are trying to figure out how many ways can they kill you as the Black potential rebel or accumulate through rape with the Three-fifths Compromise and the Thirteenth Amendment which legalizes slavery under incarceration. When you juxtapose those two women in flight, feminism is mercurial. The only thing that stabilizes it is context and the context is the democracy itself. Since the Iraqi woman asserts, "I got my card . . . I'm a US citizen now," she clearly is not on the side of struggling against a democracy that accumulates through terror, racial-chattel enslavement, and imperialism, although, she gets to the US in part because of imperialism.

When you see the second woman embodied in "A Political Statement from the Black Underground," in 1976/1977, it is very clear the conditions under which Black communities seek not just survival within but freedom from a predatory democracy.[4] In that clarity of sight, that is the feminism I choose. Am I a liberation leader? Absolutely not. I describe myself as a "librarian." But as a librarian, I'm an archivist of the Captive Maternal. I see their manifestations—from the teenager who dies in a hail of bullets because prison guards have a mandate of "no escapes, no matter who you kill," so they shoot up a van of barter-exchange hostages, to people wearing T-shirts with slogans: "I'm one of her daughters." Which leads me to ask, "Which one?" The one who was doing sickle cell testing in Harlem as a social worker, who loves the people, or the one forced underground by COINTELPRO, who becomes a reincarnation of leverage against a violent state? That underground feminism of rebellion and self-defense against a violent state does not register as much on the T-shirt as the above-ground rebel icon as "social worker," which is compatible with what President Joe Biden is doing right now; throw a bunch of money at y'all to get you more services, and then hopefully, nobody remembers what we were actually asking for and demanding: freedom, decent wages, stop polluting the environment, rein in the billionaires.

The Captive Maternals, in my understanding, are phenomena of complicity and resistance. On the first level, we/they/you can work the system, but you stabilize it at the same time. You accept modest gains or the individual gains for your child or family or yourself, which become paltry accumulations. You never accumulate on the level of Jeff Bezos and Warren Buffett and everybody else in the billionaire club, millionaire club, and the state. On the second level, you protest because you understand this is a 360-degree merry-go-round and you're not going anywhere in terms of sustainable freedom movements tied to justice. For those of us who are parents, we know that you can put your child in the preppy school with all the rich kids so they're on the "right track"; but then the indignity and the dishonor of not having the right clothes or being the right race follows: the humiliation that tells you that you and your children are supposed to defer to this sort of imperial caste does harm in itself. Or, you can leave your kid in the local under-resourced school that has metal detectors and cops roaming the halls, and students who are going into illicit underground economies—they're not going to self-regulate because underground economies are just as predatory as above-ground economies, if not more so; there, as you know, the blood is on the floor, not through the stock exchange. Either way, it's harm because you never control the environment. You force your child to adapt into hostile territory.

The next stage is: "I'm gonna protest this." Moving from the conflicted or celebratory zone of "Yay, my kid got into Harvard!"—which is a think tank for imperialism—you transition to the protest zone. Protests are not the same as a movement but you meet, organize, and negotiate with the state or the bureaucracy. There are no real negotiations though that shift power to the mass because the structure has not been revolutionized or transformed. So that leads to movement. We're out in the streets. We take over territory, or we might burn something down. From the "movement stage" of mass protests, where do you go when the movement is not organized and congealed?

You move into resistance. Think of Jonathan, a seventeen-year-old junior in high school. He must have gone through all the stages: write your brother in prison when you're around ten years old, go see him when your mom can take you; start protesting with placards for the Soledad Brothers, start marching with Angela Davis. The next stage beyond the movement would be to organize something that is a rebellion. I understand that the Panthers on the West Coast did not support the Marin County raid. Oakland Panthers saw it as a suicidal mission. Huey Newton's eulogy at Jonathan's funeral references "revolutionary suicide." You move through varied stages to reach the stage of rebellion.

Rebellion and resistance against the state are always punished. The Captive Maternal can be pacifist or militarist. The state doesn't care. It does not allow autonomous zones, particularly of or for Black freedom. What do police forces

do at Marin County on August 7, 1970? They shoot up a van.
Kill everything that moves. It's totally unnecessary. It's performative. Part of their performance or their messaging to
all Captive Maternals is: "If you ever think there is autonomy,
if you ever think your agency registers to change your reality, the material conditions, and the world towards freedom,
we have a bullet for you." Still, Captive Maternals keep doing
their thing—pacifist, militarist, spiritualist, materialist, combination of all the above. "The Womb of Western Theory"
talks about the predatory womb of Western theory writ large.
It is also talking about that unexpected by-product when you
have a breech baby that comes out the wrong way—comes
out a rebel, not a clone.

Joshua Briond I think that police violence has a similar effect to public lynching. It serves a similar ideology. In my
opinion, it represses even the potentialities of Black revolt.
Oftentimes, I see the brutality, I despise the term "police
brutality" because it's contradictory. Seeing some of the violence that we see from the state and its deputized individuals,
if that makes sense, it has to be more than just, "Hey, they
hate you because of your skin color." I'm very curious to hear
what you think about these killings. We see the brutality. Even
seeing stuff with the homeless: a video the other day went
viral showing cops brutalizing the homeless, while knowing
they're being recorded and knowing that this is all a public
spectacle of violence.

JJ   The performative nature, in my opinion, is part of
psychological warfare. It's also godlike play. Police are like:
"Yeah, you can catch me on camera brutalizing civilians but
I'm still gonna walk away." Derek Chauvin is inside though,
incarcerated for the murder of George Floyd and sentenced
to life in prison. Think, however, of the percentages in which
police predators are actually held accountable? It's really
low. I don't have the numbers, somebody can go look for the
data; and, it's really hard to find the data because police don't
report all their violence against civilians. Their performative

violence is tethered to immunity and impunity, and the indignity that our tax dollars are paying for this.

In New York City, the NYPD cracked open heads of peaceful protesters decrying the murder of George Floyd. I know young people who say, "Oh, we're gonna pay down some bills because my partner, she got X number of stitches from police attacking peaceful protests." At a televised hearing by New York State following police violence against BLM protestors, I'm looking at New York's attorney general Letitia James not even grill the head cop in New York City at the time, Dermot Shea, as the police commissioner confidently projects: "I can lie to you on camera." Most of the people speaking are middle-class or bourgeois whites. They're voters and so are considered important to politicians. The elected official—Attorney General James—was helpful in sidelining New York's governor Andrew Cuomo for his sexual predatory acts, but she is not a friend to/of the masses. I'm watching her ask the head cop questions, and he's totally confident that he can lie that the NYPD never kettled people in the Bronx and then kept them kettled, corralled with metal barricades, preventing them from leaving the enclosure until after curfew. Then police took down the barricades, rushed the protesters and observers and cracked open heads, hitting eighty-year-old journalists with green caps on (indicating that they were official observers/watchdogs)—it didn't matter. Human rights workers? Absolutely, doesn't matter. The Human Rights Watch organization makes a report[5] but the hunters—I'm gonna call the police the "hunters"—are like: "Yeah, we hunt. You have a problem with that?" Despite their brutality, they will still get a pension, vacation days—or maybe they were penalized and lost five vacation days. Whatever. They'll do overtime and make the money back. The amount of money we're gonna pay in New York City is not just for the millions of dollars in settlements for police brutality against peaceful protesters in the wake of the murder of George Floyd. Add to that the fact that the cops are going to charge overtime, which is more than basic pay. *They're charging you overtime to beat you at peaceful protests.* If you stayed within the mind space of liberalism as a zone for competent political analysis, you would either lose it or you would just have to pretend most of that violence didn't go down. This is why I think there's such mystification about violence—political violence—right now, among certain kinds of feminists, abolitionists, activists. If they analyzed the material dimensions of predatory state violence, they would realize that there is nothing in their tool kit that will remedy this.

Malcolm said: "By any means necessary." You can go either way on the spectrum with that; which means you can also say, "Get out the vote!" I don't have a problem with that. I appreciate Malcolm's candor that a lynching is a lynching; don't call it something else. Let's just call it what it is. There is little to no candor in most of today's political speechifying. Maybe I don't have to be snarky with the "speechifying," but most speechmakers have to mystify the violence to make the lynching a "non-lynching," if that makes sense. It becomes a tragedy, which it always is. It becomes a horror show, which it always is. But it is never or rarely depicted as what it is in the real material world. Which is a horror show that you have to counter by any means necessary.

Placaters will inform us that this horror movie will be over at this time; and we'll leave the theater, and then we'll all be able to figure out how to work in this system. You cannot work in this system on the stage one of the Captive Maternal to stabilize it, because it is inherently predatory and it will reproduce predation through your stabilization. The state— as white-supremacist, capitalist, shaped by misogynoir and misopedia—does have a blood lust. I don't care what they say, how many crocodile tears they shed about who died when and where, how many funerals or memorials they go to, how much money they pay out to families after they murder their kids. Those packages come out of my tax dollars. Let me pay for pre-kindergarten, okay? Or let me pay for cleaning up the environment. I don't want to pay for state/military/police murder. I don't want to do compensation for murder. But this is part of the taxing; it's part of the indignity or the dishonor that is waged against us.

If we focus on lynching, Josh, as you put it on the table, and we don't try to make it a historical artifact, then what we trace is not just the brutality, but the resistance against it. The first person who comes to mind is Ida B. Wells. Michel Foucault writes in *Discipline and Punish* that torture disappeared from the public because a guillotine was dismantled and taken out of the square.[6] No. He is wrong. The year 1892 is the height of lynching of Blacks in the US, where white crowds of up to 10,000 people come out with picnic baskets and leave with body parts. They bring their kids to the lynching "parties." They're indoctrinating the next generation to be terrorists.

Wells's resistance to that, and the clarity that she had and still has as an ancestor, created longevity in struggle. In the minds of the Black petty bourgeoisie, Wells was too tied to the grassroots. She would call terrorism as she saw it. The most militant voices that call it as they see it—terrorism—get sidelined and marginalized because we are told to mystify the violence in order to get people to perform on levels one and two of the Captive Maternal. However, the call for autonomy is only legit when you're dealing with a terrorist. If you're dealing with a democracy, then you can always reform and rehab it. My analysis of US democracy is that we have a lot of leeway to shop if we have money and to do some other stuff. But it has expressions of organized terror.

This is why Jonathan Jackson is not an elder. This is how we lose Patrice Lumumba, Che Guevara, Malcolm, Martin, Medgar Evers, Fred Hampton, Dulcie September, Chris Hani. I can't just do this rollcall all day. There's organized violence to disappear or "neutralize" leadership that trends towards rebellion for freedom.

JB   You wrote a piece a couple years ago about George Jackson entitled "Dragon Philosopher and Revolutionary

Abolitionist." You also wrote "'New Bones' Abolitionism, Communism, and Captive Maternals."[7] These are pieces about different things but in both cases you reference the Captive Maternal and Attica. To many George Jackson is a hyper-masculinist character and the Attica Prison rebellion is a reflection of the same. But you note how Angela Davis dedicated her essay "Reflections on the Black Woman's Role in a Community of Slaves" to Jackson, and you use the Attica rebellion to talk about your four stages of the Captive Maternal. Can you explain to folks how you see the Captive Maternal in relation to George Jackson and Attica?

JJ   First, I'd step back and relate George Jackson to his mother. That's the namesake, right? I believe her name was/ is Georgia Bea Jackson. There's a way in which your children can transform you. I started off talking about the hustle of getting them into good schools, keeping them away from predatory structures: school to prison pipeline, Internet (how about that one?), social media.

In order to keep them not just alive, but to allow them to thrive, you have to learn from them. It's transformative. Whether they're your fictive kin, biological, or adopted. Think about our experiences for 500 years. Under chattel slavery somebody had the idea to sell your five-year-old twins. After you finally can process that, you still adopt other children in the community and you help raise them. We're always being sold, bartered, broken apart, put in foster care, prisons. We're always being disappeared as families. If Captive Maternals function in the social order and the political order, they obviously function in the familial or family order.

When you read the "hyper-masculinist," as you call George Jackson—I'm not saying that he's not, right, but I never said the Captive Maternal was always a *nice person*—you see the way his letters in *Soledad Brother* castigate his mother.[8] For this reader, it's like, "Oh, please stop already." Kids take years off your life, just to be candid. Mrs. Jackson changes though, because of the torture, the confinement, the enslavement—also known as imprisonment—of her child. What little I know of his early childhood, George was a handful. Got it. *However, it is one thing when an individual acts out their aggression, it is another when the state does it with impunity.* You have to decide if you will align with the individual who is now treated as prey to be broken, or if you will align with the state and its punishment. Will you abandon the individual who is constantly rebelling, including against their family? Or will you find the stamina to figure out how do we move from this point to the next point so that we can be free not just from external aggressors, but also internal aggressors in the community, and our own aggressions against ourselves: our dysregulation, instability, depression, anger, rage. Our volatility. In a hostile world, you get people who can't be quiet, or won't be quiet or don't cooperate. By the time both her sons die, the mother Georgia Jackson is a militant.

Read the letters. George Jackson's letters in *Soledad Brother*. He writes to the three people he deeply loves: his mother, his brother Jonathan, and Angela Davis. George Jackson dedicates his love to them and, to their enemies, he basically dedicates his hatred. So now, the hunted will become the hunter—if you annihilate, destroy, damage, harm their kin. I would say that's not a gendered response, though men most likely are socialized to perform that endeavor. Women will do it in a different way, more verbal. If there's a hyper-masculinist presentation there's a possibility that there's a hyper-feminist presentation as well, if it's about the accumulation of power based on the dishonor or humiliation of others. I've not just experienced that from men—yes, I've got a long list on them—I've also experienced attempts to humiliate from women. I don't like hyper-masculinists. I don't really like hyper-feminists. I'm not saying that "women wanting to be free" is hyper-feminism. I'm talking about the presentation style, the code of ethics or morality that gets broken among women who want to dominate or humiliate others.

What you put out is so important, Josh, because now I have to make a choice. I'll just go for it. If I had to choose between a moral code that was principled, but not nice, and the niceties of petty-bourgeois or bourgeois or even working-class protocol, I would probably go with the ethical code that would make me whatever word you want to throw—and a lot of people have been throwing them—at me. "Nice" is probably not the first word that comes to mind. I'm not trying to be hyper anything. I'm trying to be clear.

What George said about his family kin? I cannot register with it on the level of a revolutionary because I am not one. I can definitely register though on the level of family intimacy. If you even think about harming or disappearing mine, I will dedicate the rest of my life—and that's what he said that he would do—dedicate his life—fill in the blank—to seek balance in the equation. From the different mothers that I've worked with who have had their children murdered by police forces, they are not really forgiving. Some of their demands have nothing to do with civility. Those demands sometimes may be perceived as "hyper." I'm not saying that the descriptor is inappropriate. I know a little bit about how George Jackson got inside prison. I don't think he should have been inside. I think he should have been offered the whole restorative justice, give him a lot of therapy and see how this goes.

George Jackson became a revolutionary because prison guards murdered W.L. Nolen for starting a legal petition to stop prison guards "fomenting racial strife".[9] Once you realize that they will kill you for following the rules—rules state that if you have grievances, write a petition, send it to the adjudicators and they will bring it to the state, which is what Nolen did—if they will shoot you in the yard for that? Then there are no rules. George writes that that the definition of fascism is linked to "law."[10] When I first read that in *Soledad Brother*, my skeptical mind said, "Wow. Really?" For Davis, what little bit I know about their exchanges, her position was, "No, this is not a fascist or proto-fascist state. You can work within its systems." Hence, Davis went to trial and was acquitted. I'm thinking that Jackson, who was assassinated in prison, analyzed reality from the zone he occupied—prison as a terror zone.

Even in that prison shooting in which Nolen was murdered, what little I know of that tragedy focuses on the lethal messaging. Guards shoot you, and then let the Black men bleed out in the yard, in order to tell their comrades who also loved them that, "If you even try to move them to the medical center, we will shoot you too." When you say the hyper-performative trauma it will be a guard saying, "I'm gonna make you watch your loved one bleed out in front of you; on penalty of death, I dare you to try to pick him up and take him somewhere so you can save his life." This implicates you in the murder. Once you have a regime that starts doing stuff like that, and bringing people back from the Vietnam War (now Iraq, Afghanistan) to mill into your prison forces, guard forces, and police forces, the social disorder, it's just a war zone.

What is the human, if that's what we want to be? I'm not always sure what the human is in a war zone. Sometimes a warrior, even if it facilitates your death, your brevity of life, because that becomes the only ethical choice. Malcolm could have taken the money and lived longer. You know, Martin could have. Everybody I named who got assassinated with the help of the US government, CIA, FBI, etc., they all could have taken the money but they did not; so, they had brevity, and violent endings. But then they have longevity in memory. That, obviously, is not what people were hoping for; they were hoping for more.

JW   To tack on the other point with that question, talk a little bit about Attica in relation to the Captive Maternal and their stages.

JJ   The glimpse of Attica happened last year when I was speaking on a panel with the Newburgh LGBTQ+ Center. I had been talking in part about a New York City church I attended. It had the only—or one of the few—Black trans teen night shelters/centers, in a city of eight million people.

There are probably no more than fifteen beds in the church basement. The teens had produced a cross made up of photographs of murdered Black trans women. It was six feet tall and upstairs in the sanctuary where services are held. In the sanctuary of an old church, a white alabaster angel is cradling this large cross of photographs of Black murdered women. I asked the LGBTQ+ panel, "What does security look like?" We had been having a dialogue back and forth, and conversation stopped. I don't know if they weren't ready for my question.

My little caveat: I grew up on what I call the bases of an imperial army. When my father died, he was a retired lieutenant colonel. I'm sure I'm traumatized so many times on many layers, I can't even explain it. But for me, talking about organized violence is natural. When, as a young child, I was watching my father, he's either jumping out of airplanes in the 101st Airborne Division or my siblings and I are picking up bullet casings—we all survived it—off of firing ranges for play. Violence is everywhere and the US is highly skilled in organized violence. So, I asked the moderator and panelists, "What's the security plan?" I'm stunned when people respond "We don't have a plan for security." My thoughts are: "What do you mean you don't have a plan? Everybody has a plan." But no, that is not true. Civilians usually don't have plans for organized predatory violence.

By default, either they rely on the police forces or therapeutic interventions and care. The therapeutic does good things, but it is not made for a war zone. Unless you're a trauma center and then they keep recycling the wounded into you. You have to stop the war. I start to think during the panel, "Where's this conversation going?" Then I said, "Okay, you asked me to talk about Attica. Let me try with the Captive Maternal."

Stage one. You're a trustee in prison. What do you do? You clean, you mop, you cook. You garden. You deliver towels, books, work in the library and on low-level administrative tasks. Your labor stabilizes the prison structure. You're reproducing the zone of terror not because you want to but because you got captured. Maybe it's out of boredom, or you need a job for commissary; they pay you twenty-seven cents or a dollar and twenty cents an hour. Some perks. But that labor of caring for yourself and the other incarcerated with whom you forge a community—some are your adversaries and predators—that labor, your labor, is stolen. Just like enslaved labor. The Thirteenth Amendment, it's actually enslaved labor. Your labor is stolen to preserve the structure that holds you as prey.

Stage two. As with Attica in September 1971, you start protesting as if we were humans. Attica people said they were "men." My understanding is that everybody inside the prison didn't probably identify as male, or self-identify as such, but the prison administration would classify your gender and then send you to the men's prison. It's 1971, not 2022. You start protesting, start asserting your rights, arguing that you're tired of forced "free" labor, slave labor. Labor which actually on the outside, in the "regular" world disproportionately would be done by women. Since the prison is "same gender" there is no gender difference per se. All of the labor that is feminized outside as domestic labor, wages for housework—or non-wages inside prison for the same chores—is now performed by people perceived as male. You start to protest: "Don't pay me twenty-seven cents. Don't call me the N-word. Stop terrorizing." From that protest stage, either the prison administration listens to you or they don't. But nothing changes. What follows next is the movement, or stage three.

Part of the Attica movement stage, of course, was George Jackson's murder. His "assassination," which is what Foucault calls it, and I'll go with that. The incarcerated were reading George Jackson inside, they were reading *Soledad Brother*, which was written between 1964 and 1970. Back to George as a Captive Maternal. The Captive Maternal is anybody who loves others and the people as a communal mass. They're not narcissists, per se, and they're definitely not sociopaths or psychopaths, which some people probably labeled George as. They love people so much that they're willing to sacrifice for them or to focus on them in order to deliver care.

It's not just that the prison tells you to clean, and cook. You care about yourself and others, so you're doing it for them and community, to which you all belong. When you reach this stage of protests, especially after the murder of George Jackson, if you were reading *Soledad Brother,* you probably thought that George was speaking to you through the text. You probably generated an emotional relationship with the militant author and fighter, one which I would call "love." When I read Octavia Butler, whether or not she's speaking to me, in my mind it is like: "This writer cares about me." They're in my head. Their narratives and experiences let me know that I'm not crazy because they're talking to me. It's not me as "the problem." I am jacked up, but it's also the predatory structure that repro-duces chaos, violence, and death. The writer loves me enough to tell me the truth. Jackson's book was edited heavily by his attorney Fay Stender and the book editor Gregory Armstrong because they wanted him to look more liberal and acceptable to general society in order to spare his life and free him from prison. Still, you could see that George cared for Black people and for captives. When the state murders someone with whom you have a relationship—even if it's just cerebral, emotional kinship and you've never met them—you're moving towards a stage of the Captive Maternal where rebellion is more likely to happen because you've been traumatized by the death on the other side of a continent.

And so, the rules don't apply. They were always proto-fa-scistic to begin with; but now as a captive inside the prison you're not going to clean. There's a strike, a work stoppage to some extent. Or some refuse to eat, they don't pick up their utensils, everybody and everything is frozen. Time is frozen. It's on pause, because what's the next stage after they murder your kin?

At Attica, the next stage is rebellion, stage four. The captives take over. Two trustees die, killed by the incarcerated. That, of course, is a tragedy as well. The hostages now are the prison guards. In that stage—past conflicted caretaker, past protest, past movement—the incarcerated are in maroonage. They build a maroon camp inside prison walls. How bold. I mean, come on. That's the max. Historically, we just ran for the hills or the swamps. But not now: inside the fortress, captives build a media site, an education site, health delivery, food delivery, waste removal, they form security so that everybody stays in check. There is culture. The anthropologist Orisanmi Burton is writing a book on Attica, *Tip of the Spear*, you may want to meet with him. He talks about the incarcerated singing doo-wop songs to each other in order to calm and care for each other. Now they are in full-blown rebellion.

What is the state's relationship to maroonage? I'm not a historian. These are the facts I remember. Governor Nelson Rockefeller ends up in a conversation with President Richard Nixon. Sometime later, the National Guard comes in. They have hardware from the Vietnam War, military hardware, it's counterinsurgency. A human rights struggle is seen as a declaration of war against the state. What does the state do? They shoot through white prison guards to kill mostly Black rebels. According to Burton, after the state retook the prison—I was aware of the torture—the guards then just murdered additional leaders.

So, those are the stages. From stage one, complicit in the reproduction and stabilizing of the predatory formation because it's the only way to stay alive—"I have to do what they say or they will beat me, put me in solitary, deny food. I'm forced to cooperate." Despite fear, we move to the next stage, stage two, protest. State violence or repression is so off the hook that we need to organize the movement, stage three. Eventually, the movement's gone to stage four, full rebellion. We create a container for ourselves. Build a maroon camp.

The Attica rebels try to reach the outside world, the *New York Times* journalist Tom Wicker, they asked the Black Panther leader Bobby Seale to show up, the attorney William Kunstler is on the scene with others.

State warfare comes to respond to the move towards freedom because we (Black, rebel, queer) are not supposed to be free. We are captives, right? So, to restore capture, the state goes into full-blown war, which was not necessary. I've shown in my classes *Eyes on the Prize: A Nation of Law? (1968–1971)*, the fifty-minute documentary. Wicker, the white bourgeois journalist from the *New York Times*, states on camera that the state "didn't have to come in like that" given that the cold and diminishing food supplies meant that the incarcerated would have given in or surrendered. Back to what Josh said about performative terror. The mindset of state authorities was: "We do not want you to surrender. We want to massacre you." They are messaging with lethal militarism. They're doing psychological warfare. If captives surrender, then you don't have the spectacle to display the state's godlike powers in terror. The question became for me, as I was talking to other people, what happens after the troops come in? What happens after the executions?

The memory stays alive. Through *Big Black: Stand at Attica*, the 2020 graphic novel that Frank "Big Black" Smith— spokesperson for the rebellion, who was tortured and sexually assaulted in the retaking of the prison—authored with Jared Reinmuth; through the 2021 documentary *Attica* by Traci Curry and Stanley Nelson.[11] People keep talking about Attica because they need to, emotionally and politically. Actually, it is a library. What I said before in terms of being librarians and archivists, it's a library, just as your podcast is itself a library. We have to remember or we don't understand reality. There's betrayal. It is betrayal for those who forget. It's the betrayal by those who want to clean up Attica and say, "Well, we can prevent this happening in the future." No, we can't. We have not sufficiently strategized and organized to prevent future atrocities. It's the betrayal that's shaped by fear and shaped by accumulations. It's not just white people who betray you. Anybody can betray, anybody who cannot stomach the reality of the zones in which we live, but also the uniqueness of the prison zone. It is sheer, sheer war.

In a recent conversation with Max Parthas of the Abolish Slavery National Network, we were talking about activists inside who are on a prison hit list initiated by the guards/administration.[12] I think of it as an assassination list. COINTELPRO never ended. Most of the leadership that's focusing on voting haven't told you, one, that this is a war, and, two, that its manifestations from decades ago have become more clandestine. They've diversified by having people of color and LGBTQ+ people join the CIA. The nature of the warfare is the same, it just has different faces.

JW   I've been reflecting on your essay "Airbrushing Revolution for the Sake of Abolition."[13] The first time I read it, I was frustrated by it on a couple of levels. One, I felt like it had some very scintillating details that are kind of dropped in about the CIA and Gloria Steinem and their relationships to Angela Davis's defense campaign and then maybe also in regard to Critical Resistance. But I wanted more. I've gone back to it a few times, and there's a lot within it that I really do find super generative. For me, it was a question of whether it's a critique of a kind of liberal alliance, or whether it's a suggestion of a sort of complicity in an act of counterinsurgency. I think maybe those things are one and the same. This idea of trial strategy and campaign strategy specifically related to political prisoners is something that comes up all the time. I work around and try to support campaigns related to political prisoners. There's a lot of people that I tremendously respect and we want to get freedom for all of them.

I was at a conference where Margaret Burnham spoke. She was on Dr. Davis's legal team during her campaign, and her parents are Louis and Dorothy Burnham who were also in the CPUSA. There were two statements that she read at this conference from Angela Davis's pretrial. I'm just gonna read quick excerpts from the first one, made right after she was arrested. Davis stated: "The reactionary pig forces of this country have chosen to persecute me because I am a communist revolutionary participating together with millions of oppressed people in a revolutionary movement to overthrow all the conditions that stand in the way of our freedom."

Burnham noted that every word of Davis's statement was true, but that it wouldn't play with the jury in Santa Clara County. Burnham went on to reference a statement made on the eve of Davis's trial, where Davis articulated: "The need to ensure judicial fairness and bail in order that I may better prepare my defense becomes increasingly urgent." Davis added: "While we may disagree on many things, we are surely united in our affirmation on principles of due process, and equality before the law. Millions of people throughout the world of all political persuasions and national and racial origin have voiced their concern over the fairness of my trial." Burnham discussed at this conference the distance that Davis had traveled rhetorically from her capture to the eve of her trial, with the intent of securing her innocence through the apparatus of the US legal system.

Conversely, obviously, we could talk about strategies of other political prisoners. We could talk about—and should talk about—Ruchell Magee, who as you mentioned is still incarcerated fifty-plus years later, the longest-held US political prisoner. We've had folks on the podcast before, Sekou Odinga, Jalil Muntaqim, other people within the BLA—I know Davis was not in the BLA—but people who were in the BLA. They took the stance, some of them, that they had a legal right to rebellion under international law, right? They were combatants, and so they should be treated as prisoners of war under the Geneva Convention. The US of course, doesn't recognize this right, and just treats them as criminals. But it's important to think about these distinctions. Because obviously, none of us want to be in prison for life, right? So the appeal to innocence, if you can get it, makes sense. It's the thing that you would do as a trial strategy. Your lawyers would tell you to do it. But then it's a huge issue with social movements, because if your movement is actually in a revolutionary phase or in a revolutionary state, then you can't be innocent. There is no innocence in that. As far as the state's concerned. I am interested in your thoughts on that.

J J   There's a lot going on there. As you know, "Airbrushing Revolution for the Sake of Abolition" obviously was controversial. It was first published on a liberal blog called *Black Perspectives*, which is part of the African American Intellectual History Society (AAIHS). That it even got out probably surprised a lot of people. It was sparked by a conversation with a doctoral student at an elite university. I was hearing how doctoral students—at least from this perspective, but I've heard it from other people, too—were being pressured to do their research within a certain ideological format that would not be perceived as too militant or too radical. The academy, if it's a public university, shares the ideology of the government, because it is a state entity. If it's somewhere where I taught, like Brown University, where I edited those anthologies on political prisoners to the consternation of my colleagues, the university has the ideology of the corporation. It's private capital or it's state.

Neither space is actually built for truth-telling about repression, nor to give you an adequate context for understanding why these rebellions keep happening. If you don't have political context, then the rebellions are simply criminal. I had also been hearing from other people that they were not allowed to talk about war. You could talk about war as a metaphor or an abstraction. But I've spent this time with you (maybe it's my filter growing up on military bases) saying that I think the material conditions justify this descriptor "war." War can only be a metaphor under a certain kind of politics, because if the state is at war with you, then you don't play by state rules, and it will imprison or kill you for that disobedience. Jonathan Jackson, George Jackson, and the other political prisoners did not play by the state's rules. Because the state was hunting, it was predatory. It had killed a number of people, and nobody went to jail for those killings. You can give Fred Hampton and Mark Clark's families $1.8 million, compared to $12 million for Breonna Taylor's murder, I don't know if you adjust for inflation . . . the point is you still have dead people. People that you loved, and who nobody can bring back. There's no justice because nobody has been held accountable.

In this particular instance with academics, I'm listening to doctoral students saying that there's a way in which their work is being influenced or infiltrated so that it's compatible with the hegemonic narrative of progressivism, which is, in my estimation, not grassroots radicalism.

On another level though, the Black Revolutionary Guard (BRG) did a statement.[14] I'm not on social media, but people send me stuff. BRG had strong descriptors about Davis and they were largely negative. If you're reading my work and expecting me to pinpoint somebody as something, you should read somebody else. I already told you, I'm not a journalist. I don't do exposés. I'm an analyst. I'm trained in political philosophy and, for whatever reasons, by Jesuits and Republicans—I was forced to study the Europeans. However, I think my ethical commitments are based on my organizing. It has nothing to do with the academics that I spent years in graduate school. I always rebelled in graduate school.

I read BRG describing Davis, who I know a little bit. I thought: I'm going to disagree with some of their analysis, but I'm going to tell what I see in terms of structure and history. The data I referenced about Steinem's work with the CIA and Steinem being recruited to head the fundraising component of Davis's defense campaign has been out for years.[15] It's largely written by white, bourgeois academics such as Hugh Wilford,[16] and nobody reads those white authors' work. But when a Black woman who says, "I'm also a feminist" relies on scholarship and analysis, it's like all hell breaks loose. It's funny but this isn't really a joke. The inside admonishment line is that you can't critique Black feminists or Black feminism unless they go rogue. Going rogue to do scholarship and analyze radical politics means that I'm a "librarian" attempting to discern and preserve factual knowledge.

Some of the dominant or popular resistance narratives do not make sense. Let's try to break this down. First, people don't necessarily have to be working officially for the Feds to further their agenda. My understanding is Steinem definitely did work for the CIA through the National Student Association, based on the historical data and her own confessions to mainstream media.[17] And everybody knew that from the *Ramparts* exposé releasing that information in 1967 after a whistleblower alerted them about the National Student Association operating as a CIA front. By 1971–72, Steinem is made the head of Davis's fundraising committee. That was a decision by the CPUSA and I believe, by Stanley Levison, who had a meeting in Manhattan, and Steinem was invited in to assist Davis's defense: "We want you to do this." So why would an (anti-communist) bourgeois white woman who basically says that she only worked with the "liberal" faction of the CIA—and then that statement was largely scrubbed from the media, you cannot really find that clip anymore—why would she agree to defend Angela Davis and raise money for her defense committee? I don't know. Figure it out yourself. I'm the librarian. I put the book on the table. Read it or don't. I don't care. I brought it to your attention. If you've been reading, you would have figured it out anyway. Usually when some folks "figure it out," language becomes hyperbolic. I'm going back to what Josh said about "hyper-masculinist" responses such as, "We're going to tear down Steinem, and feminism." That was not my goal. I've met Steinem decades ago when I was a grad student. The whole package, lovely person. Then you look at her politics and it's like, "Oh . . . ?" If you met Hillary Clinton, it's like, lovely persona, then you ask: "What are your policies? Oh, empire?" It's state feminism.

One of the things to think about is, if this is already public knowledge, what's the big deal when it appears on an academic Black history blog in 2020? Because it's destabilizing the perception of what Black leadership and intellectualism should be? What does it mean to be aligned with state feminism? You don't have to be a state feminist. You just need to be part of the revenue stream that funds and furthers it. Whether or not you're ideologically aligned, the revenue stream is promoting your work.

Consider Ms. Foundation's *Ms. Magazine*. There are a couple of articles to think about: Davis writing on Joan Little after Little killed the white prison guard who was raping her in 1974.[18] A Black woman defense attorney successfully defended Little in court, but Davis's piece in *Ms. Magazine* was foundational. Little was a civilian not a political combatant, until that act of self-defense, which became reframed as political phenomena.

I would argue, akin to what happened in 1991 with Clarence Thomas and Anita Hill, that the Black woman becomes representational for white women's suffering and/or amplifies gender victimization. I'm sure some women would want to have that level of retaliation and defense against their rapists which Joan Little wielded. There is an analogue: Joan Little works as an anti-rape figure for affluent and non-Black women and girls. If Joan Little was pre-politicized and did a guerrilla act against a police precinct, that would *not* be in *Ms. Magazine*. Even if her rapist was the cop in the precinct, it still would not be permissible, because it's an act against state violence. I know it may sound a little confusing. She killed a local prison guard, so isn't he the state? No, he was just a local expendable flunky, who—if he's going to be a serial rapist—should have thought about the possible consequences if there's ever blowback. He never did. But in that era, in the 1970s, Little's use of lethal force could work within a feminist modality because it could be writ large over bourgeois white women as the victims of male patriarchy and sexual violence, which are real.

Rape doesn't often reach the level of reality that you end up in a tussle with your white jailer, stabbing him with his own ice pick. That is rare. That's the anomaly. But the self-defense becomes the right of *all* women. That's why the assault on Joan Little is "useful" for feminism writ large. Same with Anita Hill being sexually harassed. Anita Hill is useful at the rallies for white feminists. She's Black, but the charge is shaped by gender; its racial component is no longer central. People don't ask, "What was Anita Hill doing with Clarence Thomas, besides being harassed by him in the office?" They both were working in the Reagan administration in the Equal Employment Opportunity Commission to basically toss out job complaints against racist discrimination, sexist discrimination, homophobic discrimination. Workers' rights were being trashed not just by Clarence Thomas, but also by Anita Hill. I stand by Anita Hill's right not to be sexually harassed, but I am not going to forget the fact that her job—which nobody forced her to take in the Reagan administration—was to eviscerate civil rights. She became reborn after the feminists championed her because, as a prototype, she was useful, although she had publicly stated that the anti-abortion judge Robert Bork was cheated of a seat on the US Supreme Court.[19]

Ms. Magazine launched the writings of Alice Walker, Angela Davis, Toni Morrison, Michele Wallace, all key Black feminists. I've learned from all their writings. But *Ms. Magazine* is an extension of Clay Felker. Steinem worked for him first at *New York* magazine. Both had allegiances with the state (CIA) during the Cold War. So how might you win the Cold War when the CIA can't kill everybody? Win hearts and minds, get publications. Produce a kind of feminism that's going to be loyal to the state. Hillary Clinton was a feminist. She was also an imperialist. These alignments between Black feminists—who don't have that much money, or clout, or platforms—with white feminists—who do have means—are usually transactional. Eventually, some Black feminists garner wealth, stature, influence leveraged through such partnerships.

State feminists can now claim that they have women of color, are rainbow, nobody can say they're "racist." The key question is, what's the position on US foreign policy? Can we talk about US imperialism? If we cannot critique US imperialism, then the transactional politics work for the *state* feminists. They may leverage the influence, raise the profile, sell more books, raise the honoraria and speaking fees for others, launch people as writers. But those individual accumulations are not mass accumulations for Black people, unless you're personally cutting everybody a check. You might be. I don't know how people do their donations. How many books did you sell? It is not for Black freedom or reparations. But for state feminists, what they gain is amazing: the persona of being anti-racist and non-racist because they're rainbow. But it's not the Rainbow Coalition that Fred Hampton talked about, right?[20] It's different from the rainbow coalition of bourgeois and petty-bourgeois feminism. Yes, we/they're diverse: we're lesbians, we're trans, we're multi-ethnic, multi-national, we're Indigenous, etc. Okay, but tell me about your position on US policy? Not just denouncing it like you denounce lynching with, "Oh, this is horrifying!" I want to know the nitty-gritty, what's the plan to confront predatory violence, and the hunter? State feminists will agree that there is chauvinism, patriarchy, sexism, homophobia. They will *not* agree, in my understanding of them, that the state is a hunter, that imperialism is a zone of terror. Once they acknowledge these facts the funding and power networks dry up.

"Airbrushing" tells you enough that if you want to know more, you find out the rest for yourself. It tells you a few facts that the only people who knew were the people at that conference, but there were thousands of people who attended the 1998 CU-Boulder "Unfinished Liberation" conference (see above, pp. 34–7). What I'm gesturing to is how labor in the academy can be exploited. Especially the labor of younger people, students, grad students, and junior faculty who are doing what they believe to be ethical. Accumulations are not going to the incarcerated but to the people who *speak about* the incarcerated and accumulate the persona of being informed, caring, and right there on the edge of serious politics. What is the relationship between us as academics and the incarcerated? How can the incarcerated check our power when we use their stories and narratives? They cannot. The incarcerated cannot deny you tenure. The incarcerated cannot stop a multi-million-dollar grant coming in the wake of George Floyd protests. There's a lot of money generated from suffering inflicted upon the Black working class/poor when violence becomes a spectacle.

Living in zones of terror/captivity, under-resourced communities are reliant upon people outside to act in good faith. But what is good faith if it is not disciplined by a political code of resistance? I can't read these codes of resistance without seeing them corrupted by bourgeois funders, if they are not seen as relevant on the street in the terms of people who are actually mobilizing.

Concerning Margaret Burnham, we met a couple of times. I also met her mother Dorothy Burnham through the CPUSA-aligned Women for Racial and Economic Equality. Communist women and Black militants in New York City trained me. Margaret's mother Dorothy was amazing, incredibly lovely and gracious. I remember our conversations were always informative and they helped me. I also met Charlene Mitchell, who was Angela Davis's mentor. It was Charlene Mitchell who told me to go to the Schomburg Center in Harlem and read all of W.E.B. Du Bois's memoirs. That's why I wrote the critique of the talented tenth.[21] The academy will corrupt you. That's the short version. The academy and the petty bourgeoisie will betray Black mass militancy. That's what happened to Du Bois. As he became more communist-minded he was forced out of the NAACP. His position in his memoirs was, "I wish I had a militant ally." I read that and thought: "Wait! You had Ida B. Wells as a grassroots militant and you blew her off." These are the cycles of refusal, rejection, and betrayal that we go through given the mystification of violence.

The language Davis was using after her capture differed during her trial as you noted in your observations earlier. Her initial denunciation of the state as persecuting her because she was a Black communist revolutionary was not coming from the CPUSA, the first organization she officially joined. If the CPUSA was paying for that expensive six-attorney legal defense, you are going to use their language. Also, the language is compatible with the state. When you say we need our legal rights under the state you're saying that this state can function for Blacks (not just Black elites). George Jackson said that US law is fascist, which means it will never function for us. If I wanted to get off on a murder charge, I would have changed my language, too; but you can't pretend that the criminal (in)justice system is representative of a resistant movement. It's not. It is about the individual being able not to spend the rest of their life or decades in jail.

Ruchell Magee could not do that, given his assertion: "I'm a captured slave. And I have the right to be a maroon." (As noted above, Magee, the former co-defendant with Angela Davis, is over eighty-three years old and remains incarcerated.) This was also the position of the Attica people. You have the right—if people are torturing you, if you're being raped, if you've been starved and beaten, if you've been thrown in the hole so that you can have a nervous breakdown or become psychotic—you get to run. I know it's illegal, but that's just the law of ethics.

If you have a torturer, you get to try to leave the enclosure. Granted, they'll shoot you for it. But I can't judge you if they're torturing and beating you, and there's blood on the floor. Do what you need to do, because it's a war zone. Figure out what works best for physical, spiritual, psychological, intellectual, emotional survival.

Geronimo Pratt was on trial during the same period as Angela Davis. It's painful and traumatic. I've never been in jail.

Davis was incarcerated for over sixteen months. Incredibly depressing. Pratt did twenty-seven *years*.[22] When I wrote about his imprisonment after he was framed by the FBI and Los Angeles Police, I said that he was held captive as long as Mandela. A prominent Black academic historian indignantly responded with, "How dare you compare Pratt to Mandela!" My counter is that it's not like either one of us as (elite) academics has been incarcerated in prison. Mandela also was probably a capitalist. (If you want to talk to me about the communist leader Chris Hani, I would love to learn more.) I know Mandela suffered. If I know correctly, he also was cutting unilateral deals with the Apartheid regime. Twenty-seven years for Geronimo is real. He was framed under COINTELPRO and by the US government.

I reference the Black Panther leader Kathleen Cleaver because she was always there in the heart of revolutionary struggle. She got the law degree from Yale. As attorneys, Cleaver, Stuart Hanlon, and Johnnie Cochran just kept at it, petitioning and litigating until they were able to get Geronimo out of prison after twenty-seven years, with some financial settlement financed through taxes that cannot pay compensation for all those years.

When I asked the tenured academics as an assistant professor at CU-Boulder, "Can we invite Geronimo, too," they flinched. That's not the profile they wanted. Geronimo Pratt did not have that European polish. He was not a woman. He was not clearly a feminist. He was not accepted by the bourgeois mainstream, at all. He was not accepted by whites unless they're white militants. The academic vibe is: "Do not bring that kind of persona up on campus. We plan on having a great conference without him." Academics chose, not necessarily based on gender, it's in part about ideology—and what the funders want. That is why all the revolutionaries I know are broke.

Notes to Chapter 16

1   James, "The Womb of Western Theory," 257.

2   See Jericho Movement, "Magee, Ruchell Cinque," accessed October 12, 2022, https://www.thejerichomovement.com/profile /magee-ruchell-cinque.

3   Zainab Salbi, "How Do People Live and Cope in the Midst of Violent Conflict?," *TED Radio Hour*, NPR, February 11, 2016, https://www.ted .com/talks/zainab_salbi_women_wartime_and_the_dream_of_peace.

4   Coordinating Committee, Black Liberation Army [Assata Shakur], "A Political Statement from the Black Underground," 1976/77; available online, http://www.assatashakur.org/message.htm, accessed October 12, 2022.

5   Human Rights Watch, "US: New York Police Planned Assault on Bronx Protesters," September 30, 2022, https://www.hrw.org/news/2020/09 /30/us-new-york-police-planned-assault-bronx-protesters.

6   Michel Foucault, *Discipline and Punish: The Birth of the Prison*, trans. Alan Sheridan (New York: Vintage, 1977), 8.

7   James, "George Jackson: Dragon Philosopher"; James, "'New Bones' Abolitionism."

8   Jackson, *Soledad Brother*.

9   "newafrikan77," "January 13th 1970 Soledad Assassination of W.L. Nolen, Cleveland Edwards, Alvin Miller, Soledad Prison Riot," *newafrikan77 blog*, January 13, 2018, https://newafrikan77.wordpress .com/2018/01/13/january-13th-1970-soledad-assassination-of-w-l -nolen-cleveland-edwards-alvin-miller-soledad-prison-riot/.

10 "[T]he definition of fascism is: a police state wherein the political ascendancy is tied into and protects the interests of the upper class— characterized by militarism, racism, and imperialism": Jackson, *Soledad Brother*, 18.

11 Frank "Big Black" Smith, Jared Reinmuth, and Améziane, *Big Black: Stand at Attica* (Los Angeles, CA: BOOM! Studios, 2020); Traci Curry and Stanley Nelson, dirs, *Attica* (Showtime, 2021).

12 See Max Parthas with Joy James, *Rebel Intellectuals*, season 2, episode 26, https://www.blogtalkradio.com/abolitiontoday/2021/06/27 /s2-e26-rebel-intellectuals-with-guest-professor-joy-james.

13 James, "Airbrushing Revolution."

14 Black Like Mao [formerly Black Revolutionary Guard], "Was Angela Davis a Panther".

15 See e.g. Stephen Rohde, "Spying on Students," *Los Angeles Review of Books*, May 4, 2015, https://lareviewofbooks.org/article/spying-on-students/; Louis Menand, "A Friend of the Devil," *New Yorker*, March 16, 2015, https: //www.newyorker.com/magazine/2015/03/23/a-friend-of-the-devil.

16 See e.g. Hugh Wilford, *The Mighty Wurlitzer: How the CIA Played America* (Harvard, MA: Harvard University Press, 2009); and Karen Paget, *Patriotic Betrayal: The Inside Story of the CIA's Secret Campaign to Enroll American Students in the Crusade against Communism* (New Haven, CT: Yale University Press, 2015).

17 See Redstockings, "Redstockings' Statement," *Off Our Backs* 5, no. 6 (July 1975); and Menand, "A Friend of the Devil."

18 Angela Davis, "Joan Little: The Dialectics of Rape," *Ms. Magazine*, June 1975; available online, https://overthrowpalacehome.files .wordpress.com/2019/02/ms.-magazine-from-the-archives.pdf, accessed October 12, 2022; see also James Reston Jr., "The Joan Little Case," *New York Times*, April 6, 1975, https://www.nytimes.com /1975/04/06/archives/the-joan-little-case-in-a-small-southern-town -the-night-jailer-is.html.

19 Sarah Pruitt, "How Robert Bork's Failed Nomination Led to a Changed Supreme Court," *History*, September 21, 2018, https://www.history .com/news/robert-bork-ronald-reagan-supreme-court-nominations.

20 Serrato, "Fifty Years of Fred Hampton's Rainbow Coalition."

21 James, *Transcending the Talented Tenth*.

22 Greve, "Geronimo Pratt (1947–2011)."

17

We Remember
the Attempts to Be Free: Part II

With Joshua Briond and Jared Ware of
Millennials Are Killing Capitalism, 2021

Joshua Briond In the introduction to *Warfare in the American Homeland* you write:

> Erasing a genealogy mapped by the "wretched of the earth" allows the non-wretched to print over their (our?) texts, to use insurgent narratives as recyclables. This is a practice of the police machinery and its technologies of warfare. Professed allies, "radical" theorists, are selective because they have that right and privilege. In one narrative, Foucault disappears all impoverished and imprisoned black/brown bodies, yet in another he presents, in painstaking delineation, the corpse of the revolutionary icon and prison rebel George Jackson; that killing in a California prison thirty years ago sparked the Attica rebellion and additional killings in a prison on the other side of the continent.[1]

In the interview you did for *Groundings* (see chapter 14) you spend time struggling over the role of the intellectual—as opposed to the "guerilla intellectual"—as you talk about the more liberal and/or academic forms of abolitionist thought that have emerged in the aftermath of the more radical potentialities of social movements. Can you talk a little about this watering-down of revolutionary struggle to mere abstracts and terms of liberal academic institutional discourse?

Joy James I'll try not to be repetitive. The "New Bones" piece is based on my reading and teaching of Amílcar Cabral's *Return to The Source*.[2] I knew about *Return to The Source* because

I have a friend who was in the Harlem Panthers. NYC Panthers were very different from California Panthers—West Coast Panthers would have been the Panthers that Davis aligned with; the East Coast had a militant ideological trajectory. From NYC, you get Dhoruba Bin Wahad, and others, and the people largely who wrote that 2020 letter that I referenced in "Airbrushing."[3] The "New Bones" argument that I was putting forward followed being influenced by Cabral and—like everybody else—traumatized by what seems like the planned ineptitude around the COVID-19 pandemic which led to loss of life, livelihoods, and housing for so many people.

What's the source of new bones for new thinking? The concept of "new bones" came from the poem by Lucille Clifton.[4] New growth, the source agency in my mind cannot be the academy. It is a source of accumulation. I said that earlier. I'm not bashing anybody, because I'm bashing myself. Inherently, if most of the people you're quoting are academics, and you're saying that academics politicized you, including me, that's going to be interesting. It's going to be "interesting," because if we've been able to keep our jobs this long, or get these honorary titles, we are compatible with the structure even if we are seen as contrarians or mavericks within it. We are still compatible with accumulation, within an empire with imperial DNA shot through it. For academics who survive as long as, say, I have, the way we risk is modified; it's shaped by our distance from physical terror. The risks taken by the incarcerated when they go on strike look nothing like the risks academics take concerning whether or not we will be published.

Warfare originally had a different title that led the editors at Duke University Press to ask, "Are you declaring war on the United States?" I said, "*Of course not*." Then we had to play around with the title. It was my last year at Brown where I was demoralized because of the department's hostile response to my work with political prisoners.

Previously, I had gotten Palgrave Macmillan to mail fifty copies of the anthology that came out of the 1998

CU-Boulder "Unfinished Liberation" conference. One political prisoner had been in the BPP and the BLA; they wrote back that the book I sent them, which I was so happy to share, wasn't really relevant. When I went to Brown I anthologized political prisoners for years, but I caught hell. Directly from Black colleagues: "You need to go. How uncomfortable can we make it here for you so you will leave?" Eventually, I did. Ironically, the academy under capital is so adaptive, a decade or two later, it's fine to write on political rebels and political prisoners. The people that I anthologized in *Imprisoned Intellectuals*[5]—George Jackson's image is on the book cover— are now having their books and writings in print by respectable academic publishers. In 2003, I'm getting called into the "principal's office," my colleagues are mocking me. I'm having a nervous breakdown. My contributors are either dying from cancer—Marilyn Buck, the white revolutionary who worked with the BLA; Philip Berrigan, one of the Catholic pacifist anti-war Berrigan brothers[6]—or are murdered. The trauma is secondary or tertiary. It is nothing like being inside prison. But the worries are real: Marilyn's got cancer, how long does she have; why didn't I visit? There's this constant worry and fear. This is textual and it's painful. I've never been caged like that. I never did enough to help those inside.

The Attica people felt while reading George. I feel. I was reading these folks in real time; they were inside, I'm writing to them, and then sometimes my letters come back because I'm sending contraband or because I'm becoming too politicized. It's always secondary, tertiary, but I know the trauma is real.

I don't care if people say I'm lying. I wasn't trying to accumulate. I was already a full professor at Brown. It was just "the right thing to do." The person who put me on this journey was the BLA prisoner going into their fortieth year, close to fifty years incarcerated before they get out. None of that was respectable then. But years later, somehow, it's respectable.

I was working with students to create a conference that brought in former political prisoners from across the spectrum: Weather Underground, American Indian Movement, Panthers, the Republic of New Afrika,[7] Puerto Rican Nationalists. Brown recruited me with $10,000 in research funds, which I hear now is not even *real* money. I spent that money, not on my research, but I'm bringing all these people to campus.

Academics increasingly write about political prisoners now. Some people are paying some costs. But when did the state agree to leverage the identity of the rebels? During the time of the Attica Prison rebellion, they just killed leaders during the takeover and then later quietly snuffed others out after the National Guard left. Why is it textually okay to have them appear now? Perhaps because of the way they are being interpreted and how they are being taught.

You cannot teach rebellion to the children of the ruling class, or to that scholarship kid who's not going to be a worker, but well paid for by the elites, and someone who hopefully joins the elites, or becomes a colored version or first generation of them. Universities are ideological factories. So how did they expand to include the rebels? They turned rebels into commodities.

When academia thought rebellion was possibly real or likely, meaning that there will be material organizing in response to comprehension, with a growth of "new bones" out of these students, it was a threat. Some weeks before the national conference,[8] the Brown administration mandated a student gathering for everybody on financial aid at the same time as our conference. The students were so smart—again, this is hearsay based on what they told me: they attended the mandatory meeting, signed their names on the attendance sheet because if they did not show up there appeared to be threats that their aid packets could be cut—capital will hurt you in the pocketbook. Then students filtered out one by one from the mandatory meeting and silently filed into the radical gathering of rebel vets and former political prisoners. Our empty auditorium with rebels teaching—as people

kept quietly opening the door—grew to its full capacity.
Students were young, brilliant. They did nothing illegal. For
Imprisoned Intellectuals, they did the research for the bios, and
wrote the research editor notes for chapters on Black anarchists, Quaker peace resistors, Plowshares people,[9] Chicano
activists, Indigenous resistors, Black Panthers. Students
were also very clear: "When we finish this work, we're going
to walk into elite law schools, or my dad will pay for Harvard
grad." There's a boundary here, right, they, as well as elite
faculty, are not giving up capital or privilege. My response
was, "Fine, just do what you think is useful." They offered
technical skills. Nowadays, there's a place of more confusion.
There's a disconnect between this kind of theory or accumulation in the academy, and the resistance to the extent it
exists on the ground. It's not just a disconnect. It's like those
birds, cuckoos, brood parasites, that come into your nest
and kick out your eggs, and then they lay their own eggs
so they look like your eggs. You come back home and sit
on their eggs. When they hatch, you're bewildered: "What is
this? What did I just hatch?"

The product of your labor is used by capital to create the
edgy, militant-minded academic. That doesn't mean they are
not ethical. But, if you do not have an organic connection to
radical resistance, there is no way for incarcerated radicals—
nonradicals who are incarcerated also deserve support—to
have peerage, not just to give their stories so you can write
the book. The imprisoned/captives should have peerage with
you, and be able to check you. If not, there is no balance of
power here.

We are taking the power of the state university, or the
private-corporate university and college, and leveraging it as
a gift to those who face the most dire conditions of repression.
That is not "new bones." That is not a "return to the source."
That is an excavation of the source. That is extraction from
the source. That is accumulation from the source. Goodwill
is not sufficient to replace an organized resistance, one that

understands that however you want to describe what we're doing, or trying to do, we still need a security apparatus, not just for our emotions through therapy; we actually need to figure out how to protect each other. One Black pastor in Rochester said after George Floyd's murder that if you kill us, we will kill your economy. I read that as a call for some form of strike or boycott of purchasing. I'd be interested in trying to change all my buying behaviors.

When I grew up on military bases, I was socialized. I was in the Reserve Officers' Training Corps in high school and university. I decided that I was not going to be my dad. But I learned a lot. You can learn a lot in the academy. You can even get a gig as an academic. But if you accept the culture without a critique, that is like growing up, in some ways, on a military base, and being indoctrinated and thinking that whatever you do is a liberation endeavor. This is why we tell the troops, "Thank you for your service." In my brain I add, "And for the empire." Thank you for your service of accumulation of knowledge for whom, for what, and to what degree?

JW   I want to talk a little bit about Jailhouse Lawyers Speak (JLS), an organization that I've worked with to support, mainly around publishing their thinking, specifically in relation to the 2018 prison strike.[10] They've publicly spoken out about abolitionists, which we could think of as those who supported Joe Biden for president, given his history of mass incarceration, his pro-police, pro-prison policies. We're all seeing that play out right now in terms of a renewed crime scare, a lot of which is just based on bad data. There wasn't a lot of crime happening when everybody was required to stay inside. Still, a lot of it could be attributed to all kinds of social factors around COVID-19 and not having enough support.

We just saw that Biden's immigration detention is double what it was when he took office.

JLS also has in the past vocalized support for prisoner escapes, including early in the COVID-19 pandemic when some people were just running away from jails or low-security prisons, and highlighted the strength of the movement that existed in the 1970s and early 1980s, when things like the liberation of Assata Shakur were possible. Dissidents and prisoners were taking those sorts of risks. They have also been attacked by the far right, including the right-wing Fox News commentator Tucker Carlson for trying to seek out Kyle Rittenhouse's location inside. These are all positions that I think on some level Josh and I probably would agree with, but they are also positions that liberals and self-described radical organizations will not or cannot publicly endorse. They are prohibited thought to a certain degree, particularly within a lot of the academic abolitionist lens. They built large coalitions when they're striking around their demands; 300 organizations expressed solidarity in 2018. But these statements caused them to lose support. Also, they've noticed a lot of support has diminished since President Biden was elected. People were just walking away because there is a Democrat in office. With relation to Tucker Carlson, the left doesn't have any sort of meaningful counterpunch. If an organization like theirs gets vilified on a platform like that, then all of these far-right folks start to attack JLS's ability to fundraise or organize. There is no left platform that can stand up to that, because we don't have the reach.

JJ   There is a lot there because this is not abstract. It's totally grounded. Let's start with the low-hanging fruit, Kyle Rittenhouse. As part of a platform, I was asked by feminist philosophers in Europe about "mothering." I used the example of Rittenhouse, out on bail, in that restaurant with his mother and white supremacists. He was, according to the press, throwing up white power signs and she, his mother, according to the press, was grinning, after he'd shot three people—anti-racist demonstrators—and killed two.[11] I raised the query as to whether this might be a "teenage serial killer," who can get a $2 million bounty bail, because he has a political function. He becomes a symbolic register, an extension of the state. He had a license to have that weapon? He drove out of state? Police earlier gave him bottled water and let him walk away after he shot three people? The state/police forces are structured for that kind of aggression. When I say "hunter," I seriously mean "hunter." What people often don't talk about is that the three people he shot were white males at a Black Lives Matter protest. Part of the "threat" messaging is for anti-racist whites. White supremacists indicate: "Our first target is Blacks, but we definitely have capacity to intimidate whites from supporting, in any real meaningful way, anti-white-supremacist liberation struggles, and escapes from terror zones into sanctuaries without police forces invading." Rittenhouse provides a free commercial for the extension of the state investment in white supremacy and terrorism. He is protected by the state, and the state is protected by reactionaries.

Your allies are not your allies, unless they show up when you really need them. That is a really painful reality. In a generalized environment where everybody is out on the street, millions are marching for George Floyd. What happens after people get off the streets? Are there above-ground and underground networks organizing? Mutual aid funds? Is everybody tithing now? Do we practice self-defense? Self-defense is not just about technology. It's that communal circle that encloses you; a 360-degree wrap of community will tell you who your core is and who is always going to be there. It's not going to be a lot of people, which is painful because folks flock to you when it seems appropriate to them, not to you. We have to strengthen the alliances to build stability and the commitment to sacrifice.

Back to Jonathan. I am not saying he should have done the Marin County raid. I can tell you I probably would not have done it. I just would be depressed, knowing that I couldn't stop my brother's torture or murder and then I would go through high school, college, get a graduate degree. That is the norm. Jonathan was the anomaly.

Sacrifice is inherent in community. Without the sacrifice, you don't have real allies. If folks are not willing to sacrifice anything, they are not your real allies. That does not mean that in those concentric circles, they can't be useful. Also, you do not have to tell people everything you are doing.

Concerning locating Rittenhouse while he is briefly held in prison before he is acquitted at trial, I don't know if that's a distraction. I am not saying don't do it because *your funders don't like it*, but I do not understand the political prioritization. Rittenhouse is gonna get off or be in a protected area if convicted. I do not know much about prison culture or life but what little I know is that if cops sentenced to prison are given a kind of enclosure within an enclosure, it is because cops run the prisons. Rittenhouse is not police but he is upheld by them and wants to be them.

In terms of the right to flee: if you translate prison violence to domestic violence (i.e., the state = abusive patriarch) there is no way you are morally denied that right. In civilian partner-battering there is a risk that the violator will look for you or drown your kids; or, do something in retaliation against your flight. I was talking with Criola, a Brazilian activist NGO in Rio de Janeiro, like last weekend.[12] I was using Latin phrases that did not translate well in Portuguese, *in loco parentis* and *parens patriae*, which mean "in place of the parent" and the "state as parent." The parental authority as state or law is (proto-)fascist.

When the state becomes the parent, it invades all levels of family and communal cohesion. There is no intimacy that this state cannot encroach upon. That's a parallel construct to the invitation for me to speak with international/Brazilian Black feminists about anti-rape organizing. I said that we cannot do sustained anti-rape organizing because it doesn't work within the proto-fascist machine; so we have to simultaneously do antifascist organizing. This means, dismantle the *parens patria*, the state as paternal father, authoritarian figure. The prison embodies that more than anything else. If the prison is beating you, that is a form of violence, including domestic violence. At home, the "mundaneness" of the terror is that since you burnt the casserole the violator wants to break your jaw in a domestic violence zone.

If the prison assaults you, physically accosts you, it is the same nature of violence. The domestic abuser acts like the prison warden or the prison guard to the point that they could disappear you and say it was justified self-defense (akin to "justified police homicide" in the case of twelve-year-old Tamir Rice, who was playing with a plastic toy gun in Ohio).[13] Or, the abuser says that they could damage you and not leave a mark on you, and that no one would be able to trace the violence back to them. Marissa Alexander comes to mind.[14] When she tried to defend herself against a domestic aggressor, she went to prison—the "stand your ground" defense does not work for Blacks or Black women. The special prosecutor in the Trayvon Martin[15] case was Angela Corey, who also prosecuted Alexander, but Corey could not successfully prosecute George Zimmerman for murdering Martin when Zimmerman used that "rationalization." The "stand your ground" defense doesn't work for women (of whatever ethnicity); I have not seen many cases concerning rich white women. Circle back to the incarcerated who are violated. They, you, have the right not to be tortured. You have the right not to be raped. You have the ethical right to sanctuary. Just because the state is acting like the patriarchal, authoritarian father, who can beat you, or rape you, or disappear you, doesn't mean it's legit. This is when George Jackson is right. This is when law is fascism. So, either you give us a zone of containment to "protect society," a zone without torture, medical handcuffs, humiliation, solitary confinement, beatdowns, psychological intimidation. You create those zones, and I will agree to *parens patria*. If you do a 180 and simply reproduce terror that I am already trying to fight in my own community or family, you are just another adversary. It is what Safiya Bukhari said at the Brown conference, on a panel with Frank Wilderson and Jared Sexton, when she described death squads coming from Huey P. Newton to kill NYC Panthers and the COINTELPRO FBI trying to kill or cage Panthers: Black militants were caught between "a rock and a hard place."[16] We are all caught between a rock and a hard place—between civilian violence and state violence.

What you do to survive it, I cannot judge you, which is why I'm not really a harsh critic of George Jackson. Maybe I should be. But I cannot find the moral high ground to look down upon him. I am not for the death penalty, either by the state or by freelancers or civilians. I believe life is precious. I do not believe that anybody should endure torture and be told that is the only life they deserve.

It is incumbent on the people outside to support the people inside on every metric. On some level, you start getting implicated and then you could be inside, which then becomes a problem. The only thing I can think to address that would be if we took the time, like the pastor, to figure out a bold strategy in real time. Money is the "god" of this empire. If it's all about making the trains run on time, meaning deportations that increasingly seem to focus on Haitians and Africans, because the cherubic phenotype of the babies the US wishes to receive don't really look Black. It's not just Joe Biden. It is also Kamala Harris supporting these deportations. The Black-feminist role model and the nice-white-guy role model coexist. But the violence continues as the reactionary white-supremacist underground comes above ground; and their modality has changed about the rapture—now it's "Jesus wants a genocide." They want ethnic cleansing. So now I've got to keep one eye on white supremacists and an eye on the state that is not really policing them if Kyle got out on bail and later was acquitted for three shootings and two executions. It is really more than two places that we are caught between, but that is why everything has to be communal. Sacrifice is inevitable, hopefully not with our lives. But the priority of care would be for those who are most at risk of torture and death.

Those with the lowest priority in terms of their feelings—this is going to win me a lot of votes—are privileged academics and intellectuals who are quite wealthy, and quite beloved by the (petty) bourgeoisie, who are not being tortured and so claim that this is a stable society. This is *not* a stable society.

J B   In your essay on "New Bones," you talk about Cabral as a type of abolitionist source of inspiration. What is it is specifically about Cabral and the liberation struggle of the African Party for the Independence of Guinea and Cape Verde that resonates? There are lots of anti-colonial or socialist revolutionary movements that we could point to, but Cabral specifically seems to stand out among a lot of folks grappling with the concept of abolitionism.

J J   Cabral was honest. That is how I feel about George Jackson. It is not like I agree with everything they said. But there is an honesty to them. I found that in Fannie Lou Hamer, even when she was angry with an earlier Martin Luther King, when he leveraged a compromise with the Democratic Party to nullify or void the Mississippi Freedom Democratic Party's attempts to secure voting rights.[17] Miss Hamer is significant; the people who deeply influenced me are never academics. I read, study, and learn from academics. The people who make me change are the people who have experiential knowledge of the struggle, because they were on the ground and in those struggles. The sacrifices are just stunning. We leave children behind.

Everybody is leaving children behind. Martin Luther King, Walter Rodney, and el-Hajj Malik el-Shabazz. Malcolm had four daughters (Betty Shabazz was pregnant with twins when he was killed). The whole natality thing was corrupted for us. You want to see your children grow up. Mamie Till-Mobley and others had to bury their children. The children of assassinated activists have to preside over their parents generations before they should. Cabral for me stabilizes these zones of grief. The trauma can paralyze you or push you into shopping or public persona, where you pretend to know what you don't know, which is how we could get free or dial down the terror arrayed against us.

When Cabral says that, within a decade or so, they were able to control most of the Angolan countryside, I thought I understood part of that. Those were the people who worked the land, who lived on the land along with their allies—not the petty bourgeoisie or bureaucrats under the colonial order— who engineered and sustained the revolutionary struggle. That does not mean that all of the petty bourgeoisie have to go to re-education camps. (Probably I need to go to one, too; hopefully it'll be a nice one.) It means that the petty bourgeoisie are not organic. They have dual loyalties—Captive Maternal, stage one. By the time the people who work the land, those who had to deal with raids, predators kidnapping their children, forcing them to be child soldiers, or combatants raping their kids—by the time *they* say "Resist," you know it's time to resist.

There is nowhere else to go. The communal land, that's the last refuge; that's the last sanctuary against incursions. Cabral's *Return to the Source* is composed of speeches.[18] When you talk to people rather than write academic treatises, you're actually in conversation with people. Academics and non-academic intellectuals—the Africa Information Service— collected and edited Malcolm's speeches, and they were published by Grove Press after he was assassinated in 1965.[19]

You hear not just Cabral speaking in the text. You can hear the people that he's speaking with, in your mind's mind. It's painful to read/hear. I also see beauty. It's different from reading Eric Williams's *From Columbus to Castro: The History of the Caribbean*.[20] It is different from reading Walter Rodney, who with his brother was blown up in a car bomb for organizing for dignity and resources for the mass.[21] It's different because it's a conversation. When I read Cabral, I'm saying, "Wait, what did you just say?" Then I reread him, because he is repeating what he said and I am debating him. I'm trying to figure it out. But everywhere in his writings—it's what I've talked about in serving on the planning committee for the "We Still Charge Genocide" tribunal in October 2021[22]—I see and I hear Revolutionary Love.

I hear love in Amílcar Cabral. It's less like George's love but it is still love. George's love was real. I challenge anybody to prove George did not love. You may not have liked what he did, but he definitely loved. In Cabral's love of community, community is loving him back and grieving. Cabral went to the UN with wry, satirical knowledge, shot through with loss. It is similar in some ways to going to official bodies, or local progressive nonprofits, that publicly say they exist to support us. But do not respond when we say what we need, they are not just flowery statements or more narratives about our suffering, or posters about our mutilations and death, what we need is *material aid*.

We don't need more words unless those words are accompanied by deeds—and the deeds step outside of the political order that reproduces like a machine the terror and the containment with which we grapple. Cabral is one of my teachers. I came late. I was told years ago by a Panther to read him. I just started reading *Return to the Source* when I had to teach him. He's a wonderful teacher, as were Fannie Lou Hamer, Ella Baker, people too many to name including those still inside: Mutulu Shakur, Sundiata Acoli, Joy Powell, Leonard Peltier.[23] These are all teachers.

With Cabral there is a gentleness. I think he knew the inevitability that there would not be longevity for him despite the fierce battles to create space for life. Despite those battles and knowing that you would not be able to see the mutations that happened later, including the gains for freedom, despite all those contradictions, he was steady because the love was steady.

He was incredibly—in my mind—disciplined by love. Now, what does that mean as we find out about people's personal lives, about how they might have cheated on their partner or were mean to their children? Yeah, we're all rough. We're all imperfect. But I would like to think that when I hear somebody speak with that kind of commitment to *us*, that I also hear love. It becomes tangible, not mystical. If I refuse to mystify violence, I refuse to mystify love. It's Revolutionary Love that transcends the family, the personal partner or partners, the self-love or self-loathing—on whatever day it is and however you are feeling about yourself.

It is that love of us collectively, and the better us, and the right to live without extraction and exploitation and intimidation. That is what I hear from Cabral. That's the source; and I need, I need Cabral. I need a source. It's spiritual. I can find it in the religions, the "greater religions," manifestations of spirit in body. I can see it in terms of his political phenomena.

Cabral's not the only one. But he's the one during these last months that soothes me, and then makes me get up and think about what am I going to try to do today or tomorrow in order to contribute to the material conditions that enable Revolutionary Love to be the norm and not the aberration.

Notes to Chapter 17

1 James, ed., *Warfare in the American Homeland*, 9.

2 James, "'New Bones' Abolitionism"; Cabral, *Return to the Source*.

3 James, "Airbrushing Revolution."

4 Lucille Clifton, "New Bones," in *The Collected Poems of Lucille Clifton 1965–2010* (Rochester, NY: BOA Editions, 2013); available online, https://thefreeblackwomanslibrary.tumblr.com/post/647893839835791360/new-bones-by-lucille-clifton-we-will-wear-new, accessed October 12, 2022; see also the forthcoming book, Joy James, *New Bones Abolition: Captive Maternal Agency and the Afterlife of Erica Garner* (Brooklyn, NY: Common Notions, 2023).

5 James, ed., *Imprisoned Intellectuals*.

6 See Friends of Marilyn Buck, "Marilyn Buck: December 13, 1947–August 3, 2010," accessed October 13, 2022, http://marilynbuck.com/about .html; and Jacques Kelly and Carl Schoettler, "Philip Berrigan, Apostle of Peace, Dies at Age 79," *Baltimore Sun*, December 7, 2002, https://www .baltimoresun.com/news/bs-xpm-2002-12-07-0212070391-story.html.

7 See Berger, "'Free the Land!'"

8 "Imprisoned Intellectuals: A Dialogue with Scholars, Activists, and (Former) US Political Prisoners on War, Dissent, and Social Justice" conference, Brown University, 2002; see Joy James, ed., "War, Dissent, and Justice: A Dialogue with Scholars, Activists, and (Former) US Political Prisoners," *Social Justice* 30, no. 2 (2003); and Joy James, "Imprisoned Intellectuals: War, Dissent, and Social Justice," *Radical History Review* 85 (winter 2003).

9 See Elise Swain, "Anti-Nuclear Pacifists Get Federal Prison Terms for Nonviolent Protest," *The Intercept*, November 16, 2020, https://theintercept.com/2020/11/16/nonviolent-protest-plowshares-nuclear/.

10   See https://www.jailhouselawyersspeak.com/; and Incarcerated Workers Organizing Committee, "Prison Strike 2018," accessed October 13, 2022, https://incarceratedworkers.org/campaigns/prison-strike-2018; and Incarcerated Workers Organizing Committee, "Prison Strike Updates—Roundup and Next Steps," October 15, 2018, https://incarceratedworkers.org/news/prison-strike-updates-roundup-and -next-steps.

11   Wilson Wong, "Kyle Rittenhouse, out on Bail, Flashed White Power Signs at a Bar, Prosecutors Say," *NBC News*, January 14, 2021, https://www.nbcnews.com/news/us-news/kyle-rittenhouse-out-bail-flashed -white-power-signs-bar-prosecutors-n1254250.

12   See https://www.fundobrasil.org.br/en/projeto/criola/.

13   See Harrison, James, and Rice, "'Justifiable Police Homicide.'"

14   See Barnard Center for Research on Women, "Marissa Alexander: Survived and Punished," accessed October 13, 2022, https://bcrw .barnard.edu/videos/marissa-alexander-survived-and-punished/.

15   See Blair Hickman and Eli Hager, "Trayvon Martin Was Killed Four Years Ago Today," *The Marshall Project*, February 26, 2016, https://www .themarshallproject.org/tag/trayvon-martin.

16   "Imprisoned Intellectuals" conference, Brown University, author's notes.

17   Chana Kai Lee, *For Freedom's Sake: The Life of Fannie Lou Hamer*, (Champaign, IL: University of Illinois Press, 1999).

18   Cabral, *Return to the Source*.

19   Malcolm X, *Malcolm X Speaks* (New York: Merit, 1965). On Malcolm's assassination, see Sydney Trent, "Malcolm X's Family Reveals Letter They Say Shows NYPD, FBI Assassination Involvement," *Washington Post*, February 22, 2021, https://www.washingtonpost.com /history/2021/02/22/malcolm-x-assassination-letter-nypd-fbi/; and Ashley Southall and Jonah E. Bromwich, "2 Men Convicted of Killing Malcolm X Will Be Exonerated after Decades," *New York Times*, November 17, 2021, https://www.nytimes.com/2021/11/17/nyregion /malcolm-x-killing-exonerated.html.

20   Eric Williams, *From Columbus to Castro: The History of the Caribbean* (New York: Harper & Row, 1971).

21   See Gray, "The Death of Walter Rodney."

22   See Special to Workers World, "International Tribunal Finds US Guilty of Crimes against Humanity," *Workers World*, November 1, 2021, https://www.workers.org/2021/11/59858/.

23   See Jericho Movement, "Shakur, Mutulu," accessed October 13, 2022, https://thejerichomovement.com/profile/shakur-mutulu; Jericho Movement, "Acoli, Sundiata (Clark Squire)," accessed October 13, 2022, https://www.thejerichomovement.com/profile/acoli-sundiata -clark-squire (Acoli was released in May 2022); Jericho Movement, "Powell, Rev. Joy," accessed October 13, 2022, https:// thejerichomovement.com/profile/powell-rev-joy; Jericho Movement, "Peltier, Leonard," accessed October 13, 2022, https://www .thejerichomovement.com/profile/peltier-leonard.

Open Letter To My Mom and Dad- From Peaches,

Political Prisoner

Mom, Dad,

I'm communicating this way to you because it would take too much time and emotion on my part to do so through glass windows and ear phones.

Mom and Dad, you both have always wanted me to be someone you, others and most of all myself can look up to and respect. All my life I've been taught that people were people. All my life you have told me that no matter what I was or how I was, be the best.

Mom and Dad, I am a Panther, I am a revolutionary woman. I am willing to fight and die for the rights of myself, my people and all oppressed people in general. What greater pride can one have? How much dignity can one feel? How much respect can one receive, if he/she takes the initiative to go after and fight for a goal.

Mom and Dad, I love you both for striving and working and sweating so that I may have the things that I needed. I love you both for what you've taught me.

Sure, I could go out and hold any job I desire. Have all the luxuries in life, get set, and die of "natural" death.

"PEACHES" – POLITICAL PRISONER

But to me there is more life than that. There are the people. People who need to be helped and loved. Not stepped on, used, and misled as "we" have been for so long.

I have found what I've wanted out of life. I didn't find it in the streets, or through dope, or through luxuries. I found what I wanted through the Black Panther Party. And that is to "Love and Serve the People."

Please, Mom and Dad, I love you for what you are, and what you do. Can't you love me for what I am, and what I want to do?

LOVE—Your only child
"Peaches"

Text and photo originally appeared in the *Black Panther Paper*, 1969.

Conclusion: The Agape of Peaches

As a political prisoner of the United States government, and a member of the Black Panther Party, a young woman known as "Peaches" wrote a 1969 open letter to her parents; the letter highlights and clarifies revolutionary struggle. An anonymous Captive Maternal, Peaches refused to accept the blood of the slaughter as a permanent fixture and so she joined the Black Panther Party in Southern California, just as the LAPD was engineering SWAT and testing it on the Panthers. A member of a Black revolutionary party targeted by an imperial state's police forces, the young, anonymous Black woman becomes the embodiment of the Black revolutionary who embraces agape but disappears from history. Peaches rejects the cynicism and the "luxuries" of bourgeois living because she has decided to "serve the people" as an expression of her political will, agape.

How might the celebrity influencer, or the Democratic Party lobbyist, initiate a dialectical dance for freedom and justice? "Peaches," a family nickname, exists in place of birth name and family or surname; no belonging beyond the Panthers appears in her brief letter; hence, her place in history is obscured or folded into Angela Davis's iconography in the reconstruction of women's contributions to liberation struggle.

The dialectic between Black submission and Black rebellion is global. The "Negro National Anthem" is now international. Its lyrics reflect the centuries of struggle endured and waged by Captive Maternals. The phrase refers to the "blood of the slaughter" as central and a fixture of Black life and death under this democracy; the lyrics also implicate the deity in our suffering or salvation: "God of our weary years / God of our silent tears." Fifty years after her captivity, when she survived a fascistic assault on the Southern California Black Panther offices, Peaches's letter to her parents survives.

Even if nothing, and no one, exists outside our circles of love and concern, the captives have to struggle to hold our attention and our hearts. This conclusion looks at the Captive Maternal's attempts through revolutionary struggle and self-defense to greet agape, the highest form of love, which endures only when braced by political will.

Juxtapose Peaches with the beloved and celebrated author and poet, Maya Angelou. When an affluent community of expats living in the highlands of Mexico asked me to speak at their church service in February 2022, in recognition of Black History Month, they chose two clips from Maya Angelou's performances. The first clip, which opened the service, featured Angelou in a packed auditorium delighting the audience with a smiling and triumphal performance of "Still I Rise."[1] The second clip, screened just before I spoke, showed Angelou painfully reciting a poem based on Paul Laurence Dunbar's "We Wear the Mask."[2] The constant refrain was our grinning, grimacing, shrinking elders reciting to us that it was only because they wore the mask, veiled their outrage, and swallowed their bile and white-supremacist violence, that the younger generation survived as a people (and continue to this day to do so). Yet, Angelou on screen after reciting poetry, and emitting the shrieks and moans that collectively emanate from us, turns exhausted from the microphone to wipe away her tears. Her back is turned to the lectern but the side cameras capture and preserve her weeping—almost as if it were part of the performance and so a capture for commodities culture.

"We Wear the Mask," the poem read by Angelou, depicts the various and contradictory stages of the Captive Maternal. In particular, "masking" our fear and rage have likely led to emotional and psychological destabilization, and muddied our politics for transformative justice. In juxtaposing Angelou's performance of that poem in which she turns from a packed auditorium audience in tears with the piercing, poetic 1969 letter of Peaches to her parents, our full vulnerability and love, not just our humiliation and pain, become revealed. In her 1969 open declaration to her parents, Peaches, a Black teenage girl, writes that her love for "the people" was her guiding light and path of discipline. There are politics here that align as well with Angelou. While Maya Angelou was living with her son in Ghana, she met and began working with Malcolm X, who would be assassinated in 1965 in the Audubon Ballroom in Harlem. Later, Angelou and Toni Morrison would also give eulogies at the funeral of the novelist and civil rights activist James Baldwin. (His funeral was held at the Cathedral of St. John the Divine in New York City. I and other seminarians walked from our classes to pay homage to Baldwin, a great lover of people and justice.) Angelou was an artist who embodied "Black Love" with an embrace that compressed it at times into Revolutionary Love or agape.

Unlike Angelou or Toni Morrison (who edited the texts of Black radicals before she published her novels), Peaches is neither author nor poet. She is one of the grunt workers/soldiers at the height of police repression of the Black radicals who expressed agape that radiated beyond their contradictions and limitations. Jail or prison highlights Black revolutionary struggle at the height of antagonism and imperialism arrayed against Black liberation. Peaches, decades after she briefly appeared, only to disappear from public, wrote a coda that interfaced Walter Rodney's instructions on genocidal race capitalism/imperialism with agape:

Open Letter to My Mom and Dad—From Peaches, Political Prisoner

Mom, Dad,

I'm communicating this way to you because it would take too much time and emotion on my part to do so through glass windows and ear phones.

Mom and Dad, you both have always wanted me to be someone you, others and most of all myself can look up to and respect. All my life I've been taught that people were people. All my life you have told me that no matter what I was or how I was, be the best.

Mom and Dad, I am a Panther, I am a revolutionary woman. I am willing to fight and die for the rights of myself, my people and all oppressed people in general. What greater pride can one have? How much dignity can one feel? How much respect can one receive, if he/she takes the initiative to go after and fight for a goal.

Mom and Dad, I love you both for striving and working and sweating so that I may have the things that I needed. I love you both for what you've taught me.

Sure, I could go out and hold any job I desire. Have all the luxuries in life, get set, and die of "natural" death.

But to me there is more life than that. There are the people. People who need to be helped and loved. Not stepped on, used, and misled as "we" have been for so long.

I have found what I've wanted out of life. I didn't find it in the streets, or through dope, or through luxuries. I found what I wanted through the Black Panther Party. And that is to "Love and Serve the People."

Please, Mom and Dad, I love you for what you are, and what you do. Can't you love me for what I am, and what I want to do?

LOVE—Your only child
"Peaches"

"Peaches" as "Panther" re-imagines and re-fashions herself through her comrades and community. No birth name, no family or surname tracks the only child who belongs to the community of care and protection as much as she belongs to her parents. Her devoted parents offered familial love. She does not need to seek "Black Love." She embodies and then transforms it through resistance to the hatred of predatory state and social and police forces. In the midst of an asymmetrical war between an imperial aggressor and an under-resourced resistance movement largely waged by Black teenagers, her political will and revolutionary family become her guides. As a Panther political prisoner, Peaches pleads for agape: the parental recognition that her political will to serve the people is an expression of divine spirit. The highest form of love and beauty, agape rejects distracting games and chooses political will in which love and sacrificial labor shape the revolutionary. How Black women carry the imprint of the anonymous captive resistors or warriors remains somewhat of a mystery.

From prologue to epilogue lies a breadcrumb trail of agape. The highest form of love, agape materializes when we put down distracting games in order to pick up political will. Then, the sacrificial labor for Revolutionary Love as the norm—not the aberration. Ethical lovers follow mutations of political will. Despite enslavement, segregation, exploitation, poverty, imprisonment, wars and genocides, poisoned land, water, air, this time, or next time, or (never) on time, returnees to freedom movements do more than pursue Revolutionary Love. In exodus, they design maps, paths, bridges for the maroonage that cradles Revolutionary Love.

Notes to Conclusion

1   Literature Today—and Yesterday, "'Still I Rise' by Maya Angelou (Live Performance)," accessed October 17, 2022, YouTube video, https://www .youtube.com/watch?v=qviM_GnJbOM.

2   tparbs, "Maya Angelou, We Wear the Mask," accessed October 17, 2022, YouTube video, https://www.youtube.com/watch?v=_HLol9InMlc.

Afterword

Mumia Abu-Jamal

Joy James is thinking. Of course, this is nothing new. As a child, she would climb into a treehouse, open her books, and read to her heart's content, until she heard the call for dinner. Her latest work, *In Pursuit of Revolutionary Love: Precarity, Power, Communities*, is a brilliant exploration of American life at the first quarter of the twenty-first century.

I must say more: after reading this text, I found it not only brilliant, but groundbreaking, incisive, heartbreaking, critical, chilling, eye-opening, honest, and sobering. She questions, challenges, and critiques her profession, the site in which she works, herself even, as well as the ideas circulating in her academic milieu, such as feminism—specifically that as practiced by what she calls "imperial feminists," who are apologists for war(s).

She is groundbreaking in this respect: she introduces the concept of the Captive Maternal, born of her conversations, observations, and interactions with Black mothers (and Brazilian ones!) who have lost their children to the impunities of state/police violence. These women have braved the threats and intimidations of state/police, who offer pay-outs for killed children, to which the mothers reply: "Return my child!" The Captive Maternal, James explains, is not an entity, so much as a social function, which performs as a source of love, caring, and nurturance of the oppressed, downtrodden, and dispossessed.

She begins her text with an almost poetic preface that centers on the Yoruba goddess-figure of Oshun, ruler of the rivers and waters, who implores the Creator God, Olodumare, to let the waters of the heavens flow because her beloved humans are suffering from aching thirsts and hunger because of drought. The Creator God, moved by her sacrifice as she soars close to the heat of the sun, singeing her feathers to serve others, relents, and orders the waters to fall and flow again.

Here, James as thinker and writer imagines the Yoruba goddess as embodiment of the Captive Maternal ethic. James sees this form of expression (i.e., the Captive Maternal) as agender, or not any specific gender, but I thought the most impressive exemplar of the Captive Maternal was the freedom fighter we remember as Harriet Tubman, whom captives in the slave South knew as "Gen'ral Moses." Tubman, born Araminta Ross, to this writer's recollection, had no children of her flesh, but her loving and caring—and freedom works!—freed not only her mother, father, and most of her siblings, but literally hundreds of other captives of the slave South through her numerous treks there, perhaps most spectacularly during the Combahee River Raid in South Carolina during the heat of the US Civil War, when several hundred Black captives—men, women, and children—escaped from the clutches of their southern prison-state.[1] How many thousands, perhaps tens of thousands, are still living in US cities today because of the love and care of "Gen'ral Moses"?

Captive Maternals, James explains, are those who believe deeply in what she terms "Revolutionary Love." James explains that "Revolutionary Love is difficult to define," but its elements are that it secures "basic needs" for other oppressed persons (quoting Malcolm X here) "by any means necessary." Captive Maternals are also those who live and practice Revolutionary Love , the "portal" to which is "lifelong education." James isn't here signifying her (or any other) university or college, but she intuits that her educators, her teachers, are people engaged in deep freedom struggles like mothers of state-slain children, political prisoners of the Empire, and those who resist white supremacy and racial capitalism. Captive Maternals are teachers—but not necessarily academics, she argues. James examines W.E.B. Du Bois's classic work, *The Souls of Black Folk*, and finds a basis of disagreement with his preference for what he called "the talented tenth," or the 10 percent of educated Black elites who were to work for the "uplift" of Black Americans.

This analysis, which was based on a racial—as opposed to a class—analysis, ignored the simple fact that elites seek places close to other elites, for they aspire to the appurtenances of wealth and class rise, not to service. She shatters this shibboleth by the sheer power of her analysis.

Although the book contains several works written by her, she especially shines when she is in conversation with a wide array of thinkers—from feminists to nationalists to neo-radicals—who all seek her counsel and intellectual perspectives on the burning issues of the day. These conversations form the bulk of the text.

In some respects, James echoes the daunting tasks facing Black people as noted in the Afropessimism discourse, but she is not one for hopelessness. She hopes for a clarity that girds Black children, and awakens them to the life awaiting them in an anti-Black colonial settler-state (America). She finds strength, and political will, in the example(s) made by the Oakland-based Black Panther Party, which taught thousands of teens to live and work together in sometimes altruistic communes. Young men and women exemplified the Captive Maternal by feeding young schoolboys and girls across the country on a daily basis.

James does not bite her tongue; nor does she assume she knows the answer to every question. But after decades of work in America's elite colleges and universities, and continuing her studies in America's racial demimonde, she is still not afraid to say in live/taped conversations those three magical words: "I don't know." When was the last time you heard such a phrase from an academic?

James writes and especially speaks with a delightfully refreshing vibration. Her study of Revolutionary Love is a valuable contribution to radicals and revolutionaries looking for a way to survive the repression of the white-supremacist fear-state of America. Just don't depend on the current political system. As presently designed, it is frankly incapable of doing more than placing dark faces in high places, with the illusion of representation its highest goal. James makes abundantly clear that both major political parties are imperialist, racist, and performative only in furtherance of corporate control and undying service. When it comes to subaltern movements, they are virtually useless, as she makes quite clear in her articles and discussions regarding the Black Lives Matter movement(s).

Finally, some thoughts about Revolutionary Love, which she regards as the highest form; she borrows here from the Greek theological idea of agape, "the love of others." This love is expressed not by sweet words, or gestures, but by sacrifice for others. She cites the bold, revolutionary attack of Jonathan Jackson, for his big brother George, upon the Marin County Courthouse in San Rafael, California, on a sweltering day in August, 1970. Jon, then seventeen years of age, carried several weapons in, and brought several men out, in a bid to win freedom for his brother. The plot failed when cops opened fire on the van in the parking lot, killing everyone inside, including a judge being held hostage, as well as crippling an assistant district attorney. Jonathan, James argues, was a Captive Maternal, moved by great feelings of love to secure freedom for George and other brothers. She names other Captive Maternals, who exhibit several examples of extraordinary Revolutionary Love.

Revolutionary Love is umph-degree love; or love beyond measure. It is anything love. It is love without reckoning. It is love that dares all things, beyond which others may find the spirit-force to survive; to live to fight another day. Such love is also fighting itself, for the sake of ensuring that others may live.

It wasn't easy for Joy James to see, dream, and then speak of this function radiating in her mind's eye. But she spit it forth; and we are all the richer for it. May it be so.

Notes to Afterword

1   See Helen Leichner, "Combahee River Raid (June 2, 1863)," *BlackPast*, December 21, 2012, https://www.blackpast.org/african-american-history /combahee-river-raid-june-2-1863/.

Acknowledgments

My thanks to all who supported and contributed to this collection. Collective thinking and dialogue with communities, organizers, spiritual leaders, and intellectuals allowed this book to appear in print. The editors of a small European press convinced me that working with them would be generative when they told me that they sell books from the trunk of their car as they travel to independent, feminist, and progressive bookstores. As they spoke on the Jitsi meet-and-greet, I could only think of Octavia Butler selling her brilliant and fierce sci-fi novels from the trunk of her car in the Bay Area of California. Butler bequeathed a rich and loving legacy for freedom struggles to shape our imaginations and organizations. Although not O.B., the contributors to this collection of essays and conversations also offer their gifts for principled struggles against injustice.

Intellectual communities and communal thinkers created the dialogues within this book that helped me to evolve as a thinker and an organizer. Appreciation for the intellectualism and transformative politics of: K. Kim Holder; Carlotta Hartmann of People for Womxn* in Philosophy; Chris Time Steele of *Time Talks*; Too Black and Ryan of *The Black Myths Podcast* (Black Power Media); Paris Hatcher of Black Feminist Future; Momodou Taal of *The Malcolm Effect* and Khadijah Anabah Diskin; Felicia Denaud and Devyn Springer of the *Groundings* podcast; George Yancy and *Truthout*; Jason Myles and Pascal Robert of *This Is Revolution* (The Real News Network); Jared Ware and Joshua Briond of *Millennials Are Killing Capitalism*; Rebecca A. Wilcox of the Political Theology Network; and Roberto Sirvent of the *Black Agenda Report*.

Mumia Abu-Jamal graciously offered to write the afterword to this book, but prison authorities made it difficult for him to receive a copy of the manuscript. The assistance of the theologian and activist Mark Lewis Taylor and the attorney Noelle Hanrahan, the founder of Prison Radio, proved invaluable in allowing Mumia's voice to be heard. Hanrahan works to dismantle walls so that the imprisoned have access to the world. In 1992, Hanrahan recorded Abu-Jamal's first commentary for Prison Radio at SCI Huntingdon; in 1994, she helped to introduce his first book, *Live from Death Row*, to the public through National Public Radio and ATC before censorship. Mumia Abu-Jamal's trilogy *Murder Incorporated: Empire, Genocide, Manifest Destiny* is published by Prison Radio.

I am grateful to all who teach. I still have much to learn.

"Revolutionary Love Resists Democracy" first appeared as "Black Revolutionary Love Reimagines Democracy," *Truthout,* February 18, 2021, https://truthout.org/articles /i-trust-the-black-legacy-of-revolutionary-love-over-us -democracy/; copyright *Truthout.org*; reprinted with permission. "'Sorrow, Tears, and Blood' Disavows the Talented Tenth" first appeared as "'Sorrow, Tears, and Blood': Black Activism, Fractionation, and the Talented Tenth," *Viewpoint,* January 26, 2015, https://viewpointmag.com/2015/01/26 /sorrow-tears-and-blood-black-activism-fractionation-and -the-talented-tenth/. An earlier version of "Seven Lessons in One Abolitionist Notebook: On Airbrushing Revolution" appeared as "7 Lessons in 1 Abolitionist Notebook," *Abolition Collective Blog,* June 25, 2015, https://abolitionjournal .org/joy-james-7-lessons-in-1-abolitionist-notebook/. Parts of "Anti-Racist Algorithms in Abolition Alchemy" first appeared in "The Algorithm of AntiRacism," *Logos: A Journal of Modern Society & Culture* (summer 2021), http://logosjournal. com/2021/the-algorithm-of-antiracism/ and "The Alchemy of Abolitionisms," in *The Routledge International Handbook of Penal Abolition,* ed. Michael J. Coyle and David Scott (New York: Routledge, 2021). The latter is reproduced by permission of Taylor and Francis Group, LLC, a division of Informa plc. "The Limitations of Black Studies" first appeared in Joy James and K. Kim Holder, "Building Critical Radical Communities: Liberation Pedagogies and the Origins of Black Studies," in *Making Citizenship Work: Culture and Community*, ed. Rodolfo Rosales (New York: Routledge, 2022). Reproduced by permission of Taylor and Francis Group, LLC, a division of Informa plc. "Power and the Contradictions of Communal Socialism" first appeared in Joy James and K. Kim Holder, "The Evolution of Black (Communal) Socialism," in *An Inheritance for Our Times: Principles and Politics of Democratic Socialism*, ed. Gregory Smulewicz-Zucker and Michael J. Thompson (New York: OR Books, 2020). "Reaching beyond 'Black Faces in High Places'" was first published as George Yancy, "Reaching beyond 'Black Faces in High Places': An Interview With Joy James," *Truthout*, February 1, 2021, https://truthout.org/articles/reaching -beyond-black-faces-in-high-places-an-interview-with-joy -james/, copyright *Truthout.org*; reprinted with permission. "Political Theory in the Academy" first appeared as the podcast "The Limits of Academia with Professor Joy James," *African(a) and South Asian Philosophies*, November 23, 2021, https://live2.podcasts.ox.ac.uk/episode-7-limits-academia -professor-joy-james. "Captive Maternals, the Exonerated Central Park Five, and Abolition" first appeared as the podcast "Joy James on the Academy, Captive Maternal, Central Park Five, Prison Abolition, and Simulacra," *Time Talks*, June 30, 2019, https://timetalks.libsyn.com/joy-james -on-the-academy-captive-maternal-central-park-five-prison -abolition-and-simulacra. "(Re)Thinking the Black Feminist Canon" is an edited transcript of Paris Hatcher's interview with Joy James as part of "Canon: Theorizing and Resisting in Black Feminisms," Black Feminist Future, summer 2021. "How the University (De)Radicalizes Social Movements" is an edited transcript of "How the University De-Radicalizes Students, Professors & Social Movements: A Conversation with Joy James and Rebecca Wilcox," the Political Theology Network, Villanova University, January 28, 2022, https:// www.youtube.com/watch?v=IjeWk4VGNGk. "Angela Davis

Was a Black Panther (AKA 'Pragmatism vs Revolutionary Love')" first appeared as the podcast "Myth: Angela Davis was a Black Panther Pt. 2 (w/ Dr. Joy James)," *The Black Myths Podcast*, August 25, 2021, https://blackmyths.libsyn.com/myth -angela-davis-was-a-black-panther-0. "Troubling Black Feminisms" first appeared as the podcast "What Are Our Sources for Struggle?—Dr. Joy James & Khadijah Diskin," *The Malcolm Effect*, June 20, 2021, https:// kultural.podbean.com/e/39-what-are-our-sources-for -struggle-drjoy-james-khadijah-diskin/. "The Plurality of Abolitionism" first appeared as the podcast "The Plurality of Abolitionism," *Groundings*, January 1, 2021, https:// groundings.simplecast.com/episodes/joy-james. "On the Rise of the Black Bourgeoisie" first appeared as the podcast "From 'Welfare Queen' to 'Black Girl Magic': Neoliberalism and the Rise of the Black Bourgeoisie," *This Is Revolution*, The Real News Network, April 5, 2022, https://therealnews.com/from -welfare-queen-to-black-girl-magic-neoliberalism-and-the -rise-of-the-black-bourgeoisie. "We Remember the Attempts to Be Free: Part I" and "We Remember the Attempts to Be Free: Part II" first appeared as the podcast "'We Remember the Attempts to Be Free': Joy James on Black August and the Captive Maternal," *Millennials Are Killing Capitalism*, August 12, 2021, https://millennialsarekillingcapitalism .libsyn.com/we-remember-the-attempts-to-be-free-joy -james-on-black-august-and-the-captive-maternal.

Transcripts have been edited for clarity and brevity.

Glossary

Afropessimism   lens of interpretation that accounts for civil society's dependence on anti-Black violence: a regime of violence that positions Black people as internal enemies of civil society, and which cannot be analogized with the regimes of violence that discipline non-Black workers, women, natives, queers, immigrants, etc. Afropessimism argues that the Black (or slave) is an unspoken and/or unthought sentience for whom the transformative powers of discursive capacity are foreclosed from the beginning.

BLA   Black Liberation Army, underground far-left Black nationalist revolutionary paramilitary organization active in the US from 1970 to 1981.

BPP   Black Panther Party, originally the Black Panther Party for Self-Defense, Marxist–Leninist Black-nationalist political organization active in the US from 1966 to 1982.

Captive Maternal   an ungendered function that cares for children and elders to keep them stable and protected. Often its labor is used to stabilize the very structures that prey on Black lives and honor in schools, hospitals, jobs, and prisons. Generative powers stolen and repurposed by the state and capital for accumulation can also be stolen back for rebellions.

COINTELPRO   Counterintelligence Program of the FBI which between 1956 and 1971 conducted illegal and covert projects of surveillance and infiltration with the aim of discrediting and undermining domestic American political groups.

Convict leasing system   system of forced penal labor in the Southern United States, becoming common in 1865 and ending only in the early decades of the twentieth century, under which prisoners, overwhelmingly African-American, were leased by states to private parties such as corporations and plantation owners.

CPUSA   Communist Party of the United States of America, established 1919.

Critical Resistance   social movement that aims to dismantle the prison–industrial complex, founded by Angela Davis, Rose Braz, Ruth Wilson Gilmore and others in 1997.

FBP   free breakfast program, BPP-run community service, established in 1969, with the aim of feeding hungry children before school.

Fourteenth Amendment   1868 amendment to the US Constitution that defined national citizenship and forbade states from restricting the basic rights of citizens.

HBCUs   historically Black colleges and universities, higher-education institutions established in the United States to serve the African-American community prior to the Civil Rights Act of 1964.

NAACP   National Association for the Advancement of Colored People, American civil rights organization founded in 1909 by a group including W.E.B. Du Bois and Ida B. Wells with the aim of advancing justice for African Americans.

Reconstruction   period 1863–77 following the American Civil War in which slavery was abolished constitutionally via amendments, except as punishment for a crime (see convict leasing system).

Sharecropping   beginning during Reconstruction, a system in which landowners permitted freedmen and women to farm small plots of land in return for a portion of their crop, severely restricting the economic mobility of the laborers, who did not control the crop prices and were often indebted to landowners for the use of tools, fertilizers, etc. Such practices meant sharecropping often bound farmers to the land/owner as had slavery. The practice diminished in the 1940s due to mechanization.

SNCC   Student Nonviolent Coordinating Committee, founded in 1960 in the Southern US by young people dedicated to nonviolent direct-action tactics and active until 1976.

Thirteenth Amendment   1865 amendment to the US Constitution that formally abolished slavery.

Bibliography

A&S Communications Staff. "Police 'Unprepared' and Possibly 'Complicit' in Capitol Breach." The College of Arts & Sciences, Cornell University, January 7, 2021. https://as.cornell.edu/news/police-unprepared-and-possibly-complicit-capitol-breach.

ACLU. "Leaked FBI Documents Raise Concerns about Targeting Black People under 'Black Identity Extremist' and Newer Labels." August 9, 2019. https://www.aclu.org/press-releases/leaked-fbi-documents-raise-concerns-about-targeting-black-people-under-black-identi-1.

Akuno, Kali. "Joining BSA: Kali Akuno." Black Socialists in America, March 28, 2019. https://blacksocialists.us/news/joining-bsa-kali-akuno.

Alexander, Ian. "Incarcerated Abolitionist Stephen Wilson on Hunger Strike against Retaliation for Speaking Out about COVID-19." *ShadowProof*, April 14, 2020. https://shadowproof.com/2020/04/14/incarcerated-abolitionist-stephen-wilson-on-hunger-strike-against-retaliation-for-speaking-out-about-covid-19/.

Anderson, Keziah. "'On the Forty Acres That the Government Give Me': Independent Freedpeople of the Five Slaveholding Tribes as Landholders, Indigenous Land Allotment Policy, and the Disruption of Racial, Gender, and Class Hierarchies in Jim Crow Oklahoma." Undergraduate senior thesis, Columbia University, 2020. Available online, https://history.columbia.edu/wp-content/uploads/sites/20/2020/05/Anderson-Keziah_SNR-Thesis_web.pdf, accessed October 26, 2022.

Annie E. Casey Foundation. "New Child Poverty Data Illustrate the Powerful Impact of America's Safety Net Programs." Blogpost, September 20, 2021. https://www.aecf.org/blog/new-child-poverty-data-illustrates-the-powerful-impact-of-americas-safety-net-programs.

Anon. "A Brief History of Alchemy." University of Bristol School of Chemistry, accessed October 26, 2022. http://www.chm.bris.ac.uk/webprojects2002/crabb/history.html.

Anon. "Sandra Izsadore and Fela." *Fela*, accessed September 29, 2022. https://felakuti.com/us/news/sandra-izadore.

Associated Press. "Trial Set for Texas Officer Who Shot Black Woman in Her Home." PBS *News Hour*, November 16, 2021. https://www.pbs.org/newshour/nation/trial-set-for-texas-officer-who-shot-black-woman-in-her-home.

Attica Prison Liberation Faction. "Manifesto of Demands." 1971. Available online, https://libcom.org/article/attica-prison-liberation-faction-manifesto-demands-1971, accessed July 22, 2022.

Bal, Rajan. "The Perils of 'Parens Patriae.'" *Georgetown Journal on Poverty Law & Policy* blog, November 21, 2017. https://www.law.georgetown.edu/poverty-journal/blog/the-perils-of-parens-patriae/.

Ball, Jared and Dhoruba Bin Wahad. "The Story of Kamau Sadiki, Assata Shakur and the Black Liberation Army." Black Power Media, accessed October 17, 2022. YouTube video. https://www.youtube.com/watch?v=UK0Onr8gDSU.

Barnard Center for Research on Women. "Marissa Alexander: Survived and Punished." Accessed October 13, 2022. https://bcrw.barnard.edu/videos /marissa-alexander-survived-and-punished/.

Bell, Derrick. *And We Are Not Saved: The Elusive Quest for Racial Justice.* New York: Basic Books, 1987.

— *Faces at the Bottom of the Well: The Permanence of Racism.* New York: Basic Books, 1993.

Benjamin, Jesse and Devyn Springer. "*Groundings*: A Revolutionary Pan-African Pedagogy for Guerrilla Intellectuals." In *Critical Understanding in Education, Volume 1: Keywords in Radical Philosophy and Education—Common Concepts for Contemporary Movements*, edited by Derek R. Ford, 220–55. Leiden: Brill, 2019.

Berger, Dan. "'Free the Land!': Fifty Years of the Republic of New Afrika." *Black Perspectives* blog, AAIHS, April 10, 2018. https://www.aaihs.org /free-the-land-fifty-years-of-the-republic-of-new-afrika/.

— "'Imagining a New World without Cages': An Interview with Stephen Wilson." *Black Perspectives* blog, AAIHS, August 28, 2020. https://www.aaihs.org /imagining-a-new-world-without-cages-an-interview-with-stephen-wilson/.

Black Alliance for Peace. "For Biden Administration, Black Lives Don't Matter in Haiti!—A BAP Statement on Haiti." February 12, 2021. https:// blackallianceforpeace.com/bapstatements/bidendoesntcareabouthaiti.

Black Like Mao [formerly Black Revolutionary Guard]. "Was Angela Davis a Panther." Blogpost, July 8, 2020. https://blacklikemao.medium.com /was-angela-davis-a-panther-8b16c6269023.

Black Power Media. "Dhoruba Bin Wahad on Assata Shakur, Angela Davis and COINTELPRO." Accessed December 5, 2022. YouTube video. https:// www.youtube.com/watch?v=qwMISdg0JAs.

— "Sandra Izsadore the Woman Who Gave Fela Kuti His Politics and Shaped Afrobeat." Accessed September 29, 2022. YouTube video. https://www .youtube.com/watch?v=kyw-LWA5FPk.

Bond, Julian and Angela Davis. "Reflections on Brown." UVA Arts and Sciences. Accessed October 3, 2022. https://blackleadership.virginia.edu /transcript/davis-angela.

Braswell, Sean. "US Higher Education's Great Robber Barons." *OZY,* September 5, 2014.

Brown, Vincent. *Tacky's Revolt: The Story of an Atlantic Slave War.* Cambridge, MA: Harvard University Press, 2020).

Bryant, Miranda. "'I'm Back on Food Stamps': Nurse Who Exposed 'Uterus Collector' Still Faces Consequences." *Guardian*, October 17, 2022. https:// www.theguardian.com/us-news/2022/oct/17/whistleblower-uterus -collector-repercussions-ice-detained-immigrant-women.

Bukhari, Safiya. *The War Before: The True Life Story of Becoming a Black Panther, Keeping Faith in Prison, and Fighting for Those Left Behind.* New York: Feminist Press, 2010.

Burton, Orisanmi. *Tip of the Spear* (Berkeley, CA: University of California Press, 2023).

Cabral, Amílcar. "The Weapon of Theory." Address delivered to the first Tricontinental Conference of the Peoples of Asia, Africa and Latin America,

Havana, January 1966. Available online, https://www.marxists.org/subject /africa/cabral/1966/weapon-theory.htm, accessed October 26, 2022.

— *Return to the Source: Selected Speeches by Amílcar Cabral*, edited by Africa Information Service. New York and London: Monthly Review Press and Africa Information Service, 1973.

Carlson, Tucker. "Tucker Takes On Cornel West over Democratic Socialism." Fox News, accessed October 17, 2022. YouTube video, https://www.youtube .com/watch?v=kuc6C2_Txmw.

Chicago Tribune staff. "Jon Burge and Chicago's Legacy of Police Torture." *Chicago Tribune*, September 12, 2018. https://www.chicagotribune.com /news/ct-jon-burge-chicago-police-torture-timeline-20180919-htmlstory .html.

Choctaw-Chickasaw Freedmen. "Deb Haaland: Stand against Modern-Day Jim Crow in Indian Country." change.org petition, accessed October 7, 2022. https://www.change.org/p/debra-haaland-deb-haaland-stand-against -modern-day-jim-crow-in-indian-country.

Chrisinger, David. "The Surge Nobody's Talking About: The US War in Somalia." *The War Horse*, June 25, 2020. https://thewarhorse.org /the-surge-nobodys-talking-about-the-u-s-war-in-somalia/.

Christian, Barbara. "The Race for Theory." *Cultural Critique* 6 (spring 1987): 51–63.

Civil Rights Congress. *We Charge Genocide: The Historic Petition to the United Nations for Relief from a Crime of the United States Government against the Negro People*. New York: Civil Rights Congress, 1951. Available online, https://babel.hathitrust.org/cgi/pt?id=mdp.39015074197859, accessed 8 July 2022.

Cleaver, Kathleen and George Katsiaficas, eds. *Liberation, Imagination and the Black Panther Party: A New Look at the Black Panthers and Their Legacy*. New York: Routledge, 2001.

Cleaver, Kathleen, Sekou Odinga, Cleo Silvers, Jamal Joseph, Yasmeen Majid, Victor Houston, Paula Peebles, Bilal Sunni Ali, Jihad Abdulmumit, Dhoruba Bin Wahad, K. Kim Holder, Harold Welton, Harold Taylor, Arthur League, Rashad Byrdsong, Khalid Raheem, and Ashanti Alston. "An Open Letter from the Original Black Panther Party." June 26, 2020. https://abolitionjournal.org/an-open-letter-from-the-original-black -panther-party/.

Cleveland Municipal Court. "Judgment Entry on the Tamir Rice Case." Cleveland, Ohio, June 11, 2015. https://www.scribd.com/document /268410100/Judgment-entry-on-Tamir-Rice-case.

Clifton, Lucille. "New Bones." In *The Collected Poems of Lucille Clifton 1965– 2010*. Rochester, NY: BOA Editions, 2013. Available online, https:// thefreeblackwomanslibrary.tumblr.com/post/647893839835791360 /new-bones-by-lucille-clifton-we-will-wear-new, accessed October 12, 2022.

Co-ordinating Committee, Black Liberation Army [Assata Shakur]. "A Political Statement from the Black Underground." 1976/77. Available online, http://www.assatashakur.org/message.htm, accessed October 12, 2022

Coates, Ta-Nehisi. "The Arrest of Henry Louis Gates." *The Atlantic*, August 12, 2010. https://www.theatlantic.com/national/archive/2010/08/the-arrest-of-henry-louis-gates/61365/.

Color of Change. "Stop Hate for Profit." Accessed July 20, 2022. https://colorofchange.org/stop-hate-for-profit/.

Conway, Eddie. "'The State Targeted the Panthers Because We Were Socialists, Not Because We Were Armed'—Eddie Conway on Reality Asserts Itself (4/12)." The Real News Network, September 14, 2014. https://therealnews.com/econway140904raipt4.

— "The Government Murdered Fred Hampton: Will It Ever Be Held Accountable?" The Real News Network, February 15, 2021. YouTube video. https://www.youtube.com/watch?v=YQvNcrcYa3A.

Cook, Jeremy and Jason Long. "How the Tulsa Race Massacre Caused Decades of Harm." *The Atlantic*, May 24, 2021. https://www.theatlantic.com/ideas/archive/2021/05/1921-tulsa-race-massacre-economic-census-survivors/618968/.

Coulon, Beau Patrick, dir. "The Coup: The Guillotine." 2012. Music video. https://www.youtube.com/watch?v=acT_PSAZ7BQ.

Cruse, Harold. *Rebellion or Revolution?* New York: Morrow, 1968.

— *The Crisis of the Negro Intellectual*. New York: Morrow, 1967.

Curry, Traci and Stanley Nelson, dirs. *Attica*. Showtime, 2021.

Darcy, Oliver. "Bezos Donates $100 Million Each to CNN Contributor Van Jones and Chef Jose Andres." *CNN Business*, July 21, 2021. https://www.cnn.com/2021/07/20/media/van-jones-bezos-100-million/index.html.

Davis, Angela. "Joan Little: The Dialectics of Rape." *Ms. Magazine*, June 1975. Available online, https://overthrowpalacehome.files.wordpress.com/2019/02/ms.-magazine-from-the-archives.pdf, accessed October 12, 2022.

— "Reflections on the Black Woman's Role in a Community of Slaves." *The Black Scholar* (December 1971): 3–15.

— *Angela Davis: An Autobiography*. New York: Random House, 1974.

Democracy Now!. "Cornel West & Rev. Traci Blackmon: Clergy in Charlottesville Were Trapped by Torch-Wielding Nazis." August 14, 2017. YouTube video. https://www.youtube.com/watch?v=R4i61_12SGY.

— "'This Is How Black People Get Killed': Dr. Susan Moore Dies of COVID after Decrying Racist Care." December 30, 2020. YouTube video. https://www.youtube.com/watch?v=7v1Oyp_bBGk.

Dowling, M. "When Susan Rice Wouldn't Label a Massacre of 8,000 People 'Genocide' for Political Reasons." *Independent Sentinel*, April 10, 2017. https://www.independentsentinel.com/susan-rice-wouldnt-label-massacre-8000-people-genocide-political-reasons/.

Drobnic Holan, Angie. "Obama Campaign Financed by Large Donors, Too." *PolitiFact*, April 22, 2010. https://www.politifact.com/factchecks/2010/apr/22/barack-obama/obama-campaign-financed-large-donors-too/.

Du Bois, W.E.B. *Black Reconstruction in America: 1860–1880*. New York: Free Press, 1999; originally pub. 1935.

— *The Philadelphia Negro*. Philadelphia, PA: University of Pennsylvania Press, 1899.

— *The Souls of Black Folk*, edited by Brent Hayes Edwards. Oxford: Oxford World's Classics, 2008; originally pub. 1903.

Editors of the *Encyclopaedia Britannica*. "Funmilayo Ransome-Kuti." *Encyclopaedia Britannica*, October 21, 2022. https://www.britannica.com/biography/Funmilayo-Ransome-Kuti.

Editors of the *King Encyclopedia*. "Congress of Racial Equality (CORE)." *Martin Luther King Jr. Encyclopedia*, accessed October 6, 2022. https://kinginstitute.stanford.edu/encyclopedia/congress-racial-equality-core.

Ehrenreich, Barbara and John. "The Professional-Managerial Class." In *Between Labor and Capital*, edited by Pat Walker, 5–45. Boston, MA: South End Press, 1979.

Ervin, Lorenzo Kom'boa. *Anarchism and the Black Revolution*. London: Pluto Press, 2021.

Esperance, Pierre. "An Appeal to President Biden: Change Course on Haiti Now." *Just Security*, July 9, 2021. https://www.justsecurity.org/77374/an-appeal-to-president-biden-change-course-on-haiti-now/.

Fabian, Jordan. "White House Meets with Koch Officials on Criminal Justice Reform." *The Hill*, December 10, 2015. https://thehill.com/homenews/administration/262895-white-house-meets-with-koch-officials-on-criminal-justice-reform/.

Fanon, Frantz. *The Wretched of the Earth*, translated by Constance Farrington. New York: Grove Weidenfeld, 1991; originally pub. 1963.

Farrell, Mary Cronk. "The Woman Who Birthed the Civil Rights Movement." Personal blogpost, May 12, 2019. https://www.marycronkfarrell.net/blog/woman-who-birthed-the-civil-rights-movement.

Federal Bureau of Prisons. "Inmate Race." September 24, 2022. https://www.bop.gov/about/statistics/statistics_inmate_race.jsp.

Felber, Garrett and Stephen Wilson. "The Makings of a Forum: 'Imprisoned Black Radical Tradition.'" *Black Perspectives* blog, AAIHS, August 24, 2020. https://www.aaihs.org/the-makings-of-a-forum-imprisoned-black-radical-tradition/.

Fierce, Tasha. "Sister Soldiers: On Black Women, Police Brutality, and the True Meaning of Black Liberation." *bitchmedia*, February 11, 2015. https://www.bitchmedia.org/article/sister-soldiers-black-lives-matter-women-activism.

Flannery, Mary Ellen. "'We Stepped Up and Fought Back': Behind the Explosive Growth of New Faculty Unions." *neaToday*, November 29, 2020. https://www.nea.org/advocating-for-change/new-from-nea/we-stepped-and-fought-back-behind-explosive-growth-new-faculty.

Foner, Philip S. ed. *The Black Panthers Speak*. Philadelphia, PA: Lippincott, 1970.

Forman Jr., James. *Locking Up Our Own: Crime and Punishment in Black America*. New York: Farrar, Straus and Giroux, 2017.

Foucault, Michel. *Discipline and Punish: The Birth of the Prison*, translated by Alan Sheridan. New York: Vintage, 1977.

— Foucault, Michel, Catharine von Bülow, and Daniel Defert. "The Masked Assassination," translated by Sirene Harb. In *Warfare in the American Homeland: Policing and Prison in a Penal Democracy*, edited by Joy James, 140–60. Durham, NC: Duke University Press, 2007.

316 joy james

Frazier, E. Franklin. *Black Bourgeoisie*. New York: Free Press, 1957.

Frazier, Harold. "Chairman Harold Frazier Statement on Governor Kristi Noem Letter Regarding Health Checkpoints on Reservation." *indianz.com*, May 8, 2020. https://www.indianz.com/covid19/2020/05/08/chairman-harold-frazier-cheyenne-river-sioux-tribe-2/.

Freedom Archives. "The 50th Anniversary of the August 7th Marin County Courthouse Rebellion." Accessed October 26, 2022. https://freedomarchives.org/projects/the-50th-anniversary-of-the-august-7th-marin-county-courthouse-rebellion/.

Freire, Paolo. *The Politics of Education: Culture, Power, and Liberation*, translated by Donaldo Macedo. Westport, CT: Bergin & Garvey, 1985.

Friends of Marilyn Buck. "Marilyn Buck: December 13, 1947–August 3, 2010." Accessed October 13, 2022. http://marilynbuck.com/about.html.

Frizell, Sam. "Here's How Bernie Sanders Explained Democratic Socialism." *Time*, November 19, 2015. https://time.com/4121126/bernie-sanders-democratic-socialism/.

Gonnerman, Jennifer. "Kalief Browder, 1993–2015." *New Yorker*, June 7, 2015. https://www.newyorker.com/news/news-desk/kalief-browder-1993-2015.

Gramlich, John. "How Trump Compares with other Recent Presidents in Appointing Federal Judges." *Pew Research Center*, January 13, 2021. https://www.pewresearch.org/fact-tank/2021/01/13/how-trump-compares-with-other-recent-presidents-in-appointing-federal-judges/.

Gray, Richard. "The Death of Walter Rodney." *History Today* 30, no. 9 (September 1980). https://www.historytoday.com/archive/death-walter-rodney.

Greenlee, Sam. *The Spook Who Sat by the Door*. London: Allison & Busby, 1969.

Greve, Eric. "Geronimo Pratt (1947–2011)." *BlackPast*, April 1, 2012, https://www.blackpast.org/african-american-history/pratt-geronimo-1947-2011/.

Hamer, Fannie Lou. "I'm Sick and Tired of Being Sick and Tired." Speech delivered at rally at the Williams Institutional CME Church, Harlem, New York, in support of the Mississippi Freedom Democratic Party's congressional challenge, December 20, 1964. Available online, https://awpc.cattcenter.iastate.edu/2019/08/09/im-sick-and-tired-of-being-sick-and-tired-dec-20-1964/, accessed November 3, 2022.

Harris, Cheryl. "Whiteness as Property." *Harvard Law Review* 106, no. 8 (June 1993): 1,707–91.

Harris, Elizabeth A. and Julia Jacobs. "Linda Fairstein Dropped by Her Publisher after TV Series on the Central Park 5." *New York Times*, June 7, 2019. https://www.nytimes.com/2019/06/07/arts/linda-fairstein-when-they-see-us.html.

Harrison, Da'Shaun, Joy James, and Samaria Rice. "'Justifiable Police Homicide' and the Ruse of American Justice." *Scalawag*, March 8, 2022. https://scalawagmagazine.org/2022/03/doj-tamir-rice-civil-rights-investigation/.

Henry, Imani. "Lesbians Sentenced for Self-Defense: All-White Jury Convicts Black Women." *Workers World*, June 21, 2007. https://www.workers.org/2007/us/nj4-0628/.

Hickman, Blair and Eli Hager. "Trayvon Martin Was Killed Four Years Ago Today." The Marshall Project, February 26, 2016. https://www

.themarshallproject.org/tag/trayvon-martin.

Higginbotham, Evelyn Brooks. *Righteous Discontent: The Women's Movement in the Black Baptist Church, 1880–1920.* Cambridge, MA: Harvard University Press, 1994.

Hightower, Jim. "J.P. Morgan: The Man and the Bank." *Progressive Magazine,* November 29, 2013.

History.com editors. "Scottsboro Boys." *History,* February 22, 2018. https://www.history.com/topics/great-depression/scottsboro-boys.

— "This Day in History: December 04 1969—Police Kill Two Members of the Black Panther Party." *History,* November 13, 2009. https://www.history.com/this-day-in-history/police-kill-two-members-of-the-black-panther-party.

Hoag, Alexis. "Derrick Bell's Interest Convergence and the Permanence of Racism: A Reflection on Resistance." *Harvard Law Review Blog,* August 24, 2020. https://blog.harvardlawreview.org/derrick-bells-interest-convergence-and-the-permanence-of-racism-a-reflection-on-resistance/.

Holder, K. Kim. "The History of the Black Panther Party, 1966–1971: A Curriculum Tool for Afrikan-American Studies." PhD dissertation, University of Massachusetts Amherst, 1990.

House of Representatives Committee on Internal Security. *Black Panther Party Part 4: National Office Operations and Investigation of Activities in Des Moines, Iowa, and Omaha, Nebr. (Hearings before the Committee on Internal Security, House of Representatives, Ninety-first Congress, Second Session, October 6, 7, 8, 13, 14, 15, and November 17, 1970).* Washington, DC: US Government Printing Office, 1971.

Human Rights Watch. "US: New York Police Planned Assault on Bronx Protesters." September 30, 2022. https://www.hrw.org/news/2020/09/30/us-new-york-police-planned-assault-bronx-protesters.

Husaini, Sa'eed. "The Socialist Agronomist Who Helped End Portuguese Colonialism: An Interview with Peter Karibe Mendy." *Jacobin,* October 17, 2019. https://jacobin.com/2019/10/amilcar-cabral-portuguese-colonialism-biography.

Incarcerated Workers Organizing Committee. "Prison Strike 2018." Accessed October 13, 2022. https://incarceratedworkers.org/campaigns/prison-strike-2018.

Incarcerated Workers Organizing Committee. "Prison Strike Updates—Roundup and Next Steps." October 15, 2018. https://incarceratedworkers.org/news/prison-strike-updates-roundup-and-next-steps.

Innocence Project New Orleans. "Mass Incarceration and Racial Oppression." Accessed September 29, 2022. https://ip-no.org/what-we-do/advocate-for-change/mass-incarceration-and-racial-oppression/.

Jackson, George. *Soledad Brother: The Prison Letters of George Jackson.* New York: Bantam, 1970. Available online, https://www.historyisaweapon.com/defcon1/soledadbro.html, accessed July 22, 2022.

James, Joy. "Afrarealism and the Black Matrix: Maroon Philosophy at Democracy's Border." *The Black Scholar* 43, no. 4 (2013): 124–31.

— "American 'Prison Notebooks.'" *Race & Class* 45, no. 3 (January 2004): 35–47.

— "Anita Hill: Martyr Heroism and Gender Abstractions." *The Black Scholar* 22, nos 1–2 (1992): 17–20. Available online, https://sites.williams.edu/jjames/files/2019/06/Anita-Hill-Martyr-Heroism-Gender-Abstractions.pdf, accessed November 1, 2022.

— "George Jackson: Dragon Philosopher and Revolutionary Abolitionist." *Black Perspectives* blog, AAIHS, August 21, 2018. https://www.aaihs.org/george-jackson-dragon-philosopher-and-revolutionary-abolitionist/.

— "Imprisoned Intellectuals: War, Dissent, and Social Justice." *Radical History Review* 85 (winter 2003): 74–81.

— "Killmonger's Captive Maternal Is M.I.A: *Black Panther*'s Family Drama, Imperial Masters and Portraits of Freedom." *Reading Wakanda: Reconciling Black Radical Imaginations with Hollywood Fantasies*, Southern California Library, May 1, 2019. Available online, https://sites.williams.edu/jjames/files/2019/05/WakandaCaptiveMaternal2019.pdf, accessed October 11, 2022.

— "Radicalizing Black Feminism." *Race and Class* 40 (1999): 15–31.

— "Searching for a Tradition: African-American Women Writers, Activists, and Interracial Rape Cases." In *Black Women in America*, edited by Kim Marie Vaz, 131–55. Thousand Oaks, CA: SAGE, 1995. Available online, https://sites.williams.edu/jjames/files/2019/05/Black-Women-in-America.pdf, accessed October 26, 2022.

— "The Architects of Abolitionism: George Jackson, Angela Davis, and the Deradicalization of Prison Struggles." Paper given at Brown University, April 8, 2019. Available online, https://youtu.be/z9rvRsWKDx0, accessed October 6, 2022.

— "The Quartet in the Political Persona of Ida B. Wells." In *The Oxford Handbook of Philosophy and Race*, edited by Naomi Zack, 309–18. Oxford: Oxford University Press, 2017. Available online, https://sites.williams.edu/jjames/files/2019/05/The-Quartet-in-Ida-B.-Wells-1.pdf, accessed October 26, 2022.

— "The Womb of Western Theory: Trauma, Time Theft, and the Captive Maternal." *Carceral Notebooks* 12 (2016): 253–96. Available online, https://www.thecarceral.org/cn12/14_Womb_of_Western_Theory.pdf, accessed October 26, 2022.

— "Until the Next (Up)Rising." Keynote address at "Imagining Abolition: Beyond Prisons, Wars, and Borders" virtual gathering, April 14, 2021. Available online, https://www.youtube.com/watch?v=giq5oABfI7s, accessed October 11, 2022.

— *Contextualizing Angela Davis*. Forthcoming.

— *New Bones Abolition: Captive Maternal Agency and the Afterlife of Erica Garner*. New York: Common Notions, 2023.

— *Resisting State Violence: Radicalism, Gender, and Race in US Culture*. Minneapolis, MN: University of Minnesota Press, 1996.

— *Seeking the Beloved Community: A Feminist Race Reader*. Albany, NY: SUNY Press, 2013.

— *Transcending the Talented Tenth: Black Leaders and American Intellectualism*. New York: Routledge, 1996.

James, Joy, ed. "War, Dissent, and Justice: A Dialogue with Scholars, Activists, and (Former) US Political Prisoners." *Social Justice* 30, no. 2 (2003).

— *Imprisoned Intellectuals: America's Political Prisoners Write on Life, Liberation, and Rebellion.* Lanham, MD: Rowman & Littlefield, 2003. Available online, https://repositories.lib.utexas.edu/handle/2152/7098, accessed October 6, 2022.

— *States of Confinement: Policing, Detention, and Prisons.* New York: Palgrave, 2002.

— *The Angela Y. Davis Reader.* Hoboken, NJ: Wiley, 1998.

— *The New Abolitionists: (Neo)Slave Narratives and Contemporary Prison Writings.* New York: SUNY Press, 2005.

— *Warfare in the American Homeland: Policing and Prison in a Penal Democracy.* Durham, NC: Duke University Press, 2007. Available online, https://abolitionjournal.org/wp-content/uploads/2020/06/Joy-James-ed.-Warfare-in-the-American-Homeland_-Policing-and-Prison-in-a-Penal-Democracy-Duke-University-Press-2007.pdf, accessed October 12, 2022.

James, Joy and T. Denean Sharpley-Whiting, eds. *The Black Feminist Reader.* Hoboken, NJ: Wiley, 2000.

Jericho Movement. "About." Accessed October 3, 2022. https://www.thejerichomovement.com/about.

— "Acoli, Sundiata (Clark Squire)." Accessed October 13, 2022. https://www.thejerichomovement.com/profile/acoli-sundiata-clark-squire.

— "Kuwasi Balagoon 1946–1986." Accessed October 26, 2022. https://www.thejerichomovement.com/profile/kuwasi-balagoon-1946-1986.

— "Magee, Ruchell Cinque." Accessed October 12, 2022. https://www.thejerichomovement.com/profile/magee-ruchell-cinque.

— "Peltier, Leonard." Accessed October 13, 2022. https://www.thejerichomovement.com/profile/peltier-leonard.

— "Powell, Rev. Joy." Accessed October 13, 2022. https://thejerichomovement.com/profile/powell-rev-joy.

— "Shakur, Mutulu." Accessed October 13, 2022. https://thejerichomovement.com/profile/shakur-mutulu.

Jilani, Zaid. "Martin Luther King Jr. Celebrations Overlook His Critiques of Capitalism and Militarism." *The Intercept,* January 18, 2016. https://theintercept.com/2016/01/18/martin-luther-king-jr-celebrations-overlook-his-critiques-of-capitalism-and-militarism/.

Jong-Fast, Molly. "What Working Mothers Heard in Judge Jackson's Words." *The Atlantic,* March 23, 2022. https://www.theatlantic.com/family/archive/2022/03/ketanji-brown-jackson-hearing-working-mom-guilt/627595/.

Katz, Jonathan M. "Who Was Naive about Bernie Sanders Meeting the Sandinistas?" *Mother Jones,* May 30, 2019. https://www.motherjones.com/politics/2019/05/who-was-naive-about-bernie-sanders-meeting-the-sandinistas/.

Kelly, Jacques and Carl Schoettler. "Philip Berrigan, Apostle of Peace, Dies at Age 79." *Baltimore Sun,* December 7, 2002. https://www.baltimoresun.com/news/bs-xpm-2002-12-07-0212070391-story.html

King Jr., Martin Luther. "Letter from a Birmingham Jail." April 16, 1963.

Available online, https://www.africa.upenn.edu/Articles_Gen/Letter _Birmingham.html, accessed July 22, 2022.

King, David Howard. "With 'Raise the Age,' Cuomo Continues Push to Reform Juvenile Justice." *Gotham Gazette*, February 19, 2015. https://www.gothamgazette.com/government/5583-with-raise-the-age-cuomo-continues-push-to-reform-juvenile-justice.

Kirkpatrick, Michael. "'Chickens Coming Home To Roost' | Malcolm X." Accessed October 17, 2022. YouTube video. https://www.youtube.com/watch?v=oD6aX3dHR2k.

Klein, Naomi. "The Battle for Paradise: Naomi Klein Reports from Puerto Rico." *The Intercept*, April 7, 2018. YouTube video. https://www.youtube.com/watch?v=pTiZtYaB3Zo.

Kolenz, Kristen A., Krista L. Benson, Judy Tzu-Chun Wu, Leslie Bow, Avtar Brah, Mishuana Goeman, Diane Harriford, Shari M. Huhndorf, Analouise Keating, Yi-Chun Tricia Lin, Laura Pérez, Zenaida Peterson, Becky Thompson, and Tiffany Willoughby-Herard. "Combahee River Collective Statement: A Fortieth Anniversary Retrospective." *Frontiers: A Journal of Women Studies* 38, no. 3 (2017): 164–89.

Kornbluh, Peter. "The Death of Che Guevara: Declassified." National Security Archive, George Washington University, accessed October 6, 2022. https://nsarchive2.gwu.edu/NSAEBB/NSAEBB5/.

Kratz, Jessie. "LBJ and MLK." *Pieces of History* blog, National Archives, February 28, 2018. https://prologue.blogs.archives.gov/2018/02/28/lbj-and-mlk/.

Kupendua, Marpessa. "Who Are the MOVE 9?" December 7, 1997. https://theanarchistlibrary.org/library/marpessa-kupendua-who-are-the-move-9.

Kuti, Fela. "Sorrow Tears & Blood (Original Extended Version)." Accessed October 17, 2022. YouTube video. https://www.youtube.com/watch?v=tj1wpNuQRaM&ab.

Lau, Tim. "Citizens United Explained." Brennan Center for Justice, December 12, 2019. https://www.brennancenter.org/our-work/research-reports/citizens-united-explained.

Lee, Chana Kai. *For Freedom's Sake: The Life of Fannie Lou Hamer*. Champaign, IL: University of Illinois Press, 1999.

Leichner, Helen. "Combahee River Raid (June 2, 1863)." *BlackPast*, December 21, 2012. https://www.blackpast.org/african-american-history/combahee-river-raid-june-2-1863/.

Lew-Lee, Lee, dir. *All Power to the People! The Black Panther Party and Beyond*. 1996. Available online, https://www.youtube.com/watch?v=pKvE6_s0jy0, accessed October 26, 2022.

Literature Today—and Yesterday. "'Still I Rise' by Maya Angelou (Live Performance)." Accessed October 17, 2022. YouTube video. https://www.youtube.com/watch?v=qviM_GnJbOM.

Litke, Eric. "Yes, Police Gave Kyle Rittenhouse Water and Thanked His Armed Group before Kenosha Shooting." *PolitiFact*, August 28, 2020. https://www.politifact.com/factchecks/2020/aug/28/facebook-posts/yes-police-gave-kyle-rittenhouse-water-and-thanked/.

Lorde, Audre. "The Master's Tools Will Never Dismantle the Master's

House." In *This Bridge Called My Back: Writings by Radical Women of Color*, edited by Cherríe Moraga and Gloria Anzaldúa, 98–101. New York: Kitchen Table, 1981. Available online, https://monoskop.org/images/2/2b/Lorde_Audre_1983_The_Masters_Tools_Will_Never_Dismantle_the_Masters_House.pdf, accessed October 26, 2022.

Lynch, Colum. "Genocide under Our Watch." *Foreign Policy*, April 16, 2015. https://foreignpolicy.com/2015/04/16/genocide-under-our-watch-rwanda-susan-rice-richard-clarke/.

Mafeje, Archie. "White Liberals and Black Nationalists: Strange Bedfellows." *Southern Africa Political and Economic Monthly* 11, no. 13 (December 1998): 45–8.

Malcolm X. *Malcolm X Speaks*. New York: Merit, 1965.

Malcolm X with Alex Haley. *The Autobiography of Malcolm X*. New York: Grove Press, 1965.

Manos, Nick. "Birmingham 16th Street Baptist Church Bombing (1963)." *BlackPast*, December 31, 2008. https://www.blackpast.org/african-american-history/sixteenth-street-baptist-church-bombing-1963/.

Marcetic, Branko. "The FBI's Secret War." *Jacobin*, August 31, 2016. https://jacobin.com/2016/08/fbi-cointelpro-new-left-panthers-muslim-surveillance/.

Mars, Ominira. "Dear Mariame Kaba, Hope Is Not a Discipline." *Medium*/Patreon, May 2, 2022. https://www.patreon.com/posts/dear-mariame-is-65935224.

Mayer, Jane. *Dark Money: The Hidden History of the Billionaires Behind the Rise of the Radical Right*. New York: Doubleday, 2016.

McDonell-Parry, Amelia. "Ferguson Activist Claims Son Was 'Lynched' as Police Investigate His Death as Suicide." *Rolling Stone*, November 2, 2018. https://www.rollingstone.com/culture/culture-news/ferguson-danye-jones-death-lynching-suicide-melissa-mckinnies-751275/.

Menand, Louis. "A Friend of the Devil." *New Yorker*, March 16, 2015. https://www.newyorker.com/magazine/2015/03/23/a-friend-of-the-devil.

Menkart, Deborah and Jenice L. View. "Exploring the History of Freedom Schools." *Civil Rights Teaching*, accessed October 6, 2022. https://www.civilrightsteaching.org/exploring-history-freedom-schools.

Merelli, Annalisa. "Alexandria Ocasio-Cortez Explained Democratic Socialism and Capitalism at SXSW." *Quartz*, March 20, 2019. https://qz.com/1569538/sxsw-watch-the-alexandria-ocasio-cortez-interview/.

Meyer, Jane. "New Koch." *New Yorker*, January 25, 2016. https://www.newyorker.com/magazine/2016/01/25/new-koch.

Michels, Jonathan. "The Fight for Medicare for All Made Some Important Progress in 2020." *Jacobin*, December 30, 2020. https://jacobin.com/2020/12/medicare-for-all-2020-coronavirus-progress.

Moody, Anne. *Coming of Age in Mississippi*. New York: Bantam, 1968.

Moynihan, Daniel Patrick. *The Negro Family: The Case For National Action*. Washington, DC: Office of Planning and Research, United States Department of Labor, 1965.

"mumbletheory." "Collapse of the Paradigm." *Mumble Theory*, January 14, 2021. https://mumbletheory.com/2021/01/14/collapse-of-the-paradigm/.

Myre, Greg. "Nelson Mandela's Prison Adventures." *NPR*, July 2, 2013. https://www.npr.org/sections/parallels/2013/07/01/197674511/nelson

-mandelas-prison-adventures.

Nader, Ralph. Acceptance speech. Green Party National Convention, UCLA Campus, August 19, 1996. https://www.cs.cmu.edu/afs/cs/user/jab /mosaic/pol/naccept.html.

Nation of Islam. "What the Muslims Want." Accessed October 6, 2022. https://noi.org/muslim-program/.

"newafrikan77." "January 13th 1970 Soledad Assassination of W.L. Nolen, Cleveland Edwards, Alvin Miller , Soledad Prison Riot." *newafrikan77* blog, January 13, 2018. https://newafrikan77.wordpress.com/2018/01/13 /january-13th-1970-soledad-assassination-of-w-l-nolen-cleveland -edwards-alvin-miller-soledad-prison-riot/.

Ng, Alfred. "NYPD Supporters Wear 'I Can Breathe' Hoodies at City Hall, Sparking War with Opposing Demonstrators." *New York Daily News*, December 19, 2014. https://www.nydailynews.com/new-york/nyc-crime /suspect-arrested-assault-cops-brooklyn-bridge-article-1.2051361.

O'Reilly, Kenneth. *Racial Matters: The FBI's Secret File on Black America, 1960– 1972*. New York: Free Press, 1989.

Oladipo, Gloria. "'The Revolution Is Here': Chris Smalls' Union Win Sparks a Movement at Other Amazon Warehouses." *Guardian*, April 6, 2022. https://www.theguardian.com/technology/2022/apr/06/chris -smalls-amazon-union-warehouses.

Olivares, José and John Washington. "'A Silent Pandemic': Nurse at ICE Facility Blows the Whistle on Coronavirus Dangers." *The Intercept*, September 14, 2020. https://theintercept.com/2020/09/14/ice-detention -center-nurse-whistleblower/.

Olssen, Göran Henrik, dir. *The Black Power Mixtape 1967–1975*. 2011. Available online, https://www.youtube.com/watch?v=O_dCL2F571Q, accessed October 11, 2022.

Onyenacho, Tracey. "Black August: Marin County Courthouse Rebellion." *ColorLines*, August 14, 2020. https://www.colorlines.com/articles/black -august-marin-county-courthouse-rebellion.

Oprah.com editors. "The Importance of Ancestry." *Oprah.com*, March 9, 2010. https://www.oprah.com/oprahshow/dr-henry-louis-gates-jr-start -your-ancestry-search/all.

Ortiz, Nicole. "The Central Park Five: How the Truth Set Them Free." *StMU Research Scholars*, November 8, 2019. https://stmuscholars.org/the -central-park-five-how-the-truth-set-them-free/.

PA Media. "Priti Patel in Fresh Bid to Push Through Strict Anti-Protest Measures." *Guardian*, May 21, 2022. https://www.theguardian.com /politics/2022/may/21/priti-patel-in-fresh-bid-to-push-through-strict -anti-protest-measures.

Paget, Karen. *Patriotic Betrayal: The Inside Story of the CIA's Secret Campaign to Enroll American Students in the Crusade against Communism*. New Haven, CT: Yale University Press, 2015.

Parthas, Max with Joy James. *Rebel Intellectuals*, season 2, episode 26. https:// www.blogtalkradio.com/abolitiontoday/2021/06/27/s2-e26-rebel -intellectuals-with-guest-professor-joy-james.

Patterson, Orlando. *Slavery and Social Death: A Comparative Study*. Harvard,

MA: Harvard University Press, 1982.

PBS *Frontline*. "Interview: Kathleen Cleaver." Accessed October 6, 2022. https://www.pbs.org/wgbh/pages/frontline/shows/race/interviews /kcleaver.html.

Pengelly, Martin. "Erica Garner, Black Lives Matter Activist, Dies Aged 27." *Guardian*, December 30, 2017. https://www.theguardian.com/us-news/2017 /dec/30/erica-garner-dies-black-lives-matter-eric-garner-daughter.

Pilkington, Ed. "The Day Police Bombed a City Street: Can Scars of 1985 Move Atrocity Be Healed?" *Guardian*, May 10, 2020. https://www.theguardian.com /us-news/2020/may/10/move-1985-bombing-reconciliation-philadelphia.

Piven, Frances Fox and Richard Cloward. *Regulating the Poor: The Functions of Public Welfare*. New York: Random House, 1971.

Pratt, Gregory. "Mayor Lori Lightfoot Was Told by Staff in November 2019 that Anjanette Young Raid Was 'Pretty Bad.'" *Chicago Tribune*, December 31, 2020. https://www.chicagotribune.com/politics/ct-lightfoot-anjanette -young-raid-emails-20201230-dhnc67ikorawdhm5a2xw7s4x7u-story .html.

Pratt, Minnie Bruce. "A Look Back at the Joann Little Case." *Workers World*, March 9, 2006. https://www.workers.org/2006/us/joann-little-0316/.

ProPublica. "The NYPD Files: Investigating America's Largest Police Force." Accessed October 3 2022. https://www.propublica.org/series/the -nypd-files.

Pruitt, Sarah. "How Robert Bork's Failed Nomination Led to a Changed Supreme Court." *History*, September 21, 2018. https://www.history.com /news/robert-bork-ronald-reagan-supreme-court-nominations.

RAICES. "Black Immigrant Lives Are under Attack." Accessed October 7, 2022. https://www.raicestexas.org/2020/07/22/black-immigrant -lives-are-under-attack/.

Randolph, A. Philip and Bayard Rustin. "How the Civil-Rights Movement Aimed to End Poverty." *The Atlantic*, accessed October 12, 2022. https:// www.theatlantic.com/magazine/archive/2018/02/a-freedom-budget-for -all-americans-annotated/557024/.

Redstockings. "Redstockings' Statement." *Off Our Backs 5*, no. 6 (July 1975): 8–9.

Reston Jr., James. "The Joan Little Case." *New York Times*, April 6, 1975. https:// www.nytimes.com/1975/04/06/archives/the-joan-little-case-in-a-small -southern-town-the-night-jailer-is.html.

Rights and Dissent. "Leaked FBI Documents Show FBI Developed 'IRON FIST' to Counter 'Black Identity Extremists.'" Accessed October 3, 2022. https://www.rightsanddissent.org/news/leaked-fbi-documents-show-fbi -developed-iron-fist-to-counter-black-identity-extremists/.

Rodney, Walter. *The Groundings with My Brothers*. London: Verso, 2019; originally pub. 1969.

Rohde, Stephen. "Spying on Students." *Los Angeles Review of Books*, May 4, 2015. https://lareviewofbooks.org/article/spying-on-students/.

Romm, Tony. "Amazon, Apple, Facebook and Google Grilled on Capitol Hill over Their Market Power." *Washington Post*, July 29, 2020. https://www .washingtonpost.com/technology/2020/07/29/apple-google-facebook

-amazon-congress-hearing/.

Rosenberg, Eli. "A Law Professor Resigns as Netflix Drama about Central Park Five Continues to Dredge Up Anger." *Washington Post,* June 12, 2019. https://www.washingtonpost.com/nation/2019/06/13/law-professor -resigns-netflix-drama-about-central-park-five-continues-dredge-up -anger/.

Ryan, Hugh. "At the Women's House of Detention, the Intersecting Influences of Black and Gay Liberation Movements." August 23, 2022. http://www .hughryan.org/recent-work/2022/8/23/at-the-womens-house-of -detention-the-intersecting-influences-of-black-and-gay-liberation -movements.

Sainato, Michael. "Amazon Workers in Alabama Vote Against Forming Company's First Union." *Guardian,* April 9, 2021. https://www .theguardian.com/technology/2021/apr/09/amazon-union-vote-result -latest-news-bessemer-alabama-plant.

Salbi, Zainab. "How Do People Live and Cope in the Midst of Violent Conflict?" *TED Radio Hour,* NPR, February 11, 2016. https://www.ted.com /talks/zainab_salbi_women_wartime_and_the_dream_of_peace.

Sawyer, Wendy and Peter Wagner. "Mass Incarceration: The Whole Pie 2022." *Prison Policy Initiative,* March 14, 2022. https://www.prisonpolicy .org/reports/pie2022.html.

Schmidt, Samantha. "'Why Did You Kill My Child?' Border Patrol Shooting of Guatemalan Woman Stirs Protests." *Chicago Tribune,* May 29, 2018. https://www.chicagotribune.com/nation-world/ct-guatemala -immigrant-killed-border-patrol-20180529-story.html.

Seidman, Derek and Gin Armstrong. "Scandal-Ridden Wells Fargo Rips Off Customers while Funding the Gun Industry and Carceral State." *Truthout,* March 30, 2018. https://truthout.org/articles/scandal-ridden-wells-fargo -rips-off-customers-while-funding-the-gun-industry-and-carceral-state/.

Select Committee on Nutrition and Human Needs. *Nutrition and Human Needs—1972: Hearings Before the Select Committee on Nutrition and Human Needs of the United States Senate, Ninety-second Congress, Second Session, on Nutrition and Human Needs . . .* Washington, DC: US Government Printing Office, 1972.

Serrato, Jacqueline. "Fifty Years of Fred Hampton's Rainbow Coalition." *South Side Weekly,* September 27, 2019. https://southsideweekly.com/fifty -years-fred-hampton-rainbow-coalition-young-lords-black-panthers/.

SFgate. "1970 Marin County Courthouse Murders." Slideshow, April 18, 2017. https://www.sfgate.com/news/slideshow/1970-marin-county-courthouse -shooting-144014.php.

Shakur, Assata. *Assata: An Autobiography.* Westport, CT: L. Hill, 1987.

Shames, Stephen and Ericka Huggins. *Comrade Sisters: Women of the Black Panther Party.* Woodbrige: ACC Art Books, 2022.

Shetty, Abhishek. "Throwback Thursday: Fifty-Year Anniversary of 'Bunchy' Carter, John Huggins Shooting." *Daily Bruin,* January 17, 2019. https:// dailybruin.com/2019/01/17/throwback-thursday-fifty-year-anniversary -of-bunchy-carter-john-huggins-shooting/.

Siegel, Bill. "Why Black Farmers Don't Trust Tom Vilsack." *Agriculture,*

February 2021. https://www.agriculture.com/news/why-black-farmers-dont-trust-tom-vilsack.

Slavery and Remembrance. "Elizabeth Key (Kaye)." Accessed October 26, 2022. https://slaveryandremembrance.org/people/person/?id=PP031.

Smith II, Preston H. *Racial Democracy and the Black Metropolis: Housing Policy in Postwar Chicago.* Minneapolis, MN: University of Minnesota Press, 2012.

Smith-Morris, Carolyn. "Addressing the Epidemic of Missing & Murdered Indigenous Women and Girls." *Cultural Survival,* March 6, 2020. https://www.culturalsurvival.org/news/addressing-epidemic-missing-murdered-indigenous-women-and-girls.

Smith, Frank "Big Black", Jared Reinmuth, and Améziane. *Big Black: Stand at Attica.* Los Angeles, CA: BOOM! Studios, 2020.

Smithsonian Channel. "Malcolm X's Fiery Speech Addressing Police Brutality." February 16, 2018. YouTube video. https://www.youtube.com/watch?v=6_uYWDyYNUg.

SNCC Digital Gateway. "Freedom Schools." Accessed October 6, 2022. https://snccdigital.org/inside-sncc/culture-education/freedom-schools/.

Sokolova, Marina. "Advocacy Democracy Modes: Benefits and Limitations." *e-belarus.org,* accessed October 10, 2022. https://www.e-belarus.org/article/advocacydemocracy.html.

Southall, Ashley and Jonah E. Bromwich. "2 Men Convicted of Killing Malcolm X Will Be Exonerated after Decades." *New York Times,* November 17, 2021. https://www.nytimes.com/2021/11/17/nyregion/malcolm-x-killing-exonerated.html.

Special to Workers World. "International Tribunal Finds US Guilty of Crimes against Humanity." *Workers World,* November 1, 2021. https://www.workers.org/2021/11/59858/.

Stanley, Jason. "Movie at the Ellipse: A Study in Fascist Propaganda." *Just Security,* February 4, 2021. https://www.justsecurity.org/74504/movie-at-the-ellipse-a-study-in-fascist-propaganda/.

Strangio, Chase. "CeCe is Free But So Much Work Remains." ACLU, January 13, 2014. https://www.aclu.org/news/lgbtq-rights/cece-free-so-much-work-remains.

Sullivan, Patricia. "How Robert F. Kennedy Shaped His Brother's Response to Civil Rights." *TIME,* August 11, 2021. https://time.com/6089512/robert-kennedy-civil-rights-alabama/.

Swain, Elise. "Anti-Nuclear Pacifists Get Federal Prison Terms for Nonviolent Protest." *The Intercept,* November 16, 2020. https://theintercept.com/2020/11/16/nonviolent-protest-plowshares-nuclear/.

Swaine, Jon. "Ohio Walmart Video Reveals Moments before Officer Killed John Crawford." *Guardian,* September 25, 2014. https://www.theguardian.com/world/2014/sep/24/surveillance§-video-walmart-shooting-john-crawford-police.

Swarens, Tim. "Boys: The Silent Victims of Sex Trafficking." *USA Today,* accessed November 1, 2022. https://www.usatoday.com/story/opinion/nation-now/2018/02/08/boys-silent-victims-sex-trafficking/1073799001/.

Taibbi, Matt. *I Can't Breathe: A Killing on Bay Street.* New York: Spiegel & Grau, 2017.

Taylor, Flint and Jeff Haas. "New Documents Suggest that J. Edgar Hoover Was Involved in Fred Hampton's Murder." *Truthout*, January 19, 2021. https://truthout.org/articles/new-documents-suggest-j-edgar-hoover-was-involved-in-fred-hamptons-murder/.

Taylor, Keeanga-Yamahtta. "'Hell, Yes, We Are Subversive': The Legacy of Angela Davis." *New York Review of Books*, September 4, 2022.

The Black Myths Podcast. "Myth: Angela Davis Was a Black Panther." August 20, 2021. https://blackmyths.libsyn.com/myth-angela-davis-was-a-black-panther.

Theoharis, Jeanne. "Mrs. Parks and Black Power." *The Rebellious Life of Mrs. Rosa Parks,* accessed October 3, 2022. https://rosaparksbiography.org/bio/mrs-parks-and-black-power/.

Thich Nhat Hanh. *Teachings on Love.* Sounds True W560D. 2 x CD.

Thompson, Heather Ann and Khalil Gibran Muhammad. "Between the Lines: Heather Ann Thompson & Khalil Gibran Muhammad." Schomburg Center, September 9, 2016. https://livestream.com/schomburgcenter/events/6114428.

tparbs. "Maya Angelou, We Wear the Mask." Accessed October 17, 2022. YouTube video. https://www.youtube.com/watch?v=_HLol9InMlc.

Trent, Sydney. "Malcolm X's Family Reveals Letter They Say Shows NYPD, FBI Assassination Involvement." *Washington Post,* February 22, 2021. https://www.washingtonpost.com/history/2021/02/22/malcolm-x-assassination-letter-nypd-fbi/.

United States Department of Justice. "Memorandum: Department of Justice Report Regarding the Criminal Investigation into the Shooting Death of Michael Brown by Ferguson, Missouri Police Officer Darren Wilson." March 4, 2015. https://www.justice.gov/sites/default/files/opa/press-releases/attachments/2015/03/04/doj_report_on_shooting_of_michael_brown_1.pdf.

US Attorney's Office, Southern District of New York. "Norman Seabrook, President of Correction Officers Benevolent Association, Sentenced to 58 Months in Prison for Accepting Bribes in Exchange for Investing Union Money in New York-Based Hedge Fund." Department of Justice, February 8, 2019. https://www.justice.gov/usao-sdny/pr/norman-seabrook-president-correction-officers-benevolent-association-sentenced-58.

US National Archives. "The Treaty of Guadalupe Hidalgo." Accessed October 11, 2022. https://www.archives.gov/education/lessons/guadalupe-hidalgo.

Vice. "Genealogist Who Tracks Down Modern-Day Slavery Practices." February 27, 2018. YouTube video. https://www.youtube.com/watch?v=6OXbJHsKB3I.

Walker, David. *Walker's Appeal, in Four Articles; Together with a Preamble, to the Coloured Citizens of the World, but in Particular, and Very Expressly, to Those of the United States of America, Written in Boston, State of Massachusetts, September 28, 1829.* Boston, MA: self-published, 1830. Available online, https://docsouth.unc.edu/nc/walker/menu.html, accessed July 22, 2022.

Wells, Ida B. *Crusade for Justice: The Autobiography of Ida B. Wells,* ed. Alfreda M. Duster. 2nd edn. Chicago, IL: University of Chicago Press, 2020.

— *Southern Horrors: Lynch Law in All Its Phases.* New York: New York Age, 1892.

Wilford, Hugh. *The Mighty Wurlitzer: How the CIA Played America.* Harvard,

MA: Harvard University Press, 2009.

Wilkes, Andrew J. "Socialism in Black America?" *religioussocialism.org*, January 14, 2016. https://www.religioussocialism.org/socialism_in_black_america.

Williams, Eric. *From Columbus to Castro: The History of the Caribbean*. New York: Harper & Row, 1971.

Williams, Paige. "Kyle Rittenhouse, American Vigilante." *New Yorker*, July 5, 2021. https://www.newyorker.com/magazine/2021/07/05/kyle-rittenhouse-american-vigilante.

Wilson, Stephen, Orisanmi Burton, Toussaint Losier, et al. "The Lasting Influence of the 'Imprisoned Black Radical Tradition.'" *Black Perspectives* blog, AAIHS. August 28, 2020. https://www.aaihs.org/the-lasting-influence-of-the-imprisoned-black-radical-tradition/.

Winter, Sylvia. "No Humans Involved: An Open Letter to My Colleagues." *Forum N.H.I.: Knowledge for the 21st Century* 1, no. 1 (fall 1994): 42–73.

Wong, Wilson. "Kyle Rittenhouse, out on Bail, Flashed White Power Signs at a Bar, Prosecutors Say." *NBC News*, January 14, 2021. https://www.nbcnews.com/news/us-news/kyle-rittenhouse-out-bail-flashed-white-power-signs-bar-prosecutors-n1254250.

Woodard, Vincent. *The Delectable Negro: Human Consumption and Homoeroticism within US Slave Culture*. New York: New York University Press, 2014.

World Health Organisation. "United States of America Situation." Updated 10 October 2022. https://covid19.who.int/region/amro/country/us.

Zinn Education Project. "This Day in History—Feb. 8, 1968: Orangeburg Massacre." Accessed October 6, 2022. https://www.zinnedproject.org/news/tdih/orangeburg-massacre/.

— "This Day in History—Jan. 18, 1968: Eartha Kitt Spoke Truth at the White House." Accessed October 12, 2022. https://www.zinnedproject.org/news/tdih/eartha-kitt-spoke-at-white-house/.

— "This Day in History—March 8, 1971: FBI's COINTELPRO Exposed." Accessed October 6, 2022. https://www.zinnedproject.org/news/tdih/cointelpro-exposed/.

— "This Day in History—May 4, 1970: Kent State Massacre." Accessed October 6, 2022. https://www.zinnedproject.org/news/tdih/kent-state-massacre/.

— "This Day in History—Nov. 10, 1898: Wilmington Massacre." Accessed July 8, 2022. https://www.zinnedproject.org/news/tdih/wilmington-massacre-2.

Zinn, Howard. "Ella Baker: 'One of the Most Consequential and Yet One of the Least Honored People in America.'" April 24, 1968. Available online, https://www.howardzinn.org/collection/ella-baker-consequential-people/, accessed October 26, 2022.

Zurn, Perry and Andrew Dilts, eds. *"Challenging the Punitive Society": Carceral Notebooks* 12 (2016). Available online, https://www.thecarceral.org/journal-vol12.html, accessed October 26, 2022.

About the Contributors

Joshua Briond and Jared Ware, *Millennials Are Killing Capitalism*
https://millennialsarekillingcapitalism.libsyn.com
Our goal is to provide a platform for communists, anti-imperialists, Black liberation movements, left libertarians, LGBTQ+ activists, feminists, immigration activists, and abolitionists to discuss radical politics, radical organizing, and share their visions for a better world. We view solidarity with decolonization, Indigenous, anti-imperialist, environmentalist, socialist, and anarchist movements across the world as necessary steps toward meaningful liberation for all people. We hope that our podcast becomes a meaningful platform for organizers and activists fighting for social change to connect their local movements to broader movements centered around the fight to end imperialism, capitalism, racism, discrimination based on gender identity or sexuality, sexism, and ableism.

Felicia Denaud and Devyn Springer, *Groundings*
https://groundings.simplecast.com
Groundings is a place where organizing, theory, and history come in contact with dialogue, experience, and storytelling. It's where the past meets the present, and political education happens. The title is in honor of the revolutionary educator Walter Rodney, whose concept of "groundings" as a form of radical, political, and communal education inspires the conversations on this podcast. *Groundings*: we sit, we listen, we talk, we share, and we learn.

Khadijah Anabah Diskin
Khadijah Anabah Diskin is a PhD researcher in psychology. Her research explores the psychosocial dimension of Black students' experiences in British higher education, using Lacanian discourse analysis to interrogate the intersubjective convergences of race, coloniality, and neoliberalization.

Carlotta Hartmann, People for Womxn* in Philosophy
https://pwips.home.blog
Where people for womxn* in philosophy at Oxford validate themselves, in thought and action. We are, we think, we discern. Hexes for essays, workshops, events, mentoring, and more.

Paris Hatcher, Black Feminist Future
https://blackfeministfuture.org
Black Feminist Future is a political hub focused on the dynamic possibilities of galvanizing the social and political power of Black women, girls, and gender-expansive people towards liberation. We do this by building and nourishing the leadership of fierce Black feminists, fortifying aligned organizations and movements, and shifting cultural norms.

K. Kim Holder
K. Kim Holder is the grandfather of Andru and Isaiah Golden and father of Zora
Holder-Santiago. Born into the struggle for justice, Holder joined the Black
Panther Party, Harlem Branch, at age twelve. He earned his doctorate from
the University of Massachusetts Amherst concentrating on African-American
studies and multicultural education. Working extensively to document and
analyze the rank-and-file organizing of the BPP, as an educator Holder seeks
to develop pedagogical tools to be used by and for marginalized populations.

Jason Myles and Pascal Robert, *This Is Revolution*
https://thisisrevolutionpodcast.com
A show about politics, history, and culture with musician Jason Myles and
journalist Pascal Robert.

Chris Time Steele, *Time Talks*
https://timetalks.libsyn.com
Chris Time Steele is the creator of *Time Talks: History, Politics, Music, and Art*.
Chris is a teacher and journalist who has co-authored articles with Noam
Chomsky and is also a hip-hop artist who has worked with Common.

Momodou Taal, *The Malcolm Effect*
https://kultural.podbean.com
The Malcolm Effect podcast is dedicated to providing political education in
an accessible manner. It is mainly interview-style and features a variety
of scholars and academics from a broad range of disciplines. As a project
it seeks to raise the level of discussion amongst a younger generation by
providing digestible responses to commonly held questions regarding race,
politics, gender, and religion.

Too Black and Ryan, *The Black Myths Podcast*
https://blackmyths.libsyn.com
The Black Myths Podcast is an informative conversational show analyzing
popular myths about Black culture of sociopolitical nature. Translation: we
debunk the bs said about Black people. Host: Too Black. Co-hosts: Shelle,
Terrell, Kam, and Ryan.

Truthout
https://truthout.org
Truthout is a nonprofit news organization dedicated to providing independent reporting and commentary on a diverse range of social justice issues.
Founded in 2001, we have anchored our work in principles of accuracy,
transparency, and independence from the influence of corporate and political forces. *Truthout* works to spark action by revealing systemic injustice
and providing a platform for progressive and transformative ideas, through
in-depth investigative reporting and critical analysis.

Rebecca A. Wilcox, the Political Theology Network
https://politicaltheology.com
The Political Theology Network is an organizing network for scholars, activists, and community leaders who are interested in promoting the publicly engaged, interdisciplinary study of religion and politics. The field of political theology attends to the connections between religious and political ideas and practices, placing scholarship on religion in dialogue with scholarship from the fields of politics, philosophy, ethics, cultural studies, and critical theory.

George Yancy
George Yancy, the Samuel Candler Dobbs Professor of Philosophy at Emory University and a Montgomery Fellow at Dartmouth College, works primarily in the areas of critical philosophy of race, critical whiteness studies, critical phenomenology (especially, on racial embodiment), and philosophy of the Black experience. Yancy received his BA (Cum Laude) in philosophy from the University of Pittsburgh, where he wrote his undergraduate philosophy honors thesis under the direction of Wilfrid Sellars. He received his first MA in philosophy from Yale University and his second MA from New York University in Africana Studies. He received his PhD in philosophy from Duquesne University (with distinction).

About the Author

The political theorist Joy James teaches at Williams College, Williamstown, Massachusetts. Editor of *The Angela Y. Davis Reader* (Blackwell, 1998), *Imprisoned Intellectuals* (Rowman & Littlefield, 2003), *The New Abolitionists* (SUNY Press, 2005), and *Warfare in the American Homeland* (Duke University Press, 2007), James is also the author of *Resisting State Violence* (University of Minnesota Press, 1996), *Transcending the Talented Tenth* (Routledge, 1997), *Seeking the Beloved Community* (SUNY Press, 2013), *New Bones Abolition: Captive Maternal Agency and the Afterlife of Erica Garner* (Common Notions, 2023), and the forthcoming *Contextualizing Angela Davis*.